D1244536

International financial markets

DEREK HONEYGOLD

International financial markets

NICHOLS PUBLISHING COMPANY
New York

Published in the United States of America by
Nichols Publishing Company,
PO Box 96, New York, NY 10024, USA

Published in Great Britain by
Woodhead-Faulkner Limited,
Simon & Schuster International Group,
Fitzwilliam House, 32 Trumpington Street,
Cambridge CB2 1QY, England

First published 1989

Library of Congress Cataloging-in-Publication Data
Honeygold, Derek
International financial markets/Derek Honeygold.
p.   cm.
ISBN 0–89397–343–2 : $34.95
1. International finance.   2. Financial institutions,
International.   3. Securities.   4. Money market.   5. Foreign
exchange.   6. Options (Finance)   I. Title.
HG3821.H63   1989
332.6'5—dc19
89–2896
CIP

*HG
3821
.H63
1989*

Designed by Geoff Green
Typeset by Goodfellow & Egan Phototypesetting Ltd., Cambridge
Printed in Great Britain by A. Wheaton and Co. Ltd., Exeter

Contents

Preface

The need for a book such as this became clear to me soon after I was invited to deliver a course of lectures on International Financial Markets to the fourth-year undergraduate students of the European Business School in Regent's Park, London. This was in 1985, at a time when the City of London was still preparing for its 'Big Bang' on 27 October 1986. There were other books available, but none seemed to embrace the scope of the course that I had in mind. Several were in existence which dealt with the theory of markets in a more general way, but the only ones available which sought to describe these various markets in any detail had already become outdated by the strong wave of innovation which still persists in the wake of macroeconomic and technological change and deregulation.

This book consists of seven chapters. The two initial chapters are an attempt to cover the material which I would usually deliver in an extemporary form, as an introduction to the course. The first is an attempt at defining fairly precisely the subject of the book namely International Financial Markets. The second is comprised of a commentary upon aspects of change which have pervaded these markets in recent years. The remaining five chapters are a development of the extensive notes which are prepared prior to delivering the course for the first time and then revised and refined in subsequent years. These attempt to characterise the specific markets which coincide with the book's title, namely capital markets – those for stocks and bonds, the money markets – which serve liquidity needs, the foreign exchange markets which are inevitably involved in each and every international financial transaction, and finally, those markets in financial futures and options which are so much a creation of the 1980s. Whilst the original intention was to concentrate upon the international markets only, considerable space is also devoted to domestic financial markets in the United Kingdom, the United States and Japan.

Like many books of a similar nature this is rather inevitably a static approach, some might say an heroic one, to a dynamic process. Black Monday, 19 October 1987, the day of the crash on the world's stock markets, clearly presented problems, since by then I had already written most of the book. Some adjustments have since been made in consequence of that event. Certain personal health problems, which have now mercifully been resolved, then combined with the over-whelming burden of my responsibilities as one of a small group of councillors holding the balance of power in a large outer London borough to create an additional impediment to the progress of this work.

It is nonetheless hoped that the result will be of value to students such as those which I encounter and seek to assist at the European Business School and elsewhere. Maybe it will also be helpful to others, such as junior operatives in specific markets, in helping them better to understand the general context in which their own particular activity is set. Finally, I hope that it will be of interest to general readers, in introducing them to one of the more important economic developments in our time.

I should like, finally, to make mention of certain friends and colleagues who have been influential in the preparation of this work. First and foremost, I would mention Professor David Liston, who first introduced me to the European Business School, and who has always been an inspiration. I would then mention those colleagues from the European Business School who have from time to time made helpful suggestions, not least Dr N. D. Quy. Similar helpful comments have come from Tony Little of Panmure Gordon and various representatives of Morgan Grenfell and Schroders. Others who have at various times been sources of great encouragement when the going has seemed difficult have included Diana Taggart, Elizabeth Sidney, and Anneliese Waugh. Finally, I would pay tribute to my publishers, Woodhead–Faulkner of Cambridge, not least for their forbearance when competing commitments have frequently meant that I could not meet their production targets.

Derek Honeygold
London, England
October 1988

CHAPTER ONE

International financial markets

The perfect market

In the broadest economic sense, a market can be defined as a meeting place, geographical location or area in which buyers who wish to exchange money for well-defined goods or services, and sellers who similarly have a desire to exchange well-defined goods or services for money, can negotiate that exchange. Dependent upon the force of the relative needs of the potential buyer and seller, that is to say, through the interplay of the market forces of demand and supply, a price is determined which will clear the market.

Just as some markets are unique to a specific meeting place in a particular geographical location, others may cover an area which can be local, regional, national, supranational or worldwide. Several factors will determine the structure of these markets – not least the quality of communications, and the presence of regulations, such as fiscal, monetary and other constraints. It can be argued that the better the communications and the fewer the regulations, the greater the market area is likely to be. Even more important, perhaps, is the effect of these factors on the degree of perfection of that market, or its efficiency. After all, with better communications and fewer impediments, the easier it will be to set a price which will bring supply and demand into equilibrium and clear that market.

The perfect market describes an absolute but elusive condition in which there is a total absence of distortions, with all available information reflected in the price, and where no abnormal profit in relation to the risks involved can be obtained from utilising the available information. If the perfect market were to be sustained, it would need to achieve the ultimate in terms of other measures of efficiency, such as allocation and operation. For this reason it would generally be comprised of large numbers of both buyers and sellers, to the extent that an average deal or transaction by any of its participants would not individually influence the price. It would also require perfect freedom of entry, in that new participants could enter and deal on precisely the same terms as existing participants, along with an absence of other economic frictions, such as the costs of communication. This would clearly be a bigger problem for markets in goods than for financial markets, since markets in goods would require communications that physically transplanted goods from one location to another in addition to those which merely entailed the transmission of information.

Efficiency is a measure of the degree to which this absolute state has been achieved. Three separate considerations have been mentioned, which are worth explaining in more detail.

Allocative efficiency

The allocative efficiency of a market has to do with its ability to direct the purchaser to the most efficient seller. In general terms, of course, the price will perform this function. In primary financial markets, it is more difficult to ensure that savings are directed to the most productive firms, where returns are maximised and risks are minimised. This is often because of a shortage of information about potential borrowers. It is here that the existence of an active secondary market becomes a great advantage, since it is then more likely that those borrowers will already have been monitored on a regular basis. There are two important measures of such market activity – its depth and its breadth.

The depth of a market is generally determined by the number of potential buyers and sellers at different prices. In a financial market, this would be demonstrated by the number of buy and sell orders for a security, for example, around the last sale price.

The breadth explains the different motives of those buyers and sellers. For example, a particular financial market could appeal to a multiplicity of players all of which had different motives for wanting to hold that security. An equity in a company may be desired, for example, by another company which may anticipate a takeover, by a foreign investor who may be interested in the return in base currency terms or by another who may be interested in the return in foreign currency terms.

Operational efficiency

Operational efficiency can be measured by the difference between the cost and the selling price, that is the seller's turn or gross profit. While the presence of competition will generally ensure that, the more active the market is, the smaller the gross profit is likely to be, it is also the case that, in less active markets, the gross profit will reflect a trader's perception of the risk which he will have to carry while holding the goods in stock for a period of time. In secondary financial markets, this is measured by the so-called 'spread' between buying and selling prices. In primary financial markets, on the other hand, dealers will claim a commission, together with stamp duties or other transaction costs. It is in the interest of stimulating demand that commissions and related costs are kept low.

Another factor which influences the operational efficiency of primary financial markets is the negotiability which comes from the existence of secondary markets for a comparable security. This influences the pricing and size of new issues. If, for example, the new issue is too large in relation to comparable issues already trading on secondary markets, it will decrease the price and hence the liquidity of the old issues. Since it is precisely this liquidity which encourages lenders to subscribe to new issues, there is a great possibility that the issue would be unsuccessful. Similarly, if the price of the new issue does not immediately relate to the price of the old issues already trading on the secondary market, there will be an absence of negotiability which will undermine its attractiveness.

Information processing efficiency

In financial markets, information processing efficiency is related to the extent to which prices of securities reflect what is currently known about the likely future pay-offs from investing in them. In the efficient market, where all buyers and sellers bargain on an equal footing, it will not matter if some are better informed than others, since they will derive no advantage from it. In inefficient markets, however, those who are better informed will be able to take advantage of their superior knowledge and secure abnormal gains. Since information processing efficiency implies instant knowledge of the incidence of demand and supply within the boundary of a market, it is far more difficult to satisfy in an international market than in a domestic market.

Finally, markets may be broken down into three main sectors – markets in goods, the factor markets (which may include markets in services, such as labour, and markets in natural resources, such as land), and financial markets. The latter are, of course, a central subject of this book, and can be divided into several sub-sectors, such as capital markets and money markets, foreign exchange markets and markets for covering risks.

Characteristics of financial markets

What differentiates a financial market from other markets is that no tangible good or service is exchanged for the monetary consideration. Instead, a piece of paper, which may be broadly described as a financial claim, will generally change hands. This may be in the form of a promissory note, or a title to a future flow of income adjusted for any capital appreciation or depreciation.

Financial markets play an important part in bridging the gap between what may be described as the spendthrift economy – an economy of the here and now, where all income is spent on goods and services for current consumption and all current output is consumed – and the frugal economy – where households and firms look to the future, and as a result saving and investment occur.

There are always those in society, generally in the household sector, who hold funds in excess of immediate consumption needs. Firms fall into this category too, in the sense that they may elect not to pay out to their owners some of the profits that they have earned. Instead they may prefer to keep them in the form of reserves. The funds withheld in such cases are known as savings.

There are also those in a society with immediate investment or consumption needs greater than the funds they currently hold available, usually in the business and government sectors. Just as there will always be a price which the latter will be prepared to pay in return for borrowing the savers' surplus funds, so there will generally be a price at which the saver will be prepared to forego those funds for a period of time, rather than keeping them in cash. The fundamental function of financial markets is to facilitate this process.

There are, however, two problems. Firstly, the periods of time over which the savers are prepared to forego the use of their funds will not usually coincide with the periods over which the borrowers require them. That is to say, there is a maturity mismatch. Secondly, the sums which individual savers have available to lend will not usually coincide with those which the borrowers require. These two problems create the need for so-called financial intermediaries, who are generally the 'players' within financial markets. There are two basic types of financial intermediary. Those who buy and sell on their own account, and 'take positions' by risking their own financial resources in performing the role of smoothing out the various financial claims of others, are the market-makers. Those who enter a market to carry out transactions on a client's behalf for payment of a commission, but who bear no risk, are the brokers. Nowadays, both these categories of financial intermediary will usually be employees of a much larger institution, such as a bank, and it is more often these institutions which are referred to when using the term 'financial intermediary'.

Financial intermediaries perform several useful, indeed crucial, functions. They collect and parcel up the savings of those units within an economy which are in surplus, which are often the smaller ones, into larger loan packages which are more attractive to those units which are in deficit, generally larger ones. They will spread the risks, by taking small amounts of savings from many different savers and lending them to a 'portfolio' of firms. They will carry out that important function known as the 'transmutation of claims'. This is the process of borrowing money on a short-term basis and lending it on a longer-term basis. And because of their geographical position, they will often reduce the transaction costs of lenders and borrowers alike. Finally, they will provide financial advice and insurance services, ranging from the traditional services offered by stockbroking firms to private investors to advice on the benefits and otherwise of a range of products offered by the insurance and mortgage brokers.

This book is about the markets in which these players operate, which fall into several categories. There are equity markets, in which the capital of companies or corporations are traded in the form of stocks and shares which actually confer a portion of ownership of a part of that company or corporation on the purchaser of the security. There are debt markets, in which governments and other public bodies, as well as corporations, will borrow funds in return for a reward, known as interest, but which do not confer ownership. These, in turn, can be broken down into two sub-categories. There are the bond markets, which generally trade in medium- to long-term loans and, along with equities, are of a capital or longer-term investment nature, and there are the money markets, which are essentially concerned with meeting short-term liquidity needs.

The importance of the negotiability which the presence of secondary markets adds to markets in financial securities has already been covered. But a further word should be added here about the fundamentally different functions of primary and secondary markets. A primary market is one which deals exclusively in new issues, where transactions are essentially between a borrower and lender. Secondary market trading, in contrast, takes place between two lenders, where one will transfer his right to repayment to another.

This book also includes chapters on two other forms of financial market, namely foreign exchange markets and futures and options markets. The inclusion of the first group is clearly essential to any book which pretends to cover the whole range of international financial markets, since each international transaction must of necessity entail a foreign exchange transaction. The markets in financial futures and options fall into a different category. They are not exclusively international, but have developed in recent years from the commodities markets to perform a very similar function, namely the mitigation of risk. They operate in parallel with the other financial markets, and indeed to a large degree the transactions are linked to similar transactions on one or more of the other markets. However, it seems more appropriate to separate them for presentation purposes.

International markets

Mention has been made of two factors which strongly influence the structure and efficiency of markets – communications and regulations. It might perhaps be argued that a prerequisite of the truly international market would be a maximisation of the former and a minimisation of the latter. This is because, by definition, international markets involve transactions which transcend national frontiers, and the operation of these could only be impeded by the existence of regulatory measures, generally of government imposition, such as exchange and fiscal controls. The existence of simultaneous communication facilities for market information will, on the other hand, greatly assist the efficiency of those markets.

In the ultimate sense, international markets might be expected to adhere to the concept of a single global seamless market operating on a twenty-four hour basis at different financial centres in several time zones around the world. But, in reality, this happens relatively infrequently. An obvious exception are the closely related markets for foreign exchange and short-term deposits in the various Euro-currencies which, as one might expect, are the harbingers of inter-nationalisation. After all, at the front end of every international transaction is a related transaction in foreign exchange, with mature markets for the United States dollar and an increasing number of other major currencies existing around the globe. But at the other extreme, although there are an increasing number of international equities which are traded at more than one financial centre in the various time zones around the world, and while the markets in which they trade are frequently accorded the description 'global equities markets', in reality this is rather a grand title for markets which are hardly out of their infancy. There is a huge gulf between 'international' equities markets, in the sense of satisfying the Euromoney definition – securities which are traded in one or more market outside their market of domicile – and a global seamless market. A similar reservation could be applied to the international bond and credit markets. Although far more mature in historic terms, such bonds and credits merely need to be traded exclusively in one offshore centre in order to be accorded their 'Euro-' prefix, while foreign bonds or credits are no more than loans raised in the currency of one foreign country. More often than not, so-called 'international' markets are far from global in structure.

CHAPTER TWO

Aspects of change in contemporary financial markets

The process of structural change which pervades contemporary financial markets has been under way for virtually three decades. It could be said to date from the inception, in the late 1950s, of the first truly international financial markets, the Eurocurrency and Eurobond markets, as American banks came to London to exploit the growing pool of offshore dollars which had emerged from the consecutive US balance of payments deficits following the Second World War. Before embarking on an analysis of this process, a few words can be added which emphasise its contemporary nature.

International financial markets are not an entirely new phenomenon. After all, massive investment flows from Europe to the New World, for example, had existed throughout the nineteenth century and up to the outbreak of the First World War. This process was well documented in an article appearing in the centenary issue of The Financial Times, which focused on the floating of New York State bonds in 1817 to finance the building of the 'Big Ditch', the Erie Canal. These bonds were the first issued by an American state to be quoted in London, and the greater part of the $US 7 million issue was taken up by British investors. Twenty-five years earlier, the State of Louisiana had been purchased from France on the back of a $US 11.25 million issue of stock carrying a coupon of 6 per cent and funded mainly in London, Paris and Amsterdam. Subsequent issues of bonds financed the building of railroads across the United States and then the mining of gold in California. Most investors were British, followed by the Dutch and the Germans, with France preferring to direct its savings towards areas such as Russia and Turkey where it had more direct political and economic interests. A later stage was the issue of US 'blue chip' industrial shares, such a US Steel, Eastman Kodak, General Electric and United Fruit. However, these investments largely came to a halt during the First World War, and it was another forty years before they were replaced by similar investments in the opposite direction.

In analysing the nature of this contemporary process of change, several distinct but interrelated phenomena can be identified. There is the fundamental trend towards internationalisation itself, which can be exemplified in at least three ways. It can perhaps be described most graphically through an assessment of progress towards that elusive concept of the global, seamless market which offers a broad choice of securities, all being traded through a twenty-four hour time span in a large number of financial centres in time zones stretching from the Far East through Europe to the United States and back to the Far East. Parallel to this, on the supply side of the financial equation, is a globalisation of portfolios by risk-averse investors, who recognise that a greater diversity in the trends in economic fundamentals between major countries will result in a greater need to invest in those areas. Finally, there has been an enormous increase in the presence of financial intermediaries, such as banks and other institutions, outside their home markets.

The second major theme relates directly to the changing role played by the same intermediaries in the provision of credit during the 1980s. This is illustrated by the evolution away from directly negotiated bank credits and syndicated loans towards securitisation borrowings, largely in the form of commercial paper and international bonds. A by-product of this has been a less specialised structure among credit intermediaries, as competition between banks, securities houses, other domestic institutions, and their foreign counterparts reaches new peaks each day.

The third theme has been an unprecedented propensity to product innovation, with a profusion of major new financial instruments – mostly taking the form of off balance sheet commitments. Simultaneously, certain other instruments which are by no means so newly-created have also dramatically increased their role in the financial structure.

These are the manifestations of this contemporary wave of change, but it is also important to consider the causal factors which have brought them about, that is to say the true motivators of this evolution. Macroeconomic developments since the Second World War have certainly been instrumental. After all, it was the flow of dollars out of the United States immediately after the war which brought about the Eurodollar. There has also been a marked increase in the propensity of governments to deregulate, that is to relax rules governing financial transactions across national frontiers. Unquestionably, the rationale behind this has been strongly political. In addition there has been the continuous wave of technological innovation in communications, which has come through increased use of electronic computerised techniques.

All these factors have led to a tremendous enhancement in competition and a multiplication in the volume of daily transactions on markets worldwide. In the sense that international financial markets now offer a broader and more flexible range of instruments both for borrowing as well as for hedging interest and exchange rate exposures, the result has also been an improvement in efficiency. Finally, a need has been created for all countries to take a new approach towards the regulation of conduct in internationalised markets in the interest of protecting the consumer. The United Kingdom's Financial Services Act, enacted by parliament in 1986, was a first attempt to meet this need.

Only a few years ago, financial innovation seemed to be of either actual or prospective importance, principally in North America and the London-based Euromarkets. Although Germany and Switzerland regulated_neither interest rates nor cross-border capital flows, their low inflation, universal banking, and concentrated domestic markets appeared to leave little room for financial change. In Japan, France and Italy, credit and international capital controls were thought to stifle change. But as things turned out, financial pressures were building in the latter group. This resulted in internationalisation stepping up competition in all major financial markets. In general, it may be observed that where competition is most intense, innovation is most advanced, notably in the Euro, US and UK markets. In concentrated markets where competition is less, however, innovation tends to lag.

Internationalisation

As previously mentioned, three contemporary factors seem best to exemplify the process of internationalisation in financial markets – the concept of the global market, the globalisation of portfolios, and the powerful tendency for banks and other financial institutions to set up a presence outside of their own domestic markets.

Towards the concept of a global seamless market

When discussing the global integration of financial markets over the past three decades, what is under consideration for the most part is the changed pattern of borrowing in debt financing operations through the medium of the Eurocurrency and Eurobond markets. These markets, which for simplicity may be viewed as the international equivalents of domestic bond and money markets respectively, arose out of an increasing availability to borrowers during and after the late 1950s of offshore resources of US dollars at rates which were in many cases better than those quoted on domestic markets. This trend evolved to an extent that sovereign and corporate borrowers alike, dependent on their credit ratings, could have access to virtually unlimited resources in a variety of base currencies. In fact, it was only during the 1970s and 1980s as countries deregulated, causing a convergence of interest rates between the domestic and international markets which contributed in turn to the harmonisation of issuing costs and a marked qualitative uprating of international paper, that capital raising actively moved away from those offshore centres and back towards the major financial centres. In this way an integration took place.

Because these markets were essentially developed out of a void, they were able from the start to generate their own conventions, which were outside the bounds of the various national regulatory agencies. As these markets grew, so the foreign exchange markets developed apace. For many years, of course, transactions on international credit markets were conducted almost entirely in US dollars, and it was only as national regulations were relaxed that global markets in other major currencies began to emerge. Similarly, as foreign exchange markets have become more volatile, provoked not least by the massively increased flows of capital across borders, so the risk markets have grown up.

By comparison, the international equities market has yet to develop to anything like the same extent as the debt markets. The notion of a global market for equities provokes a vision of markets linked instantly by modern communications, with corporate borrowers raising their capital from a global pool, while the investors select from a vastly expanded international range of stocks. It is true that an increasing number of equities are being distributed and traded at more than one financial centre in different time zones throughout the world. There has also been a massive increase in the resources devoted to research in foreign shares. But to describe these as global equities markets is not yet accurate. While the international diversification of investment has led to approximately 1000 shares being listed officially in at least one market outside their home country at the end of 1986, only half of these fitted the Euromoney definition that at least one of the markets of listing had to be an active liquid market. So far the international equities market is very much centred upon London, where almost all of the 500 shares which fit the Euromoney definition are quoted on the International Stock Exchange. In fact, they represent about a third of London's total turnover volume. Meanwhile, only about one half of those shares are quoted by its chief competitor, the NASDAQ system in the United States, representing only 5 per cent of NASDAQ's turnover volume. Numbers elsewhere are even smaller.

While international trading of equities is made easier by telecommunications links between exchanges – such as those which exist between SEAQ International in London and NASDAQ in New York and between the Boston and Montreal exchanges, the claim that the global equities market is still in its infancy is a just one. Despite this, there are some notable achievements to record, for example the British Telecom privatisation issue of 1984, when £0.6 billion of the total £4 billion were placed in the United States, Canada, Switzerland and Japan, and the Nestlé sale of bearer participation certificates through an international bank syndicate, the forerunner of the Euro equities market. Meanwhile trading hours have been generally extended and further telecommunications links remain under discussion.

Several governments are actively promoting their home markets as international financial centres, while some appear to have liberalised their regulations only because financial institutions and their clients have shown an ability and readiness to move to less regulated foreign markets. Governments are also now pressing the claims of their own financial institutions for 'reciprocity' or 'national treatment' in foreign markets. All these motivations featured in London's 'Big Bang' of October 1986, which had the effect of eliminating fixed commissions and many traditional barriers from the UK equities markets, and which provoked a rush of newly permitted mergers, as many UK securities firms became owned by commercial banks or foreign institutions. The current initiative now under way within the European Communities which aims to achieve a single integrated financial market by 1992 is another evolutionary process provoked by similar concerns. A number of countries allow relatively easy foreign entry into domestic markets by branching or establishing a subsidiary, but formal or informal restrictions may make expansion or profitable operation difficult. For example, even the now-liberal British share the near-universal reluctance to accept foreign takeovers of major domestic banking institutions.

The globalisation of portfolios

Closely associated with this trend towards the global integration of financial markets, there has been an increase by financial managers in the proportion of foreign currency denominated assets in their portfolios as the institutionally managed funds have pursued policies of international portfolio diversification, both active and passive. Although this evolution has been generally observed for some years, it became increasingly apparent as the 1980s progressed. It is not yet clear whether any prolonged slowdown has resulted from the stock market crash of October 1987.

The motivations behind this trend have been varied, although risk aversion has clearly been important. There is also a more deep-seated reason for this cross-border investment – the existence of huge financial imbalances between countries, which could only be financed through accumulation of foreign assets by investors in the creditor nations on the encouragement of governments.

The easing of restraints on holdings of foreign assets and lending to foreign borrowers as part of the deregulatory process has naturally played an important role, not least in so far as these rules apply to pension funds and insurance companies. In the United Kingdom, which has been a pacemaker in this respect, the abolition of exchange controls in 1979 was a crucial turning point. Holdings of foreign securities by UK pension funds, which had represented about 5 per cent of their total assets at the end of 1978, had risen to 14 per cent by the end of 1985 (an increase of $16 billion) and to nearly 25 per cent by the end of 1986. At the end of 1984, some $40 billion of funds were managed within Britain on behalf of foreign residents, of which at least 70 per cent was invested abroad. The ceiling for foreign asset holdings in the portfolios of Japanese insurance companies and pension funds was raised to 10 per cent in 1980, and such investments currently represent about $10 billion. Even in Italy, which has not been at the forefront of the deregulatory evolution, the quite recently established unit trusts are now allowed to invest up to 10 per cent of their assets abroad without the need to subscribe to the usual penal deposit at the Banca d'Italia.

The pattern of institutional investment in the United States is legally determined by the Employee Retirement Income Security Act (ERISA) of 1974, which required investments of pension funds to be prudently diversified. While it was not explicit on the subject of international diversification, its enactment was followed by increased foreign investment. However, the crucial change came after 1981, when foreign banks were permitted to hold the title of foreign assets, thereby clearing away the previous need to transfer them physically into the United States. It has been estimated that about $18 billion has been invested abroad since 1974 (of which $8 billion is managed in the United Kingdom). But this still represents only about 3 per cent of the US pension funds' investments, and it seems quite likely that dollar-based portfolio managers will increasingly be seeking to emulate their overseas counterparts in finding opportunities to increase the foreign currency component in their portfolios. To an extent, they have already been doing this, despite deep and broad dollar asset markets, and regardless of a high liability concentration in dollars.

As a general rule, it might be argued that a greater diversification of investments in portfolios should reduce the exposure to risk. At the same time, there may be reasons for believing that some asset managers deliberately increase the risk exposure of portfolios they run in order to improve performance. The point is that there are many portfolio management techniques. Some may be viewed as passive, such as those which concentrate on various global indices, while others are far more active, in the sense that they will lay more stress on selection of stocks on an international basis in the hope of maximising the return. But even then there are different strategies, such as the 'bottom up' approach, which is basically a widened version of domestic portfolio management, and the 'top down' approach, which concentrates on macroeconomic factors at the primary level and on stock selection only at the secondary stage. The point is that the different styles of the various managers will appeal to those with varying perceptions of risk. And given that their instructions extend the discretion, some portfolio managers may hedge currency risk when acquiring assets abroad, although to do so would necessarily sacrifice all or most of any potential yield gain arising from interest rate differentials.

In many cases, interest yields available in most popular alternative currencies, such as the Japanese yen, Deutschmark and Swiss franc, have been substantially lower than for dollars. However, this return could be brought up to the level of a comparable dollar asset by the use of forward foreign exchange transactions of currency swaps. It should be stressed that the latter carry transaction costs, and these may mean that the investor's all-in return is inferior to that obtainable in dollars for an equivalent credit risk. This is probably why most cross-currency investments and borrowings are frequently unhedged. This implies that investors are intentionally carrying exchange rate risks in the hope of improving long-term yields on portfolios against those attainable in the base currency alone, remaining content to monitor markets so as to determine the appropriate time to take cover. Such behaviour has been the rule rather than the exception in the context of the massive flow of financial capital into the United States in the 1980s, an overwhelming majority of which is thought to have been exposed to exchange rate risk. One can presume that a greater part of such liquidity would previously have been invested in, say, Japanese domestic markets, in which case the growth of multinational portfolios would clearly have increased aggregate exposure to market risk.

International presence of banks and other financial institutions

A third aspect of internationalisation, which has reflected the changing needs of borrowers and investors alike, is the sharply increased presence of banks and other institutions outside their home markets. This evolution has taken two forms. There are those countries where foreign institutions have been operating for many years, where the effect has been that they have grown both in number and in relative importance. At the same time, there is now a new generation of countries, such as Australia, Canada and Sweden, which have only recently permitted or liberalised the activities of foreign banks. Table 2.1 gives examples of foreign banking presence in selected countries.

Foreign establishments as a rule carry out a high proportion of their business in foreign currency with non-residents or multinational companies than do the domestically-owned banks. In this respect such establishments have often played a prominent role in developing trade-related finance in minor market centres. Moreover, since they often cannot rely on a natural deposit base in the domestic currency of the country in which they choose to operate, these banks are major participants in wholesale money markets. For example, the term

Table 2.1   Foreign banking in selected countries

Host country	1960	1970	1980	end June 1985
Number of institutions				
Belgium	14	26	51	57
Canada	0	0	0	57
Italy	1	4	26	36
Netherlands	–	23	39	40
Switzerland	8	97	99	119
United Kingdom	51	95	214	293
Number of banking offices				
France	33	58	122	147
Germany	24	77	213	287
Japan	34	38	85	112
Luxembourg	3	23	96	106
United States	–	ca.50	579	783

Source: Bank for International Settlements, April 1986

federal funds market in the United States is dominated by the agencies and branches of foreign banks, and similarly in many other centres foreign banks are large purchasers of funds in the local interbank market. Table 2.2 shows foreign banks' assets in selected countries.

Foreign establishments are also likely to transfer innovations across centres. US banks, for example, have often marketed in foreign countries new instruments – such as asset sales and packaged loans – similar to those originally developed in the United States.

With respect to the integration of domestic and international markets, foreign establishments have internationalised domestic financial activity by undertaking business abroad such as the under-writing of securities which their head offices cannot carry out in their country of origin. This can result indirectly in the development of new market instruments, as in the case of note issuance facilities (NIFs).

Securitisation

Just as one characteristic of this evolution has been the opening, integration, and internationalisation of financial markets with a grow-

Table 2.2   Foreign banks' assets in selected countries
(per cent in total assets of all banks operating in those countries)

Host country	1960	1970	1980	end June 1985
Belgium	8.2	22.5	41.5	51.0
Canada	–	–	–	6.3
France	7.2	12.3	15.0	18.2
Germany	0.5	1.4	1.9	2.4
Italy	–	–	0.9	2.4
Japan	–	1.3	3.4	3.6
Luxembourg	8.0	57.8	85.4	85.4
Netherlands	–	–	17.4	23.6
Switzerland	–	10.3	11.1	12.2
United Kingdom	6.7	37.5	55.6	62.6
United States	–	5.8	8.7	12.0

Source: Bank for International Settlements, April 1986

ing diversification of financial instruments – manifested through the concept of the global, seamless market in foreign exchange, bonds and prime industrial stocks from Tokyo through to San Francisco and back to Tokyo, making possible, and even mandatory, the global management of portfolios – so a second feature has been an adjustment in the relative importance of various channels of financial intermediation through a shift of credit flows from bank lending to marketable debt instruments. Here the large international banks, in particular, have lost their advantage relative to international securities markets as the channel for high-grade borrowing.

This process of disintermediation or securitisation has been stimulated by several specific factors. In the first place, the sharp fall in OPEC investible surpluses reduced the supply of bank deposits while the compensating contraction in syndicated bank credits restrained access to credit by major less developed borrowing countries, contributing to the international debt crisis. This certainly emphasised the desirability for liquidity and marketability in bank assets while also encouraging banks to strengthen their capital base by stepping up long-term debt issuance. At the same time, until late 1986 at least, there had been virtually no recent difficulties in the bond markets, not even with paper issued by problem debtor countries. Similarly, the switch in the role of the United States during the term of the Reagan presidency from the world's largest net provider of funds to its largest net user, combined with the growth of current account surpluses in Europe and Japan, was also consistent with the increased use of marketable debt instruments in international financial markets.

The decline in long-term interest rates from the abnormally high levels of 1974 and 1980 in particular, with a reappearance of positive real interest rates and positively sloped yield curves, has not only enhanced the appeal of longer-term bonds to investors but has also made it more attractive for market-makers to hold and trade inventories of such bonds. Finally, for a variety of reasons, mainly associated with pressures on bank balance sheets consequential upon both the debt crisis and the general deflation of the 1980s – which have taken particular toll of shipping, property, agricultural, energy and other commercial sectors – banks have seen their credit ratings slip and funding costs rise. Such changes, on top of intermediation costs associated with reserve requirements, capital and overheads, mean that it has become cheaper for prime non-bank borrowers, such as governments and corporations, to raise funds directly from investors through the securities markets at a lower cost than from banks, on the basis of borrowings free of reserve requirements and insurance fees. It should also be noted that commercial banks have themselves become major issuers and purchasers of securities as well as mere arrangers and managers of new issues.

Because this propensity of the highest quality borrowers to turn increasingly to direct credit markets has had a direct effect on the quality of the banks' loan portfolios, banks have been left with the option of either earning a reduced spread or seeking out other areas for profitable expansion. This has frequently led to new products, such as fee-based services or off balance sheet activities. While securitisation reduces demand for traditional bank loans, it can still create demand for other bank services. An example would be the potential demand for back-up facilities faced by borrowers and lenders in securitised markets who perceive rollover risks. Up until mid-1985, this demand was met by such devices as note issuance facilities (NIFs), involving medium-term bank commitments to purchase short-term paper that otherwise failed to sell within specified terms. The use of these rose rapidly until superseded by another innovation – Euro commercial paper (Euro CP), which is now normally issued without the direct back-ups and ratings which are common when selling paper in United States markets.

More generally, securitisation has been fostered by the maturing and increasing efficiency of the Eurobond markets. Initially segmented, these markets are now broad and homogeneous, with standardised trading practices. It has become common practice to issue bonds through multinational syndicates of large banks with well-developed placing power, and this increases the possibility of raising significant amounts of capital at short notice. While many debt instruments are tailored to the needs of specific investors or borrowers, most new issues are still priced according to one of only three basic formulae – fixed rate, floating rate and 'convertible' – permitting price comparisons, arbitrage and a unified price structure.

The secondary market for Eurobonds has grown so much that it now ranks second only to the US domestic market in terms of its depth and liquidity. The main market-makers are major international banks. The Eurobond market is almost entirely free of official regulation; instead it is self-regulated by the Association of International Bond Dealers (AIBD). Both the primary and secondary markets operate through standard clearing mechanisms (Euroclear and CEDEL), producing low-cost dealing and delivery.

The organisation of short-term securities markets is less clearly defined than that of the Eurobond market, but the development of new forms of back-up facilities is clearly in response to preferences of both borrowers and investors for increased flexibility. Thus the various forms of NIFs, in assuring long-term access to funds, offer the borrower the choice of when to draw and repay, how much to draw, in which form and in what currency the drawing will be made, and what reference rate will be used (LIBOR, prime rate, LIBID, CD rate, etc). For the investors, securities issued under these facilities combine relatively high yields with short maturities and therefore relatively limited price and credit risks.

The cost savings and liquidity benefits from securitisation have enabled firms worldwide to cut their reliance on direct bank financing. In the United States, for example, net commercial paper and bond issuance by private non-financial corporations eclipsed their borrowing from banks by a margin of four to one in the first half of 1986, whereas bank loans were in the lead as recently as 1984. Financial and non-financial firms in the United States are now securitising mortgages, automobile loans, and consumer credit receivables – assets which had previously been illiquid and difficult to trade. In international markets, meanwhile, securitised lending now accounts for over 80 per cent of gross new credit arranged, compared with about 50 per cent in the mid-1970s. Syndicated bank lending has declined both in value terms and as a share of total international lending.

Table 2.3   International credit and capital markets

$US billions	1981	1982	1983	1984	1985	1986	1987
International bonds and notes	44.0	71.7	72.1	108.1	164.5	221.5	175.6
of which: Floating rate notes	7.8	12.6	15.3	34.1	55.9	47.8	12.0
Convertible bonds	4.1	2.7	6.8	8.5	7.3	7.5	17.7
Syndicated Euro bank loans	96.5	100.5	51.8	36.6	19.0	29.8	87.9
of which: Managed loans	–	11.2	13.7	6.5	2.4	N/A	N/A
Euronotes (NIFs etc.)	1.0⁻	2.3	3.3	18.9	50.3	71.1	70.2
Total	141.5	174.5	127.2	163.6	233.8	322.4	333.7

Source: Bank of England *Quarterly Bulletin*

The growing use of securities markets is also producing a closer integration of some market sectors than would have been possible if the same financial flows had taken the form of bank credits. One effect has been to bring the equity and the bond markets closer together through the use of convertible bonds, bonds with equity warrants and FRNs issued by banks with features which enable them to be treated as capital for supervisory purposes. The latter have enabled banks to raise quasi-capital from a much wider range of investors.

Another effect of securitisation has been to link the capital markets more closely to the foreign exchange markets. Bonds have been issued with currency conversion options, with warrants exercisable into bonds in a different currency or with dual-currency features. In all these cases the bonds offer a combination of a capital market asset and a foreign exchange or option contract.

Product innovation

Product innovation, in the contemporary context, usually refers to the proliferation in the off balance sheet activity of banks. This is a way of describing that part of a bank's business, often fee-based, which does not generally involve booking assets and taking deposits. Examples would be the trading of swaps, options, foreign exchange forwards, standby commitments and letters of credit. This is by no means a new direction, since financial institutions have long engaged in a wide range of these activities, but trading in many such services has become markedly more active in recent years. The most important examples of these have probably been loan commitments, bankers' acceptances, forward foreign exchange transactions, financial futures, guarantees of various types and agency and fiduciary services. In addition there have been the genuine product innovations, such as note issuance facilities (NIFs) which gradually gave way to commercial paper, currency swaps and interest rate swaps, foreign currency and interest rate options, and forward rate agreements (FRAs).

Many of these instruments have the effect of unbundling and repackaging some of the characteristics of existing financial instruments – that is to say, their yield, price risk, credit risk, country risk, liquidity, marketability, pricing conventions, size, duration and so on – so as to satisfy an underlying need to hedge price, interest rate and exchange rate risks. A report commissioned by the Bank for International Settlements (the Cross Report) published in April 1986, classified these product innnovations into four groups according to their functional nature:

1. Risk-transferring innovations
   These comprise the new instruments or techniques which allow economic agents to transfer among themselves the price of credit risks inherent in financial positions.

2. Liquidity-enhancing innovations
   In general, these consist of those instruments which increase the 'moneyness', the negotiability or transferability of existing financial instruments or new instruments with enhanced liquidity properties.

3. Credit-generating (or debt-generating) innovations
   These comprise those innovations which broaden the access of economic agents to credit supplies. They may either result in a general increase in the volume of all credit or else a shift from traditional credit channels for some agents – say, bank borrowings – to non-traditional channels – say, the capital markets.

4. Equity-generating innovations
   These broaden the access of economic agents to equity finance. Some innovations may result in an observed greater leveraging in the economy; in effect a greater reliance on debt relative to equity, with consequential actual contraction of equity positions.

In general terms, the growth of these activities can be attributed to the same forces which stimulated the trend towards securitisation, that is the changing regulatory environment – technological expansion, market volatility, shifts in current account balances, and growing competition among financial institutions. More specifically, the exceptional economic circumstances of the early 1980s – high inflation, interest and exchange rate volatility and the sharp changes in creditworthiness of large economic sectors were major factors, with innovations themselves being no more than an attempt at restoring a preexisting situation. But there have been two additional influences. Firstly, certain constraints have been imposed on banks' balance sheets, notably regulatory pressure to improve capital ratios and the rate of return earned on assets. Secondly, for similar reasons, banks have sought ways to hedge interest rate risk without inflating balance sheets, as would occur with the use of the inter-bank market.

Such innovations have not only changed the nature of specific problems faced by central banks; they have also affected the policy tools which those institutions customarily employ. Policy responses need to be much more rapid under present circumstances than previously. They may also call for closer co-operation between banking authorities and those responsible for the regulation of capital markets at national and international levels. Because of the market's ability to innovate rapidly and flexibly, it can now be rather more difficult than in the past to design policy changes which are durable in terms of the results which they achieve, and which also lack unwanted side effects.

This was confirmed in the report on the supervisory implications arising from the management of the off balance sheet exposures of banks, which followed a study of the prudential aspects of banking innovation and was published by the Banks for International Settlements' Supervisors' Committee early in 1986 alongside the better-known and previously mentioned Cross Report. Besides concluding that this trend posed urgent challenges to supervisory authorities, the report recommended that central banks should concern themselves with other far-reaching policy issues that arise from the process of innovation and structural change, that is in the fields of macro-prudential policy, monetary policy, and financial reporting and statistics.

It may well be argued that a more stable environment would reduce many of the incentives for product innovation. One area where such a reduction might not apply, however, would be that of technological advance, both in terms of the 'hardware' aspects of computer and communications systems and of the 'software' aspects of sophisticated financial models and financial product designs.

The motivations for change

Macroeconomic developments

Earlier macroeconomic forces which influenced the contemporary evolution in financial markets were the sharp rise in inflation and increased short-term volatility of interest rates and exchange rates in the mid-1970s. Tables 2.4, 2.5 and 2.6 demonstrate these trends in consumer prices, three-month interest rates and exchange rates respectively.

These trends had resulted from swings in oil and commodity prices, the large current account imbalances and differing policy responses by governments to the eventual breakdown of the Bretton Woods system and the first oil shock of 1973–4. The OPEC current account surplus increased from $7.7 billion to $59.5 billion, the $8.4 billion surplus of the Group of Seven was transformed into a $13.5 billion deficit, and the $12.9 billion surplus for all the 24 OECD countries was transformed into a deficit of $25.9 billion. While the fiscal and monetary policies of both the United States and Japan were severely restrictive during 1974, and the general tendency in Europe was also restrictive, especially in monetary policy, the recession there began somewhat later and policies differed between countries. For example, both Britain and Italy ran substantial budget deficits in 1974 and they were enjoined by Germany in the following year. By the end of 1975, industrialised and oil-importing developing countries alike were prepared to allow their rates of economic growth to recover pre-oil shock levels through the use of recycled 'petrodollars'. But what was important to the development of international financial markets was that out of an estimated $317 billion cash surplus for oil exporters in the period from 1974 to 1980, $147 billion was recycled through private sector banks, largely through the Euromarkets. This preference on the part of deficit countries was borne of a desire to avoid the politically unacceptable constraints on domestic economic policies frequently imposed as a part of official rescue operations, even at the cost of higher interest charges. Table 2.7 shows current account balances in the Group of Seven, OECD, OPEC and non-oil producing developing countries between 1970 and 1980.

Table 2.4 Consumer prices

	1970	1971	1972	1973	1974	1975	1976	1977	1978	1979	1980
United States	5.9	4.3	3.3	6.2	11.0	9.1	5.8	6.5	7.7	11.3	13.5
Japan	7.7	6.1	4.5	11.7	24.5	11.8	9.3	8.1	3.8	3.6	8.0
Germany	3.4	5.3	5.5	6.9	7.0	6.0	4.5	3.7	2.7	4.1	5.5
France	5.2	5.5	6.2	7.3	13.7	11.8	9.6	9.4	9.1	10.8	13.6
United Kingdom	6.4	9.4	7.1	9.2	16.0	24.2	16.5	15.8	8.3	13.4	18.0
Italy	5.0	4.8	5.7	10.8	19.1	17.0	16.8	17.0	12.1	14.8	21.2
Canada	3.4	2.8	4.8	7.6	10.9	10.8	7.5	8.0	8.9	9.2	10.2
Group of Seven	5.7	5.0	4.3	7.5	13.3	11.0	8.0	8.0	7.0	9.3	12.2

Source: OECD *Economic Outlook*

Table 2.5 Three-month interest rates

	1970	1971	1972	1973	1974	1975	1976	1977	1978	1979	1980
United States	7.18	4.66	4.43	8.73	10.50	5.82	5.05	5.54	7.93	11.20	13.36
Japan	–	6.41	4.72	7.16	12.54	10.67	6.98	5.86	4.36	5.86	10.93
Germany	9.42	7.15	5.61	12.14	9.90	4.96	4.25	4.37	3.70	6.69	9.54
France	8.93	6.29	5.51	9.13	13.02	7.84	8.69	9.22	8.16	9.48	12.20
United Kingdom	–	–	–	–	–	10.56	11.62	8.06	3.70	13.59	16.10
Italy	7.38	5.76	5.18	6.93	14.57	10.64	15.68	14.03	11.49	11.86	17.17
Canada	5.99	3.56	3.56	5.47	7.83	7.40	8.87	7.33	8.67	11.68	12.80

Source: IMF *International Financial Statistics*

Table 2.6 Effective exchange rates (1970=100)

	1970	1971	1972	1973	1974	1975	1976	1977	1978	1979	1980
United States	100.0	97.6	90.6	83.1	85.2	84.3	88.7	88.3	80.7	79.0	79.2
Japan	100.0	102.2	114.1	122.8	114.9	111.4	116.0	128.3	157.8	146.4	140.9
Germany	100.0	103.6	106.9	119.2	125.4	127.4	133.5	143.9	153.0	162.4	164.1
France	100.0	98.3	101.4	106.1	99.0	109.1	104.3	99.6	99.6	101.9	102.9
United Kingdom	100.0	100.4	97.2	88.0	85.1	78.6	67.3	63.8	64.1	68.6	75.5
Italy	100.0	99.5	99.2	90.2	81.4	78.3	64.4	59.1	55.7	54.3	52.6
Canada	100.0	102.7	102.4	98.7	102.1	97.7	103.6	95.7	85.7	82.3	82.5

Source: IMF *International Financial Statistics*

Table 2.7 Current account balances ($US billions)

	1970	1971	1972	1973	1974	1975	1976	1977	1978	1979	1980
United States	2.3	–1.4	–5.8	7.2	2.0	18.1	4.2	–14.5	–15.4	–1.0	1.9
Japan	2.0	5.8	6.6	–0.1	–4.7	–0.7	3.7	10.9	16.5	–8.8	–10.7
Germany	–0.9	0.8	0.9	4.6	10.3	4.1	3.9	4.1	9.0	–6.0	–15.7
France	0.1	0.5	0.3	1.5	–3.9	2.7	–3.4	–0.4	7.0	5.2	–4.2
United Kingdom	2.0	2.7	0.5	–2.6	–7.9	–3.5	–1.6	–0.2	1.9	–1.6	7.2
Italy	0.8	1.6	2.0	–2.5	–8.0	–0.6	–2.8	2.5	6.2	5.5	–9.7
Canada	1.0	0.4	–0.3	0.3	–1.3	–4.6	–4.2	–4.1	–4.3	–4.2	–1.0
Group of Seven	7.3	10.4	4.2	8.4	–13.5	15.5	–0.2	–1.7	20.9	16.1	–32.2
OECD	6.5	9.5	8.2	12.9	–25.9	5.0	–15.2	–21.6	11.8	–28.9	–68.6
Non-oil producing countries	–6.7	–10.0	–6.0	–6.0	–23.5	–30.0	–17.5	–13.0	–26.0	–39.0	–60.0
OPEC	–	–	–	7.7	59.5	27.2	36.5	29.0	4.5	62.0	115.0

Source: OECD *Economic Outlook*

Then came the second oil shock of 1978–9, at a time when the outstanding debt of developing countries had already reached about $400 billion, of which about $130 billion had been in bank loans. The 1980 Annual Report of the Bank for International Settlements reported

'By contrast with 1974 banks are not starting out with relatively clean sheets but are already heavily burdened with third world risks. They may therefore have less scope than before to expand their international risk exposure more rapidly than their balance sheet totals. Conversely, the debt burdens of certain groups of countries vis-à-vis the international financial markets have increased substantially since 1974, which has certainly not helped their risk ratings.'

Despite this, by the end of 1982 the outstanding foreign currency debt of the developing countries had risen to $626 billion, of which $210 billion was to banks. A major effect was that the credit ratings of some countries completely collapsed and the debts of Mexico, Brazil and Argentina had to be rescheduled.

There are really two comments to be made here. The high incidence of imprudent lending in this period finally led to the global debt crisis of more recent years. Perhaps the most poignant observation that one can now make about this is the bizarre flow of capital away from the developing countries, which after all represent that part of the world market with the greatest growth potential, back to the developed industrialised countries. The consequences for worldwide growth are only too obvious. Secondly, it was this eight years of constant appeals for credit, above all to capital markets to meet the financial deficits, which spawned the outline of what could truly be called global financial markets. Even then, they only appeared as a patchwork of individually integrated financial instruments and channels of inter-mediation.

There followed the increased divergence of macroeconomic policies in the 1980s. The development of a large US budget deficit matched by tighter fiscal policies in Japan and Europe, with the concomitant sharp shift in the geographic pattern of net flows of international savings and investment as reflected in the distribution of current account imbalances, also generated an increase in the risk exposure of those financial intermediaries who failed to maintain a strict match in the term structure of their assets and liabilities and intensified the use of novel tools in the management of cash and interest rate risk. Exchange rate volatility has also stimulated demand for instruments to manage currency exposure.

Deregulatory measures

Another factor in the contemporary financial evolution has been the increasing propensity for national authorities to respond to inter-national pressures and join the drive towards deregulation of domestic financial markets. This process of changing the rules to suit the game, frequently described as 'moving the goalposts', came from a growing acknowledgement by governments of the declining efficiency, and even perverse consequences, of many pre-existing regulations and controls. It was perceived that a worldwide reduction of structural rigidities and other barriers to competition would stimulate a greater competitiveness between the national financial positions, and assure an equality of competitive conditions between all financial inter-mediaries, thereby decreasing costs of intermediation and making markets more efficient. The extension of banking supervision to a worldwide consolidated basis in the main industrial countries has also tended to reduce regulatory distortions in the international capital flow pattern.

The classical justification for regulation was described in a paper which was published in December 1986 by Morgan Guaranty Trust of New York in *World Financial Markets* as 'the need to protect the safety and soundness of a financial system from excessive risk-taking and mismanagement generally'. Governments recognise the need to step in and defend solvent financial institutions but demand the right to supervise and regulate them as a quid pro quo for providing lender of last resort facilities or deposit insurance.

The scope of these regulations had varied markedly between countries, mainly dependent on the philosophies of prevailing governments. They embraced various instruments of monetary policy, such as controls on interest rates and general credit, and restrictions on cross-border movements of capital. There were also reserve requirements as well as arbitrary prohibitions on the use of certain financial instruments. Some of these techniques, such as asset-holding (or reserve) requirements and differential credit limits, could also be used to help finance government deficits and fulfil a range of other preferred activities. Sometimes governments would regulate the banks, so as to prevent abuses and undue concentration, and to protect national ownership and control of financial institutions. When binding, such regulations typically prevent, or make more expensive, the extension of non-favoured loans, reduce bank competition, and lower interest rates.

Interest rate ceilings on the deposit and lending activities of key financial intermediaries had long been a problem on time deposits of less than one month maturity, for instance in the United States. In Japan their scope had extended even further. Credit controls had existed in several countries, usually only as a temporary instrument, most recently in the United Kingdom, France and Italy. Only in Japan, with its system of *ad hoc* window guidance, had they been a virtually permanent feature since shortly after the Second World War. But the most critical feature, in many respects, had been exchange controls and various other direct impediments to the market structure, such as limitations on entry of foreign players into domestic markets. There were also limitations imposed upon permitted product structures within certain domestic markets, generally a result of concern over inflationary pressures. Finally there were the fiscal impositions, such as withholding tax, which narrowed the scope of investment portfolios.

Just as the extent of previous regulations had varied widely between countries, so the nature and impetus of the deregulation in different domestic markets has differed as exchange controls have been abolished, interest rate ceilings have been phased-out, domestic markets have been opened for foreign financial institutions, product boundaries have been relaxed and taxes reduced. However, for some time after the inception of the Eurocurrency and Eurobond markets, preexisting regulations and controls still represented a considerable impediment to change. In consequence, links beween new international markets and individual domestic markets remained, in most cases, rather tenuous and incomplete.

The first powerful stimulants towards liberalisation and the eventual elimination of controls on cross-border capital movements, were really the dual shocks to the world's economy in 1973, when the Bretton Woods system broke down, entailing a move towards a flexible exchange rate regime, and then oil prices exploded for the first time. One year later, the United States took the initiative in completely dismantling their restrictions on capital inflows. While some other major oil-importing countries thought about relaxing controls on capital inflows to some extent, it was not really until 1979 and into the early 1980s that a second more prolonged and far-reaching wave of deregulation brought this about. This time it was the United Kingdom and Switzerland which scrapped their exchange controls on capital outflows. Although Japan amended its Foreign Exchange Control Act in 1980 and then revised its Banking Law in 1982, it was only really after 1984, when the US Treasury put pressure on Japan's Ministry of Finance to internationalise the yen and phase out controls on the domestic financial system, that any significant progress took place in the western world's most regulated economy. And apart from Switzerland's abolition of exchange controls in 1979–80, continental Europe had also been slow in embracing this evolution. While Germany did complete the abolition of controls on capital flows in 1981, when restrictions on purchases by non-residents of the domestic bonds and money-market instruments were lifted, it has otherwise, in company with Switzerland, proceeded at a distinctly measured pace. For example, foreign entry into the German domestic markets was not eased until 1985. The Italians showed even more reluctance to liberalise, as did the French until the Chirac government came to power intent on reversing their traditions. It remains a point of some speculation as to whether political pressures which now prevail within the European Communities, perhaps in belated recognition of potential economic gains, will result in the single integrated market in financial services by 1992 envisaged by President of the Commission Jacques Delors.

Other regulatory changes more directly related to banking than the facilitation of cross-border movements have also contributed to bringing domestic and international financial markets more closely together. In the United States the integration between the Euromarkets and domestic markets was stimulated by deregulation of domestic interest rate ceilings and the opening of International Banking Facilities (IBFs) – a means by which US banks may use their domestic offices to offer foreign customers deposit and loans services free of Federal Reserve requirements and interest rate regulations. As part of the Chirac reversal of previous traditions in 1985, France permitted banks to issue French franc and ECU certificates of deposit on the domestic market. Issues of certificates of deposit denominated in foreign currency were sanctioned later. In the Netherlands, too, deregulatory measures took effect in 1986 which allowed domestic and foreign banks to issue a wider range of financial instruments, not least certificates of deposit. Meanwhile, foreign-owned banking entities which are domiciled in Germany have been allowed to manage foreign DM bond issues, and an Italian Eurolira bond market is now operating.

Germany had offered a rare example in the area of interest rate and credit controls as early as 1967, when all interest rate controls were abolished – credit controls were already absent. Elsewhere at this time interest rates on demand deposits, and often also on time deposits, were generally regulated. It was only more recently that interest rate controls came to be viewed in many countries as unfair to small depositors while credit controls were seen as penalising private investment. Although competitive forces have militated against the continuance of both, it is the United States and Japan which appear to have been slowest in deregulating in this sector. Although there are no longer any controls on time deposits or credit in the United States, banks are still prohibited from paying interest on ordinary demand deposits of less than 30 days' maturity. Since 1983, however, negotiable order of withdrawal (NOW) and super-NOW accounts have been available to individuals. Interest rate controls and fiscal preferences of the sort which have distorted the choices of savers from the household sector still persist in both Japan and France, although both are taking action to lift them over the next few years. Credit controls are also on the wane as monetary policies increasingly rely on open-market operations.

In recent years, largely in response to pressure from domestic constituencies, regulators have allowed a greater range of new products into major financial markets. In the case of Japan, of course, the negotiations between the Ministry of Finance and the United States Treasury in 1984 were an additional crucial factor, although there was a domestic rationale in so far as the markets needed to be modernised to help finance a rising budget deficit. The most tangible results have already been mentioned. Other reforms have included the opening of a somewhat restricted offshore banking market, an easing of access by non-resident borrowers to the domestic issues market and the Euroyen bond markets, and the lifting of the *de facto* restriction on the management of Euroyen bonds issued to Japanese banks. Limits on certificate of deposit issues have been relaxed, and active short-term markets in treasury bills, money market certificates, bankers acceptances and commercial paper have all been introduced. Moreover, the Tokyo Stock Exchange has launched a futures market in government bonds. In Germany, meanwhile, the abolition in May 1985 of limitations on foreign issues within Germany to straight fixed bond rates and the subsequent sanctioning of certificates of deposit means that, with the exception of DM money market fund units, all main types of instrument, such as FRNs, zero coupon bonds and convertible bonds can now be traded on the German domestic market. Similar decisions were taken by the authorities in the Netherlands, whose markets are closely linked to those of West Germany. In line with the Chirac initiatives, France reopened the French franc Eurobond markets, permitted commercial paper, and sanctioned the launch of futures in a French government bond contract.

A number of other institutional barriers which have segmented the domestic and international sectors of the securities markets have also been broken down. The most significant step in this direction took place in the United States in 1984, when withholding taxes on interest paid to non-resident investors on government and corporate bonds were finally lifted. This was followed shortly thereafter by similar measures in the United Kingdom, France and Germany. The formal or informal restrictions that still exist in several countries, most notably in France and Italy, are also gradually fading. Finally, another change back in 1982, which brought the United States more closely in line with practices in international securities markets, is worthy of mention. This was the introduction of 'shelf registration' in lieu of registration requirements with the SEC for each new bond issue. Finally, the easing of rules applied to domestic bond issues by Japanese entities, many of which had previously found foreign channels preferable, has had a substantial effect.

Still on the agenda is the problem of the continued separation of the banks and securities houses, which in the United States comes within the purview of the Glass-Steagall Act, and in Japan is governed by Article 65 of the Securities and Exchange Law. It is true to say that there has been some slight erosion in restrictions in the United States, and several US banks have applications pending for permission to underwrite commercial paper, the full range of municipal revenue bonds, and asset-backed securities. However, even if these applications are approved, US banks would still be prohibited from underwriting corporate securities in domestic markets. Anomalously, thanks to a 'grandfather' clause, some foreign banks which entered the United States before 1978 can engage in a wider variety of activities – including securities business – than US banks. In Japan, the authorities recently allowed nine foreign banks into trust banking and several into the securities business through subsidiaries with 50 per cent foreign bank ownership. Remarkably, Japan's city and long-term credit banks cannot enter either area. The Japanese government, banks, and securities companies see that traditional demarcation lines are not viable forever, but they seem to be waiting for US abandonment of Glass-Steagall before significant amendment of their analogous Article 65.

Technological change

Another fundamental force underlying change and innovation in financial markets over the past twenty-five years has been the world-wide revolution in information processing, computing and telecommunications technology. This has come about through the development of increasingly more sophisticated computers, with their widespread application in the provision of worldwide information, which has strongly influenced progress towards greater perfection in goods and financial markets alike and led to much higher trading activity. Meanwhile, their use in the processing of transactions has lowered costs to a fraction of their earlier levels. The costs of data processing and communications themselves continue to decline dramatically, at the rates of approximately 25 per cent and 15 per cent per annum respectively, and there is certainly no end in sight.

Low-cost, instantaneous telecommunications have been vital in bringing together financial market participants worldwide to create truly global financial markets with the possibility of 24-hour trading. One of the most important results of this growth in technology has been the significant increase in the efficiency with which information is disseminated and interpreted in both cash and futures sectors of world financial markets. This brings greater breadth and depth to trading. It also encourages financial institutions to make markets in further new instruments, since providers of innovations are enabled to match up directly or indirectly with end-users who have previously only enjoyed isolated markets.

This ability for all market participants throughout the world to receive information on economic and political happenings almost as they occur has also led to a change in one of the peripheral functions of markets. At one time, when information dissemination was slower, it tended to be channelled more through the trading institutions at the centre of markets, and especially the cash markets, since these also specialised in the interpretation of information for clients. The institutions have now lost so much of their control over these processes, and an increasingly broad range of financial firms outside the central core of markets, as well as commercial firms and individual investors, has equal and ready access to timely information along with the capacity to interpret it.

These developments raise a secondary consideration – market volatility. The notion that efficient distribution and interpretation of information will stabilise markets depends upon the assumption that there will be adequate dissemination of the interpretation of new information, that is to say, that there is more than an average chance that the market will view it 'correctly'. For example, a modest increase in dollar interest rates would probably mean that the dollar itself would settle at a higher level, thereby prompting traders and investors to buy dollars and bid its value even higher in the exchanges.

The alternative hypothesis, that efficient distribution of information might destabilise markets, rests upon the notion that the process just described does not, and probably cannot, work quite so neatly. While traders and investors may get the direction of change right in many cases, they rarely get the amount right. Thus it is difficult to determine, at the time a market move starts, when it will stop or, more precisely, when it ought to stop (that is to say, when a new 'equilibrium' has been reached). Moreover, many traders believe that the market's response to any new information, at least in the short term, will first depend on how the new information compares to the market's expectations, and perhaps even more on how the other market participants are likely to interpret it rather than on what is the 'correct' interpretation. Such tendencies of traders and speculators have accumulative effects on markets, as well as making them vulnerable to the pressures of those speculators willing and able to commit sizeable amounts to speculative short-term positions. In this way, a more efficient distribution of information, simultaneously available to a larger number of speculators, will contribute to a greater rather than reduced short-term market volatility.

The practice of using 'technical analysis' (charting and related techniques) to forecast price movements can be viewed in much the same way. Technical analysts believe that better insights into future price movements will be obtained by studying how prices have behaved in the past rather than by studying why prices have acted in a certain fashion. Based on past observations, analysts derive what essentially are rules of thumb about future movements, based on methodology ranging from the fairly simple to the highly complex. Computer technology is heavily utilised in the manipulation of large volumes of data, producing charts as the end product. The fundamental idea is that markets exhibit characteristic patterns of movement which, because they repeat themselves, can be a basis for trading. Such 'rules of thumb' will generally dictate specific actions based on certain preconditions.

For present purposes, it is essential to note that current technology allows quick and efficient dissemination of the price information on which these techniques are based, and that the use of the techniques themselves has become fairly pervasive. Even those that do not have the capability to perform technical analysis themselves already have access to it through the electronic information distribution media or other sources. As with the more fundamental analyses, there tends to be some degree of similarity in the conclusions which are reached by the broad community of technical analysts and a knowledge of this among the trading community. Thus a ready belief that the predictions of technical analysts will materialise is often stimulated in a market, causing some to trade accordingly even if they are somewhat dubious of the predictions. This is a process which can generate self-fulfilling momentum to price movements and also increase the amplitude of the price movements. For example, let us suppose that it was widely reported in the market that DM2.50 was regarded by technical analysts as a 'support level' for the dollar on a typical day and that market participants with long dollar positions placed stop-loss orders at this exchange rate. If the dollar then fell through this level, large sales of dollars would be generated, and continue for a time without apparently being justified by changes in economic fundamentals, thereby increasing the volatility in the market.

There are other advantages, many of which could not have been developed but for the technological breakthroughs that massive improvements in computing and information processing have facilitated. Market-makers are now able to design and continuously price new instruments with quite complex financial structures. They are similarly able to monitor continuously those exposures which they have generated from running books in these instruments, besides both designing and carrying through the complex hedges for them. This is typically the case with financial futures and options contracts, where trading volume has multiplied in the 1980s and technological availability allows low-cost hedging of exposure to various economic risks. Because today's optimal hedging strategies require the processing of data from a wide variety of markets both at home and abroad, and trading opportunities are very often short-lived, speed is of the essence. It is for this reason, too, that the treasury managers of large corporations could never hope to monitor their complex exposures adequately without the benefits of technological advances.

Improved information flows have probably also contributed to reduced earnings and increasingly competitive pricing structures in more traditional areas of business, thereby encouraging financial institutions to pursue more innovative lines. The widespread diffusion of rate screens, for example, has significantly reduced the costs to market participants of searching for the best prevailing market price. Margins of market-makers can then be cut, enabling financial firms to be more inclined to provide a greater range of innovative, customised products that, at least in the initial stages, would otherwise trade at wider margins.

Enhanced competition

Growing competition in international financial markets is another factor which has increased the pressure for innovation and structural change. There are at least two sources of the rise in competition over and above the world-wide trend towards deregulation, and these have both direct and indirect effects in the process of innovation. Reference has just been made to the rise in competition fostered by technological change as the developers of new technology seek to exploit its advantage in as many markets as possible. The second source are the shifting patterns of savings and investment, which may place pressure on those financial institutions which are experiencing an erosion of their traditional market to innovate and compete more aggressively for a larger share of their traditional market or expand into new areas of business, and on those institutions which are resident in geographic areas with excess liquidity to seek new ways of deploying such resources.

This increased competition has come in two forms: that between different national financial systems and that between banks and non-bank financial institutions within national financial systems. Both tendencies have been supported by a global regulatory environment which has become increasingly sympathetic to deregulation and liberalisation. Technological advances have played a role here too, since telecommunications equipment and computers are now commonly available to all enterprises, regardless of their business traditions. Such facilities level the playing field of financial competition by allowing any company from any business tradition to generate and control offers of generic versions of financial services – loans, deposits, credit cards and insurance are all important examples – to the company's existing customer base. This gives rise to the concept of the 'financial supermarket', and the exploitation of such a strategy has led to intense competition around customer bases. Any company with a large existing customer base, such as a large retail outlet, is at an immediate advantage in such a contest, even if it has no tradition of financial services.

Financial institutions have moved in two directions in response. Some have concentrated on providing customised services, becoming 'boutiques' that seek to profit from exploiting relatively limited niches. Others attempt to develop new products and generate new business. Such trends are at work both in the market for international wholesale financial services and in the retail sector. This has resulted in stronger entrepreneurial attitudes in finance, possibly originating from the transplantation of new attitudes by non-financial companies diversifying into the financial sector.

Global portfolio preferences

Finally, among the forces for innovation, financial markets have had to cope with shifting global portfolio preferences. The second oil shock shifted wealth from the oil-consuming countries to the oil producers and then, in the wake of economic adjustment, back to Europe, Japan, and a few small Asian nations. OPEC portfolio holders were more attracted into short-term bank deposits, but today's Japanese investors prefer treasury bonds. These differing portfolio preferences among investors, and corresponding differences among debtors, have fostered such innovations as swaps and options, not to mention securitisation.

Benefits and challenges

The global financial evolution of the past three decades has undoubtedly brought benefits. Enhanced competition and improved technology have reduced transaction costs, and these in turn have heightened the efficiency of capital allocation, thereby increasing world output potential.

Another tangible benefit to both borrowers and investors alike, particularly in the context of hedging interest and exchange rate exposures at lower cost, has been the greatly enhanced and flexible range of financial products, not least in the area of the futures and options markets. These have made possible a separation or unbundling of risks which has further contributed to more competitive pricing and trading by redistributing the risks from risk-averse market participants to more willing and arguably more able holders. This has enabled lenders to invest in greater volume and diversify their portfolios on a global basis, while borrowers have been enabled to raise funds in quite different markets and in much more efficient ways than previously. The smaller depositors benefit too, through access to a wider and less expensive array of financial services, as well as an increased ability to earn interest rates consistent with those available on much larger wholesale markets.

Another benefit of the technology which upholds some of the newer, more complex financial products is that it facilitates the monitoring of exposures involved. More and more exposures are now being recorded immediately. This means not only that they can be revalued, or 'marked to market' instantly, but also that they may be quickly recalculated under various scenarios, thus helping managers to appreciate the potential gains and losses.

Such benefits also bring new challenges in their wake. After all, it is the most efficient markets which transmit shocks the most quickly. They exacerbate interest rate and exchange rate volatility, for instance, which has an immediate influence on the turnover volume of financial assets, creating problems for the financial institutions in terms of settlement complexities, complications for central banks in the conduct of monetary policy and, perhaps less recognisable, the need for new disciplines by governments in the exercise of their function as macroeconomic managers.

Threats to the stability of the international financial system

Contrasting presumptions have commonly been expressed concerning the effects on the stability of the global financial system of many of these changes. At the forefront have been the various assertions about the effects of futures trading on the volatility of cash prices. The most recent claims, in the wake of the October 1987 stock market crash, have tended to uphold the findings of careful studies on previous commodity markets, which suggested that financial futures and options markets would indeed be beneficial to stability.

There are undoubtedly some ways in which, if poorly handled, the processes of deregulation and financial innovation could undermine the stability of the financial system. For instance, some regulators and market participants have expressed concern that the prices prevailing on some new financial instruments inadequately compensate banks and other participants for the risks which they assume. Until the end of 1986, no difficulties sufficiently large to put such underpricing claims to a real test had occurred. Then came the crisis in the perpetual floating-rate note market, which showed that holders of securitised assets could not depend on the ready saleability of their securities on advantageous terms. Then came the general overcrowding problems in the Eurobond markets, which were not only blamed on excess supply but also on competition for mandates leading to widespread unrealistic pricing.

It has also been argued that securitisation, by reducing the profitability and quality of the bank loan market, has added to the contractionary forces on the traditional banking sector, thereby complicating its orderly rationalisation by merger or acquisition.

Yet another matter of general concern is the perceived potential of financial change to encourage excessive borrowing. Particular anxiety has surrounded the escalating United States debt/GDP ratio.However, it is not easy to determine the extent to which this is a by-product of financial change rather than US government economic policy.

A clearer concern is one which was mentioned earlier, namely that enhanced communications, in conjunction with more efficient and complex markets, may transmit shocks more rapidly and widely than ever before. Not only is our history full of precedents where runs on banks, currencies and stock markets have proved internationally contagious, but there has recently been a reminder in the form of the stock market crash of October 1987. This seemed an eloquent answer to the previously and frequently expressed concern that foreign disturbances were far more likely to spill into contemporary domestic markets before authorities could react.

Yet another area for concern is the opacity of many contemporary transactions, arising from the long chains of both bank and non-bank counterparties involved, which can make it difficult to limit the spread of defaults. In conjunction with the rapidly accelerating transaction volumes recently witnessed, these can carry great potential for breakdowns in settlement systems. One consequence of this is that large daylight overdrafts are allowed to accumulate as participants go unmonitored or inadequately monitored by regulators.

The need to cope with such risks, combined with the question of the capacity to expand in profitable markets, raises the question of capital adequacy of banks and other financial institutions. Many bank supervisors are encouraging such action, in some cases by applying or proposing risk-based adequacy requirements which endeavour to categorise on and off balance sheet activities by the degree of risk. However, much remains to be done in designing the appropriate requirements, to say nothing of the need to impose them uniformly on both countries and financial institutions. Failure to do this would invite some 'regulatory arbitrage' between different jurisdictions and certain types of more privileged institution.

Challenges for monetary policy

The challenges so far mentioned have largely been those which threaten to undermine the stability of the financial system. The complications for central banks in the pursuit of monetary policy are even more real. The process of deregulation and that of product innovation both facilitate substitution among domestic assets, and the internationalisation of markets increases substitution between assets in different countries. Both forms of substitution alter the mechanism by which monetary policy influences the overall economy.

The policy objective of a contrived contraction in money supply may be expected to be a slowing of economic activity, which will put upward pressure on exchange rates and reduce net exports. The introduction of deregulatory measures into this equation will probably increase the degree of variability necessary if this objective is to be achieved. For, while easier domestic and international substitution would probably dampen interest rate movements, this would usually be at the expense of wider exchange rate swings.

Not only does financial change of the kind that has occurred in recent years create problems for the definition of money, it also increases the unpredictability of demand for monetary aggregates, thereby hindering policy judgements and impeding the ability of countries to achieve their money growth targets. The targeting of monetary aggregates rests heavily upon the behaviour of velocity, which is the frequency of circulation of the average unit of money. In practice, it is measured by the ratio of nominal GNP to the money stock. Just as velocities vary widely among industrial economies, so the velocities of narrow and broad monies within most of them will often diverge. The point is that in the event of velocity falling, money stock has to rise commensurately in order to support a given level of nominal expenditure. Indeed, such an event has taken place in recent years, as interest rates and inflation have both declined. Since such trends were expected, it was possible to accommodate them by adjusting monetary targets in the light of experience.

More devastating for targeting are the unexpected velocity swings, of the sort which have frequently been the subject of research studies. The results of such studies have frequently cited product innovation and deregulation as significant and imperfectly quantifiable causal factors. Officials from the United States, the United Kingdom and Canada have used these findings in making policy decisions. Japanese officials, on the other hand, have been less rigid in their adherence to targets, perhaps most noticeably during 1986 when their discount rates were reduced on three separate occasions despite quite severe money growth concerns. In contrast, the Federal Republic of Germany has consistently been one of the strongest adherents to targeting, through the so-called *Zentralbankgeldmenge*.

Challenges for governments

Less easily recognisable is the associated challenge to governments in the role of macroeconomic managers. Previously, financial crises had often (some would say always) originated from shocks compounded by mistakes in macroeconomic policy. If they are to optimise the rewards and at the same time contain the risks of these new financial freedoms, governments must now observe discipline and co-ordination so as to limit the international imbalances that may arise in the pursuit of stable, non-inflationary economic growth.

Conclusions

Until the shock to the international financial system of the October 1987 stock market crash, there seemed no doubt whatsoever that the trend towards an internationalisation of financial markets and the broadening of the product structure would continue unabated. Worldwide competition among the financial institutions had steadily intensified, providing a strong incentive to product innovation, and gains in technology had consistently lowered the cost of transactions, sustaining the attractions of efficient cash management. While both interest rates and inflation rates remained generally subdued, the record external imbalances and reduced costs of hedging had seemed sure to generate a continuing strong demand for risk management products. Until these underlying trends in economic fundamentals change direction, there seems little reason to believe that this evolution of the financial system will not continue. But a note of uncertainty must now be introduced about the continuation of the trend towards diversification in international portfolios. This has been thought to be a fertile source of further stimulation in the demand for novel financial products, not least from the US and Japanese institutional investors who had always been well behind London in this particular respect, largely on account of differences in regulatory policy. However, the whole point about global portfolios is that they are constructed with the intention of spreading risk over countries which are expected to have divergent trends in their economic fundamentals. Yet the message of the days following the October 1987 stock market crash was that, with the possible exception of Japan, financial markets throughout the world were displaying a remarkable propensity to convergence in their behaviour.

In so far as deregulatory measures have a strong political motivation, it might be expected that the trend will continue. On the other hand, exposure to shocks makes everyone much more aware of the risks they are facing, and in this sense perhaps a change in direction can be expected. There were certainly at least two broad trends already under way prior to the latest shock. The first was the emergence of new domestic regulations, which were designed to match the changes in the financial services industry, and were typified by the Financial Services Act 1986. The second was the growing movement among regulatory authorities to harmonise their standards and requirements on a global level as a response to the fast growing internationalisation of the finance and investment banking business.

However, there seems to be one fundamental area outstanding on the deregulatory agenda. This is the continued existence of the restrictions of commercial banks in the United States and Japan, as manifested in the Glass-Steagall Act and its Japanese equivalent, Article 65 of the Securities and Exchange Act. Not only have these been costly and of questionable relevance to market activity, but they have also hindered the competitive viability of the commercial banks generally to the benefit only of other financial institutions or other countries' markets. Those markets with fewer regulatory constraints will generally expand relative to those elsewhere.

CHAPTER THREE

Stock exchanges

Definition

A Stock Exchange can be described as the place where a 'marriage of convenience' is enacted between those who wish to raise capital, such as companies, governments and local authorities, and those who wish to invest – largely households through the medium of institutions acting upon their behalf. But while this gives an accurate picture of a primary market, in which funds are raised through the sale of stocks and shares to outside investors, it does not cover the simultaneous presence of the secondary market, where those stocks and shares can subsequently be freely traded between two or more investors. It is only when this factor is also included that we can comprehend the full power of the pricing mechanism which is offered by the stock markets. This will enable companies to evaluate their capital, not just for a first time but on a continuing basis, by making certain presumptions about the flow of anticipated income from the wealth which is already reflected in a company's balance sheet. It is also the basis upon which the prospective buyer will judge the wisdom of a purchase.

Everything else concerned with a Stock Exchange is secondary and built around this market function. Other aspects are listed below.

Listing requirements

These fall into two distinct categories, rules surrounding applications for new listings and conditions for a continued listing. For example, applications for new listings on the International Stock Exchange in London are governed by Part IV of the Financial Services Act 1986. This requires that all applications are submitted to the Council of the

Stock Exchange for approval. The Stock Exchange Yellow Book, entitled *Admissions of Securities to Listing*, also lays down that detailed particulars must usually be made available through two national newspapers. Upon a quotation being granted, listed companies are then bound to observe certain reporting obligations with respect to information which may affect markets in their shares, the price of shares, the results of the company, and the conduct of the directors.

By comparison, the method adopted by the New York Stock Exchange merely entails the signing of a formal listing agreement, governing the company's conduct on similar matters. The basic listing requirements in Tokyo, on the other hand, are not unlike those for London, being governed by the SEL (Securities and Exchange Law), which requires that applications for an equity listing are filed with the Tokyo Stock Exchange. On being satisfied that certain standards have been observed in terms of the public interest and investor protection, that body grants a listing subject to the approval of the Ministry of Finance (MOF). The company then enters into a listing agreement with the Tokyo Stock Exchange, stating that it will abide by certain rules and regulations covering business, listing and the supervision of listed securities.

Membership, dealing and settlement rules

These are quite distinct from the previous group in that they apply to members of a stock exchange and not the companies actually quoted on it. In the United Kingdom they are ultimately governed by the requirements of Part I, Chapter III of the Financial Services Act 1986 in so far as it relates to self-regulating organisations. The self-regulatory organisation (SRO) in this context is to be known as the Securities Association. It is the result of an agreement reached in September 1986 between the International Securities Regulatory Organisation and the Council of the Stock Exchange to form an SRO and a single recognised investment exchange (RIE) within the meaning of the above Act.

In the United States these rules are governed in a similar way by two pieces of legislation dating from the 1930s, the Securities Act of 1933 and the Securities Exchange Act of 1934, through the Securities Exchange Commission (SEC), while Japan's Securities and Exchange Law (SEL), enacted in 1948, is patterned on the same United States legislation and is administered by the Ministry of Finance.

Compensation arrangements

Since 1950 the London Stock Exchange has administered its own compensation fund, with the general intention of compensating members of the public in the event of default on obligations to a client by a member firm. While the maximum claim is usually limited to £250,000, this can be increased to £500,000 when losses of more than £250,000 are attributable to misappropriation by a member firm of any securities registered. Section 54 of the Financial Services Act 1986 provides for the introduction of a central compensation fund, although it is understood that this does not apply to self-regulating organisations such as the Stock Exchange.

Every United States broker or dealer registered with the SEC must be a member of the Securities Investor Protection Corporation. This was established under the Securities Investor Protection Act of 1970 to provide financial loss insurance to customers of brokers or dealers who fail to the extent of $US 500,000 in the case of securities losses and $US 100,000 for cash losses. In Japan, however, there is no such compensation fund.

Information services

The efficiency of a stock market, in common with that of any other market, rests heavily on its information services. Given that there are a minimum of interventions in that market, its prices will depend upon the interplay of supply and demand forces. If the potential seller and the potential buyer cannot promptly convey their intentions to the market-maker, therefore, the price is likely to be distorted to some degree. The recent evolution in electronic technology as applied to communications has greatly enhanced the efficiency of stock markets, particularly on the supply side. Worldwide real-time systems such as the Reuter Monitor and the AP-Dow Jones Telerate Service have certainly contributed to this. One of the big steps taken in London was the introduction of the Stock Exchange Automated Quotations System (SEAQ), which went live for domestic equities in the context of the Big Bang of 27 October 1986 (see Appendix A). This was preceded eighteen months earlier by SEAQ International, which from its outset had been linked up with the NASDAQ system in the United States. NASDAQ itself, the National Association of Securities Dealers Automated Quotations System, had been intro-duced in the United States as early as 1971. In addition, Japan has an

OTC Automatic Quotation System and the Tokyo Stock Exchange has its own Market Information System.

The world's stock exchanges

The bourses of continental Europe

The history of the world's stock exchanges starts off in continental Europe with the inception of the German and Dutch bourses during the Renaissance. The first of these was established in Hamburg in 1538, although the transactions in those days were mainly in bills of exchange. The first actual stock market to begin operating was that in Amsterdam in 1611, supplemented by some after-hours trading in the coffee houses along Dam Square. The Amsterdam Stock Exchange was also the first to trade in the shares of public companies when, in the seventeenth century, an issue of shares by the United East India Company was made. Dutch investors played a dominant role in the financing of foreign investments in both the public and private sectors. Indeed, even up until the Second World War, the Amsterdam Stock Exchange was ranked as the third most important stock market in the world after New York and London. The reason why it became comparatively neglected thereafter lies with the preference of many continental companies to rely upon bank finance to meet their capital requirements.

Another of the oldest stock exchanges is the Vienna Stock Exchange, founded in 1771 during the reign of Empress Maria Theresa as a state institution to provide a market for state-issued bonds as well as for exchange transactions. Its first share issue was actually that of the Austrian National Bank in 1816.

It may seem surprising, considering the traditional involvement of many Italian cities in trading in currencies, precious metals and other commodities over several centuries, that it was not until 1808 that the first formal exchange, the Milan Stock Exchange, was created. This still accounts for 90 per cent of total equity volume and about 80 per cent of turnover in fixed interest securities, although nine other exchanges have since been founded.

Traditionally, the stock exchanges in France competed amongst themselves, with multiple listings of the same companies. It was not until October 1961 that the principle of a single market for a given share was established by decree, and since then the provincial exchanges have not been permitted to make markets in those securities quoted on the Paris Bourse.

The most active and most international of Spanish stock markets, the Bolsa de Madrid, was founded in 1831 and still accounts for nearly 50 per cent of total market capitalisation in both bonds and stocks. Since 1915, other exchanges have been established, principally in Barcelona but also in Bilbao and Valencia.

Stock markets in Scandinavia only really became formalised in the mid-nineteenth century with the onset of industrialisation. It was then that the Copenhagen Stock Exchange emerged. Although the Oslo Stock Exchange had been founded in 1819, it first operated solely as a foreign exchange market, commodities being introduced in 1850 and shares and bond trading in 1881. While organised trading in securities in Sweden can be traced back to 1776, the Stockholm Stock Exchange was not founded until 1864, and was only internationalised in 1901.

Geneva is the oldest of the seven stock exchanges in Switzerland, being formally organised in 1850 followed by Basle in 1876 and Zurich in 1877. Nowadays Zurich is the largest, followed by Basle and then Geneva, the others being considerably smaller.

The London Stock Exchange

The London Stock Exchange is the oldest in the English-speaking world. The merchant venturers began dealing in stocks and shares during the seventeenth century, and an informal market dealing in shares in joint venture trading companies grew up in the coffee houses of Threadneedle Street during the eighteenth century, as a way of spreading the risk to their backers. The most famous of these was Jonathans, and it was in New Jonathans in 1773 that the market became centralised. This situation was formalised in 1802 with the building of the first Stock Exchange with some 550 subscribers and 100 clerks. More than thirty local stock markets in various other parts of the United Kingdom followed as the nineteenth century progressed. These began the process towards amalgamation in 1890, with the formation of the Council of Associated Stock Exchanges. By 1967 they had grouped themselves into six regional exchanges. Finally, in 1973, they became part of The Stock Exchange of Great Britain and Ireland, with trading floors in London, Birmingham, Manchester, Liverpool, Glasgow and Dublin.

There are now more than 210 member firms of The Stock Exchange, each of which will deal for those who want to buy or sell stocks and shares. The most recent development, which was ratified by the members of the Stock Exchange in November 1986, was the previously-mentioned historic agreement with the International Securities Regulatory Association which allowed the Stock Exchange to take the steps necessary to create a truly competitive marketplace in London. One of the first moves in this connection was to change its corporate structure to form a limited liability company, The International Stock Exchange of the United Kingdom and the Republic of Ireland Ltd. This is the body which is destined to become the new RIE (Recognised Investment Exchange) within the meaning laid down in the Financial Services Act 1986, which covers markets in foreign and domestic equities, gilt edged securities and traded options.

The USM (Unlisted Securities Market), which has operated since 1980, is designed for the smaller and younger company, for which a full listing would be much too onerous. Only 10 per cent of such a company's capital must be in public hands at the time of issue, compared with 25 per cent on the main stock exchange. At the end of September 1987, 407 securities from 370 companies were traded on the USM with a total market value of £9.5 billion.

The Third Market, with rules even further modified, was launched on 26th January 1987. It was intended to become the trading centre for dealing in securities of companies that were too young for a listing on the USM but which still had good prospects for growth. It was also intended to cover some of the 230 established unquoted companies, whose shares had previously been traded off-market by Stock Exchange member firms. It was disappointing, therefore, that only 30 securities from 28 companies were being traded on the Third Market at the end of September 1987. They had a total market value of just over £300 million.

Appendix A explains in detail the 'Big Bang' which took place in the London Stock Exchange in October 1986.

North American stock exchanges

The United States, with nine major stock exchanges, several smaller ones and the NASDAQ over-the-counter system, has the largest and most diverse capital market in the world, giving every encouragement to foreign investors. Shares and bonds denominated in US dollars form a significant proportion of internationally invested portfolios throughout the world. While New York remains the most important centre, the midwestern city of Chicago has become a significant rival, and has the largest futures and options market in the world.

The New York Stock Exchange (NYSE)

Securities had been traded in the streets of New York since as early as 1700, as outdoor brokers made markets in the securities issued by the American government and by newly-created enterprises. But it was not until 1792 that twenty-four brokers subscribed to the original brokers' agreement, which formed the first organised stock market. This eventually encouraged, in 1817, the establishment of an organisation of brokers who agreed to meet regularly at set hours, drawing up a constitution which created the New York Stock and Exchange Board. Over a hundred years later, five years after the 1929 Wall Street Crash, this body gave way to the Securities Exchange Commission (SEC) which has since been responsible for the regulation of securities trading, not just for the New York Stock Exchange but throughout the United States. The character of Wall Street changed quite radically in April 1975, when fixed commissions were abolished, forcing brokerage firms to become more competitive. This evolution was to be completed two years later, when the first foreign brokers/dealers were admitted to membership.

Trading on the New York Stock Exchange is conducted on a dealer-to-dealer basis, without jobbing intermediaries. Nevertheless, the key element is the specialist, who has a dual capacity as both a dealer on his own account and as a broker, although only in stocks for which he specialises, or is registered. Of the four categories of single capacity trader, the largest are the commission brokers, who are employees of one of about 500 securities houses. They execute orders at agreed commission rates and may only act as principals, on their own account, if they are not banks. In this sense, of course, they assume a dual capacity. They may occasionally be assisted by floor brokers, who will take a portion of their commission. There are then registered traders, who only deal on their own account or as trustees. Odd-lot dealers, who would buy and sell from commission firms at prices which are based on round lots, plus or minus a differential, have been virtually extinct since the NYSE acquired computerised processing systems in 1976.

An electronic order-routeing system, Superdot 250, links member firms throughout the United States directly with the trading floor. Almost instantaneously, it routes market and limit orders directly to trading posts and members' booths, and then confirms executions to the account executives without delay. It was the use of this system by programme traders which excited much interest in the January 1988 report from the Brady Commission, which was set up by President Reagan to investigate the events surrounding the stock market crash of 19 October 1987.

American Stock Exchange (Amex)
A second generation of 'on the curb' street traders, this time in stocks and bonds not large enough to qualify for a listing on the New York Stock Exchange, had meanwhile moved indoors in 1921. They finally became known as the American Stock Exchange (Amex) in 1953. Like the New York Stock Exchange, Amex is based on a central market floor with specialist firms which have a commitment to make a market in certain issues. About 25 such firms make markets in more than 900 stocks and in options, including a good number of foreign stocks. Because its listing requirements are less stringent, Amex encourages registration of some relatively young companies. It has also gained a reputation for technological and product innovation, not least in 1985, when it introduced the first two-way electronic hook-up between primary equity markets in different countries with the Toronto Stock Exchange. This innovation gives US and Canadian investors the opportunity available price for the whole North American market, and interlisted companies a greater market liquidity.

The NASDAQ System
Through the National Association of Securities Dealers Automated Quotations System, known as NASDAQ, the United States has by far the largest OTC (over-the-counter) market in the world. Some would regard it as the harbinger of the global stock market of the future, in which investors can trade on a 24-hour basis from around the world through a fully computerised system. Introduced in 1971 to improve the efficiency of the OTC market while exploiting the 'state of the art' in terms of available technology, NASDAQ has since grown to be the third largest trading system in the world in turnover terms after the New York Stock Exchange and the Tokyo Stock Exchange.

NASDAQ was first developed as an OTC market, to help the many smaller companies which were unable to meet the stringent listing requirements and high listing costs of the major exchanges. It is regulated by the National Association of Securities Dealers, and incorporates 3000 dealers, 500 brokers and most investment bankers. Apart from dealing between major institutions, like pension funds and insurance companies, which normally hold large blocks of shares, it also provides for the private firms which make block sales by linking their customers together through computer terminals. This results in lower commission charges and a greater speed of transaction. Consequently, larger well-known companies such as Apple Computer and MCI Communications, which would otherwise qualify for listing on the NYSE or Amex, have chosen to remain on the OTC. Moreover, an increasing number of companies are switching to NASDAQ from those exchanges because they see the OTC system of competing market-makers as more advantageous to their needs. At the lower extreme of the scale, since December 1984, the instantaneous completion of orders for up to 500 shares has been possible through computer-to-computer transmission via a Small Order Execution System.

Other US stock exchanges
A third small exchange exists in New York. This is the National Stock Exchange, which opened in 1962 and deals exclusively in securities of smaller companies. However, a far more important evolution has been that of the city of Chicago as the second most important financial centre in the United States. Apart from being the home of the Midwest Stock Exchange, which originated in 1882 as the Chicago Stock Exchange and – after later amalgamations with exchanges in St Louis, Cleveland, Minneapolis-St Paul and New Orleans – is now regarded as the fastest-growing and second largest stock exchange in the United States, Chicago is also the largest centre in the world for trading in futures and options. These activities take place at two separate exchanges, the Chicago Mercantile Exchange (CME) and the Chicago Board of Trade (CBOT).

There are other major stock exchanges at Boston, Cincinnati, San Francisco (Pacific), Intermountain and Spokane. While all nine major exchanges operate separately and autonomously, they are connected through a visual electronic computerised communications system, the national tape, which is supervised and maintained by the Securities and Exchange Commission. In common with the New York exchanges, all these are regulated by the SEC. Indeed, all exchanges which cross US state lines must either be registered or classified as exempt from registration, and only the Honolulu Stock Exchange falls into the second category. In the general context of the rules explained earlier in this chapter, Exchanges have to provide full information concerning their activities, organisation, membership and rules of procedure, and prepare registration statements, new listing applications and periodic reports in accordance with the SEC requirements.

The Canadian exchanges

In terms of market capitalisation, Canada is the world's fourth largest public equity market. It comprises three significant stock exchanges, but only two of these trade in senior shares – the Toronto Stock Exchange (TSE) with 75 per cent of Canada's traded value in stocks, and the Montreal Exchange (ME), which claims 20 per cent. The Vancouver Stock Exchange is a venture capital market, dealing almost exclusively in the penny stocks of resource-based companies, and accounts for the remaining 5 per cent or so. A similar 5 per cent of trade in Canadian securities, largely in resource-based stocks, is through the small OTC market. This latter activity has benefited since 1985 from the Canadian OTC Automated Trading System (COATS), which is an electronic quotations system giving brokers immediate access to bid/offer and trading volume information besides greatly assisting surveillance and regulation.

Although the first public underwriting of corporate shares in Canada was that of the Bank of Montreal in 1817, the Montreal Exchange was not founded until 1874. Meanwhile, an association of Toronto businessmen formed a partnership in 1852 to meet for half an hour each day to exchange holdings of securities. This went on until 1878, when the Toronto Stock Exchange was incorporated by a Special Act of the Ontario legislation. The 62 members of this exchange then amalgamated with the 51 members of the rival Standard Stock and Mining Exchange in 1934 to form the Toronto Stock Exchange as it is now known.

It is not proposed to go into any detail about stock exchanges in South America and Central America, save to say that they have existed in South America since the foundation of the Buenos Aires exchange in 1854 and the organisation of an exchange on the French model in Brazil around that time. The foremost exchange in Central America is that in Mexico City, which was founded in 1894.

The stock exchanges of Japan and the Pacific Basin

Japan

Although there are stock exchanges in eight cities in Japan, the most important by far is the Tokyo Stock Exchange, which can now claim to be the world's largest stock market, both in market capitalisation and turnover terms, having overtaken the New York Stock Exchange early in 1987.

The first Japanese stock exchange was established in 1878, nearly a hundred years later than London and New York, when the Tokyo Stock Exchange Company Limited was set up as a profit-making corporation. Although the initial transactions were largely in public bonds, it was only some ten years before the equity transactions increased and the Japanese securities market began to expand rapidly.

Japanese stock exchanges suspended activity following the Second World War, and trading took place at the offices of securities companies. The present generation of exchanges was founded in 1949 following enactment of the new Securities and Exchange Law during the previous year. This was revised in 1967, with the introduction of a securities companies licensing system, improved trading rules and a stock-pool organisation. The Tokyo Stock Exchange (TSE) now handles about 83 per cent of stock exchange business in Japan, against 13 per cent and 3 per cent respectively for Osaka and Nagoya. The other five are in Kyoto, Hiroshima, Fukuoka, Niigaatta and Sapporo, sharing less than 1 per cent of total turnover between them.

All Japanese stock exchanges comprise three distinct sections. Within the first are the larger listed shares, accounting for about 96 per cent of total market capitalisation. The second section handles the newly quoted or unlisted shares which might otherwise be expected to be traded over-the-counter, while the third section is the over-the-counter market. All are similarly subject to the same Securities and Exchange Law which is administered by the Minister of Finance.

Japanese stock exchanges have two types of member – regular members and *saitori* members. The number of the former, which are securities companies whose main activity is the buying and selling of securities on the floor of the exchange, either as principal or agent, is limited to 93. These are represented on the floor of the exchange by trading clerks. The four *saitori* members, which must also be securities companies and are represented on the floor of the exchange by intermediary clerks who, as their description implies, act as intermediaries between regular members. Rather like the old stock jobbers in London, they have trading posts on the floors of exchanges from which they will deal in specific securities. There is also a similarity with the new London system, in that all transactions are input into the exchange's computer system, and then instantly disseminated to display devices installed in the offices of regular members by the Market Information System of the exchange. Apart from the unlisted shares, which are traded over-the-counter, all publicly quoted shares are listed and traded on the stock exchanges. Trading is conducted under the *zaraba* method, an open outcry procedure, and this is supplemented by special auctions to determine opening and closing prices of specific shares, usually those of widely-traded larger companies.

When foreigners first started to buy on the Tokyo market, following the Foreign Securities Firms Law of 1971, price/earnings ratios were low and growth rates high. Now, due to the huge liquidity of the markets, the reverse is the case. This is not least attributable to the popularity since 1982 of *Tokkin* funds to corporations and financial institutions seeking ways to divert their rising flow of surpluses into short-term investments in the stock market. Aggressive interventions for previous high profits have been a clever way of offsetting recent weaker operating results arising from the over-valued yen. This is a process known as *zaiteku*, financial technology. It has become possible because share investments in *Tokkin* can be kept separately from the large strategic holdings commonly held in one Japanese company by another and, since the price paid for *Tokkin* does not have to be applied to those strategic holdings, some significant capital gains tax advantages can accrue to corporations. Insurance companies have benefited in a similar way, in that through *Tokkin* funds they are able to build up hidden reserves. There was some concern during late 1987 over the Ministry of Finance's attitude to perceived valuation abuses, and new softer guidelines for insurance companies, although not corporations, were published in January 1988. The possibility of raising the proportion of assets which insurance companies can invest in *Tokkin* from 3 per cent to 5 per cent is also said to be under consideration.

Hong Kong and Singapore
Other important markets in Asia are those in Hong Kong and Singapore. Although brokers had been operating in Hong Kong since 1866, the year after the enactment of the colony's first Companies Ordinance, the Association of Stockbrokers in Hong Kong was only formed in 1891. It name was changed to the Hong Kong Stock Exchange in 1914. This is now the least restricted market in the world, having no exchange controls and no distinction between resident and non-resident investors. The stock exchange in Singapore was a later creation, with a chequered history tied up with the secession from Malaysia in the 1960s. Although the first share trading in Asia took place on an informal basis in Bombay during the 1830s,

the Indian market is no longer of any great international interest, being largely closed to foreign investors who are not of Indian origin.

Australasia

Although trading in shares has taken place in Australia since as early as 1828, the first stock exchange was not actually formed in Melbourne until 1865. This was followed in succession by Sydney (1871), Brisbane (1884), Adelaide (1887), Hobart and Perth (both in 1891). In the fifty years since 1937, these have together constituted the Australian Associated Stock Exchanges (AASE). They have now been formally amalgamated, under an Act of the Commonwealth Parliament in 1894, into the Australian Stock Exchange Ltd (ASX), with all members of the six capital city exchanges becoming members. Despite this, some 90 per cent of all trading volume is shared between Melbourne and Sydney and, not surprisingly for such a resource-rich country, more than one-third of the total capitalisation is represented by the shares of mining companies. One of these in particular, Broken Hill Proprietary (BHP), is by far the largest, both in terms of market value and turnover. Although the Australian markets are all connected by computer, there is as yet no OTC market on the lines of NASDAQ in the United States. However, there is a Second Board Market comprising smaller unlisted companies, which began in Melbourne in 1984 and has now spread throughout Australia.

The total market value of New Zealand exchanges is only about a quarter of that of their Australian counterparts. The four trading floors of the New Zealand Stock Exchange, in the four main areas of population – Auckland, Wellington, Christchurch/Invercargill and Dunedin – have been in existence since the 1870s.

Measuring the world's stock exchanges

There are approximately 20,000 companies listed on one or more of the stock exchanges around the world, with a total market value estimated at the end of 1987 at over $US 7000 billion. This estimate of capitalisation had risen to nearly $US 8000 billion before the October 1987 crash, so the effect of that event was to reduce world market value by around $US 1000 billion. It will also be seen from the following table that, measured by the market value of domestic equities alone, the share of the market enjoyed by Japanese registered companies rose from 31 per cent at the end of 1986 to 42 per cent, comfortably the largest at the end of 1987. Meanwhile, companies

Table 3.1 Comparative size of world stock markets (domestic equities only)

	Total market value ($US billions)			Percentage of world market
	end 1986	Jun 87	end 1987	
North America	2369	2950	2417	34
United States	2203	2722	2216	31
Canada	166	228	201	3
Japan	1746	2726	2978	42
Europe	1338	1672	1544	22
United Kingdom	440	696	664	9
Federal Republic of Germany	246	243	207	3
France	150	172	154	2
Italy	141	136	109	2
Switzerland	132	145	132	2
Netherlands	73	91	74	1
Sweden	49	55	49	0.7
Spain	42	48	76	1
Belgium	36	47	42	0.6
Others	30	39	37	0.5
Pacific Basin	164	220	168	2.4
Australia	78	105	83	1.2
Hong Kong	53	68	50	0.7
Singapore/Malaysia	33	47	35	0.5
Mexico	7	15	6	0.1
South Africa (gold mines)	11	27	26	0.4
World market	5648	7610	7139	100

Sources: Morgan Stanley Capital International Indices

of North American origin, whose share of the combined capitalisation of the world's equity markets only ten years ago had been well in excess of 50 per cent but which, by the end of 1986, had reduced to 42 per cent, only took 34 per cent by the end of 1987. Out of this, the share accounted for by companies registered in the United States was reduced from 39 per cent at December 1986 to 31 per cent at December 1987. The share which was enjoyed by companies of European origin, which had reduced from 24 per cent to 22 per cent during the first half of the year, stabilised in the second half of the year, while that of countries from the Pacific Basin fell from 2.9 per cent to 2.4 per cent, again largely in the first half of the year. Table 3.1 shows the comparative size of world stock markets in relation to domestic equities.

There were several factors which enabled the Japanese to eclipse their United States counterparts, in terms of market value of domestic equities, so easily during 1987. Indeed, the exceptional general growth demonstrated by Japanese shares in the first quarter, combined with a flotation in February on the Tokyo Stock Exchange of the first tranche of shares in Nippon Telegraph and Telephone, had by April already enabled them to make up the $450 billion difference and edge marginally ahead, although both still had 36 per cent of the market. To place the NTT offering in perspective, this created overnight the world's largest quoted company, at $US 164 billion. Another part issue, in November, brought its value up to $US 313 billion, and a third tranche is planned during 1988. The differential fall in equity markets following the October 1987 crash was responsible for the remaining part of the large adjustment. Meanwhile, the shares of British companies remained throughout the third largest group in the world.

So far, only one measure of the size of world stock markets has been used, and since it is based strictly on the market value of domestic equities only, it is only a very rough method of comparing stock exchanges country by country. It is also grossly inaccurate in this latter respect that it does not include the rising number of overseas equities listed. On the other hand, if these were included, there would be such an element of double counting that any objective comparison between various markets would be impossible. In common with other international comparisons, such a snapshot of market values depends heavily upon which base currency is used. For example, it was the powerful rise of the Japanese yen against the US dollar in the first quarter of 1987 which was a major factor in enabling the market value of Japanese shares to overtake those of US origin.

There are at least two other ways of measuring comparative size of the world's stock exchanges, namely by turnover and the number of listings. Table 3.2 shows, this time in measured sterling terms, that in the year 1986, the New York Stock Exchange had the highest turnover in front of the Tokyo Stock Exchange, the NASDAQ over-the-counter system and the combined West German stock markets, and that London's International Stock Exchange was only fifth largest. It also shows that, when measured in terms of companies listed, the London Stock Exchange was second only to the NASDAQ system, and quite substantially ahead of the New York Stock Exchange, the Tokyo Stock Exchange, the Australian exchanges and the Paris Bourse.

Table 3.2 also gives a clue to the extent of double count, were one to try to compare outright market values. The fact is that about 70 per

Table 3.2   Comparison of international stock exchanges: year ended December 1986

£ million	Market value domestic equity	Equity turnover	Companies listed Domestic	Overseas	Total
American	20875	14770	815	51	866
Amsterdam	46106	47446	248	227	457
Athens	2393	252	117	–	117
Australia	54532	32549	1488	40	1528
Barcelona	35782	3755	385	–	385
Basle	67394	n/a	n/a	n/a	998
Brussels	23013	6579	192	145	337
Copenhagen	10840	1206	269	8	277
Frankfurt	102579	76485	234	208	442
Geneva	63657	n/a	173	417	590
Germany	116710	123121	507	212	719
Helsinki	10642	3607	49	3	52
Hong Kong	33014	27744	264	12	276
Johannesburg	74298	5401	738	27	765
Kuala Lumpur	9807	2178	232	59	291
Kuwait	298	n/a	44	7	51
Luxembourg	n/a	94	347	171	518
Madrid	38399	18315	327	–	327
Milan	64425	19213	204	–	204
NASDAQ	208803	304444	4434	272	4706
New York	1130998	994900	1580	67	1647
Osaka	1240175	148249	1070	–	1070
Paris	92117	51754	481	202	683
Singapore	23082	6075	127	194	321
Stockholm	41156	12457	150	7	150
Tokyo	1451322	1095717	1532	88	1620
Toronto	284866	100225	1147	61	1208
UK	363170	193259	2135	523	2658
Vienna	3991	949	70	36	106
Zurich	68301	n/a	166	213	379

Source: The Stock Exchange, *Quality of Markets Quarterly* Spring 1988

cent of the world's market value is made up from about only 10 per cent, or around 2000, of listed companies. These include most of the truly 'international equities', which are the substance of the new 24-hour global market for equities from London through New York and Tokyo and back to London. Under the Euromoney definition, such a calculation embraces all those companies which have at least one

Table 3.3   Foreign equities listed on the International Stock Exchange in London

As at 31 December 1987	No of companies	Market value £m	% Total	Average market value £m
Japan	9	71,285.9	9.9	7,920.6
Germany	8	25,529.2	3.5	3,191.2
Netherlands	13	34,652.1	4.8	2,665.5
Spain	4	10,077.7	1.4	2,519.4
Netherlands Antilles	2	4,850.1		2,425.1
United States	195	461,905.2	63.8	2,368.7
Italy	1	1,379.5		1,379.5
France	5	6,661.2		1,332.2
Hong Kong	2	2,375.4		1,187.7
Canada	26	25,937.3	3.6	997.6
New Zealand	3	2,407.8		802.6
Australia	20	15,833.2	2.2	791.7
South Africa	96	25,616.6	3.5	266.8
Total	505	723,466.1	100.0	1,432.6
(as at 30 September	504	1,056,555.2		2,096.3)

Source: The Stock Exchange, *Quality of Markets Quarterly* Winter 1987/88

active, liquid market outside their home base. It has been calculated that the number of these rose from 236 in December 1985 to 496 in December 1986.

While the number of overseas equities actually listed on a stock exchange is not necessarily comparable with the number of truly 'international equities' as defined by Euromoney, it is no coincidence that, apart from the high number listed on the Basle Stock Exchange, the London Stock Exchange at 512 had by far the highest number of overseas companies listed. This is because London is not only already recognised as the most active market in foreign equities, but is also consolidating this position as the world's main trading centre. There have been two fundamental reasons for this – its SEAQ International quotation system which has already been enhanced by the link-up with NASDAQ in New York giving mutual on-screen access to the top tier of around 300 quotations in each market, and a favourable regulatory framework.

Details of the countries of origin of most of these listed companies is shown in Table 3.3, taken from a longer table listing 384 companies from 13 countries, which altogether totalled 95.2 per cent of the total market value as at 31 December 1987. Some 195 of these, representing just below two-thirds of the total market value of listed overseas equities, were from the United States. Although the next most numerous in terms of countries represented was South Africa with 96, mainly mining shares admitted prior to 1950, in market value terms the largest presence consists of Japanese, German and Dutch companies, most of which were only admitted in recent years.

There seems little point in including a list of the 196 US companies, one or two of which, such as ITT and Gillette, were admitted as early as 1950, but the much shorter list of Japanese, German, Dutch and Spanish companies as it stood at the end of 1987 is as follows:

JAPAN (9)	NETHERLANDS (13)
Fuji Bank	Aegon
Fujitsu	Akzo
Honda	Algemene Bank Nederland
NEC	English & Dutch Investment Trust
Renown	European Assets Trust
Sony	Philips Lamps Holdings
TDK	Robeco
Toray	Rolinco
Toshiba	Rorento
	Royal Dutch Petroleum
GERMANY (8)	Unilever
Allianz	Wereldhave
BASF	Wessanen (Koninklijke)
Bayer	
Commerzbank	SPAIN (4)
Deutsche Bank	Banco Central
Hoechst	Banco de Bilbao
Schering	Banco de Santander
Thyssen	Compania Telefonica National de Espana

The average daily value of this foreign equity trading in London was running at around £350 million per day in the first half of 1987, rising to £630 million per day in October, the month of the stock market crash. This represented an increase of more than 100 per cent in the eleven months year since London's 'Big Bang' of November 1986, which compared quite favourably with the comparable 80 per cent rise in domestic equities and left the foreign equities market with about a third of total turnover. In contrast to the domestic market, however, there is very little intramarket business; this represents only about 5 per cent of turnover value. Foreign equity deals are also very much larger than the average transaction in UK equities – on average about £140,000 per bargain against £24,000 for a UK equity deal – which makes these markets much more volatile. The size does vary considerably between countries of origin, however, with Japanese by far the largest at over £200,000 per bargain, followed closely by the Europeans at around £180,000 per bargain, indicating that these are very much markets for professionals and institutions, mainly from overseas. The average bargain for the US equities sector is, by comparison, only about £50,000, while those for the Australian dollar sector are even smaller at £29,000, suggesting a fair degree of private investor interest in both cases.

A point worth making is that, because not all the firms currently active in foreign equity trading in London are members of the Stock Exchange, the transactions actually reported may be understated. Towards the end of 1987, there were some 49 registered market-making firms on the SEAQ International electronic trading system, less than half of which were members. And there may be as many as 200 active dealing firms, most of which would have been members of the ISRO prior to the December 1986 merger with the Stock Exchange. It is envisaged that this situation will be rationalised with the implementation of the Financial Services Act, when all dealing firms will have to be members of the International Stock Exchange in its capacity as a Recognised Investment Exchange (RIE).

Nothwithstanding the effects which statistical inadequacies may have, some interesting further statistics are available on foreign equity trading in London. Table 3.4 relates foreign equity turnover to countries of origin of issues. The statistics differ very substantially from the proportions in terms of market value, when around two-thirds of the foreign equities quoted were of US origin, Japan represented 7.7 per cent, and Germany 3.6 per cent. In turnover terms, by contrast, nearly a half is of European origin, one-fifth from Japan, and a mere one-tenth from the United States and Canada together.

Also shown in Table 3.4 are the origins of the 194 major foreign equities for which firm dealing prices were provided by those 49 registered market-makers on the SEAQ system in mid-1987. Of these, 54 are European, 53 North American, 43 Japanese, and 44 from elsewhere. The 49 market-makers tend to be specialists, with more than half covering only one country sector and eight covering five countries or more. As a result, the Japanese sector is the biggest,

Table 3.4 Foreign equity turnover by sector

			Number of SEAQ quotes	
Europe				
France	13.8		21	
Germany	12.8		13	
Other EEC	13.7		10	
Other European	8.7	49.0	10	54
Japan		20.8		43
North America				
USA	8.2		36	
Canada	2.1	10.3	17	53
Australia		5.8		16
South Africa		5.4		15
Others		8.7		13
Total		100.0		194

Source: The Stock Exchange, *Quality of Markets Quarterly* Summer 1987

with 21 market-makers, followed by the Scandinavian sector with 18 and Germany with 14. However, these are not all the quotations carried by SEAQ International, since there are a further 600 stocks carried on an indicative basis only.

There is often a deeper market in London than in the domestic markets of some securities. Early research has indicated that the average touch on German and Dutch equities quoted on SEAQ International is about 0.7–0.8 per cent, which not only compares with those of domestic alphas but is also significantly greater than those dealt on overseas markets. The imposition of a 2 per cent turnover tax on Stockholm equity transactions has turned London into an active market in Swedish securities. Moreover, the average size of deals in German stocks in London is £150,000 compared with only £20,000 in Frankfurt.

To show that this trend towards 'internationally' liquid stocks is multilateral, Table 3.5 gives a list of stocks of United Kingdom origin which are quoted on overseas stock exchanges. It will be seen that by far the largest number are those quoted in New York in the form of American Depositary Receipts (ADRs), and that these are followed by the major European stock exchanges and then Tokyo. The table also gives a list of UK companies quoted in two or more overseas exchanges, led by ICI with nine, and BAT Industries with six.

Table 3.5   United Kingdom shares quoted on overseas stock exchanges

By country:			By company:	
United States*			Imperial Chemical Industries	9
NYSE	15		BAT Industries	6
Amex	2		British Petroleum Co	5
NASDAQ	19	36	Consolidated Gold Fields	5
Paris		14	Rio Tinto-Zinc Corporation	5
Brussels		14	Bowater Industries	4
Frankfurt		13	Courtaulds	4
Amsterdam		12	Shell Transport & Trading Co	4
Zurich		10	Bass	3
Tokyo		7	British Telecommunications	3
Johannesburg		5	GKN	3
Kuala Lumpur		4	Glaxo Holdings	3
Luxembourg		4	Marks & Spencer	3
Toronto		4	Rothmans International	3
Australia		3	Thorn EMI	3
Montreal		2	Allied-Lyons	2
New Zealand		2	Barclays	2
Singapore		2	BTR	2
Vienna		1	Charter Consolidated	2
Oslo		1	Fisons	2
Total		134	Grand Metropolitan	2
(19 stock exchanges)			Hanson Trust	2
			Lonrho	2
			National Westminster Bank	2
			Ultramar	2

*Quoted in the form of American Depository Receipts
Source: The Stock Exchange, *Quality of Markets Quarterly* Winter 1987/88

By comparison with London, trading in foreign equities in New York is relatively insignificant. In all, only 23 ADRs and 45 foreign equities were traded on the New York Stock Exchange in 1986, representing about 5 per cent of total equity trading. Meanwhile, the 88 ADRs and 178 foreign equities traded on NASDAQ were 6.6 per cent of the total.

The Euro equities market

Many of the more recent quotations of stocks on exchanges outside their country of domicile are the result of Euro equity issues. These are so-called because they are distributed or syndicated across more than one market, usually outside the country of domicile of the issuer, using Eurobond syndication techniques. They tend, therefore, to be favoured by the larger multinational corporations, which are encouraged by the benefits of a wider dissemination of their shares, the access which these techniques give them to new sources of capital, and the general opportunity to increase the awareness of the company amongst potential investors and customers in foreign countries.

The Euro equity market, which came into being during 1984, produced new issues totalling $4 billion during 1985, reached $11 billion in 1986 and then, in the first nine months of 1987, produced another $11 billion of new issues. These offerings are usually initiated by the publication of a preliminary prospectus, which is then used, by the group of banks which will have already provisionally agreed to underwrite a portion, to 'build a book' of client interest over a two to three week period. The issuing company will then conduct presentations to investors in various overseas centres so as to get a firm indication of demand. A price is then fixed and firm sales are made.

Prior to this, two distinct approaches are used in the construction of the syndicates which undertake such sales. European houses tend to favour what is known as the 'regional' approach. This is based upon a view that, because each geographical area is a separate marketplace, sales are best effected by granting leading domestic banks the exclusive distribution rights to each of those areas. It is argued that this is a means of mitigating the kind of 'flow back' to the country of origin, such as accompanied distributions of British Telecom shares in the United States. The US houses, on the other hand, whose European strength tends to be based more on the breadth of their coverage in any particular nation rather than its depth, are generally more attracted to the 'global' approach. This is based on a single 'book', run without geographical restrictions, either on approaches to investors or on the ability of investors to resell.

Most of the recent European privatisation issues have been syndicated according to the regionalist doctrine, whereas the largest European tranches of US issues, such as the $200m deal for Citicorp led by Merrill Lynch Capital Markets, have been syndicated globally. A hybrid syndication system, which united different aspects of both regional and global approaches, did however emerge during 1987, with the lead manager becoming 'global co-ordinator'. A prominent example was the $500m issue for Philips in May 1987, when Crédit Suisse First Boston was the global co-ordinator responsible for appointing four different regional managers, each of which was

Stock exchanges

Table 3.6   Euro-equity lead and co-lead managers 1984–6

	Total lead and co-lead managed		
Manager or Group	$US million	Issues	% share
Deutsche Bank	3,797.39	23	23.01
Crédit Suisse First Boston	2,049,77	59	12.42
Swiss Bank Corporation	1,130,79	43	6.85
Union Bank of Switzerland	803.67	25	4.87
Merrill Lynch	692.38	20	4.20
Morgan Stanley	619.85	21	3.76
Nomura Securities	550.31	13	3.33
Salomon Brothers	549.68	16	3.33
Shearson Lehman	529.14	17	3.21
Banque Paribas	514.66	15	3.12
Goldman Sachs	485.39	10	2.94
SG Warburg	410.72	13	2.49
Banque National de Paris	408.26	6	2.47
Dresdner Bank	358.18	7	2.17
Daiwa Securities	277.42	9	1.68
Total	13,177.61	297	

Source: Euromoney Bondware

allowed to shift shares between areas. A similar method was used for the French privatisation issues, with separate managers in the United Kingdom, Switzerland, Germany, and the rest of the world.

About five houses control some 50 per cent of current Euro equity business, and there are only about twelve of any significant size. Table 3.6 lists Euro equity lead and co-lead managers and the level of their activity in 1984–6.

There is still considerable debate among these houses about how to adapt international distribution and underwriting procedures learned in the Eurobond market to the more risky and fragmented equity markets. Issuing shares will always be a more sensitive undertaking than issuing debt, if only because, while bonds are individual commodities, new shares are fungible with all others outstanding. If a Euro equity issue fails, therefore, the entire equity base of a company can be undermined. Such risks were highlighted by the débâcle which was associated with the $2.2 billion Fiat issue led by Deutsche Bank in September 1986. Really a secondary offering of shares in that company owned by Libya, it underlined the limits to the market's ability to absorb international equity placements. Moreover, underwriters were uncertain whether the dollar denominated shares could be traded interchangeably with lira shares already quoted on Milan's Stock Exchange. Some houses used bond salesmen to sell these shares, many of whom approached the same investors quoting different prices, contributing to a sharp fall in share prices.

Evaluating stock market performance

Stock market indices, which exist for most, if not all, stock exchanges in the world, are not always a good means of comparing performance within countries, let alone between various countries. They are a minefield for the unwary. This is because they can be calculated in so many different ways – some are based on simple arithmetic averages, others are weighted in different ways. There are also differences in their composition – some are broadly-based, others narrowly-based, and they all have different base dates. Indeed, any two indices in any country can lead to a different conclusion. But they can still be useful as an average against which to judge the performances of an investment portfolio over a period of time, given that the interpreter understands their true status.

The performance of shares quoted on the London Stock Exchange is measured by a range of Financial Times Indices. Until the beginning of 1984, there were only two indicators of equity performance – the FT Ordinary Index, which consists of only 30 industrial shares, is price-related and is calculated hourly, and the FT All-Share Index, which now includes 727 equity shares and is calculated daily. An innovation at that time was the FT-SE 100 Share Index, which met the need for an index that was representative and which could be rapidly calculated, and which, generally speaking, is based upon the largest 100 companies, measured by their market valuation calculated on a minute-by-minute basis.

These FT indices are broadly analagous in terms of their popularity to the Dow Jones indices as used in the United States, of which the most frequently quoted is the Industrial Average, and provide an adequate profile of share performance because of the homogeneity of the Exchange itself. Gilt edged securities have their own performance indicators.

There are two independent groups of indices in the United States, Dow Jones and Standard and Poors (S & P), in addition to which the various stock exchanges have their own composite indices. Dow

Jones publishes four integrated averages daily in the Wall Street Journal: the Industrial Average, simply an arithmetic average of the price movements of 30 large manufacturing companies which is posted every half-hour during the trading day in the NYSE; the Transportation Average, which is a similar average of 20 transport companies; the Utility Average which takes 15 utility companies; and the Composite Average, which is a combination of the other three. The Standard and Poors Composite takes the total market value of 500 stocks, divides their weighted average market value during the period 1941 to 1943 and then multiplies by 10.

The New York Stock Exchange Composite Index and Amex Market Value Index are both measures of all common stocks traded on the respective exchanges, weighted by their market value. NYSE also publishes specialised indices for industrial, utility, transport and financial companies, all adjusted to eliminate effects of capitalisation changes, new listings and delistings. NASDAQ offers a variety of weighted average indices for the OTC market, and on 10 July 1984 introduced two new market-weighted measures, a Composite Index and an Industrial Index. The Wall Street Journal also publishes the much less sophisticated Advances and Declines Index which simply consists of two figures each day.

Japan's Nikkei Dow Jones Average is calculated on an arithmetic basis similar to the formula of the Dow Jones Average in the United States, using share prices of only 250 companies listed on the first section of the exchange relative to the basis of 4 January 1968. Although it is adjusted for rights issues and share splits, it suffers from the same shortcomings as the Dow Jones; volatile movements of smaller companies have a disproportionate effect and it is far too narrowly-based. The Tokyo Stock Exchange New Index was devised to remedy just these defects, being a weighted average of all first section listed shares and calculated retrospectively to give the same basis as the Nikkei. It is adjusted to take account of rights and split issues and also new listings. It is also supplemented by separate sub-indices for groups of small, medium and large companies defined by issued capital, for specified industrial groups, and for 300 designated shares that are traded on the second section of the exchange.

Table 3.7 is a selective list of some of the more important indices, along with their essential characteristics.

As the supply and availability of international stocks increase and as investors and institutions become more aware of and more interested in foreign investment, there follows a need to measure how well such

Table 3.7   The essential characteristics of some stock market indices

United Kingdom	FT Ordinary Index	30 blue chips, arithmetic 30'
	FT All-Share	727 shares
	FT-SE 100 Share Index	100 shares
United States	Dow Jones Industrial Average	30 blue chips, arithmetic
	Standard and Poors Composite	500 stocks, weighted average
	NYSE Composite	All, weighted
	NASDAQ OTC Composite	All, weighted
Japan	Nikkei Dow Jones	250 shares, arithmetic
	Tokyo SE New	All first section, weighted
Germany	Commerzbank	60 blue chips, weighted average
	Faz Aktien	100 shares actively traded on the Frankfurt SE
	Boersen-Zeitung	30 shares 'real-time'
France	CAC General Indication de Tendances	250 stocks, categorised
Italy	Banca Commerciale Italiana	All shares on Milan SE
Switzerland	Swiss Bank Industrial	100 actively-traded shares
Australia	All Ordinaries	250 shares, weighted
	Metals and Minerals	Approx. one-third all ordinaries
Canada	Toronto Metals & Minerals	
	Toronto Composite	300 capital-weighted shares
	Montreal Portfolio	25 stocks, arithmetic
Hong Kong	Hang Seng Bank	33 stocks, arithmetically weighted
Singapore	Straits Times	30 stocks, unweighted
World	MS Capital International	see below

investments are performing. Such measurements are now available in the form of price indices based on a selection of internationally-traded stocks. For the fifteen years up to 1987 this field had been the exclusive preserve of the Capital International World Index, which had a history going back to 1960. The index aims to synthesise data of nineteen countries worldwide, covering 1375 of the largest companies representing some 60 per cent of the world's stock market capitalisation. These components are all standardised on an identical base (1 January 1970) so as to build a world index which is a particularly valuable aid to managers of international investment portfolios, whichever discipline they prefer to use in their efforts to outperform the market – selection or currency selection.

Subsequent to the Capital International indices being bought in

Table 3.8   Global stock market indices

	Constituents	Countries	% World capitalisation
Morgan Stanley Capital International	1375	19	60
FT-Actuaries World Index	2400	23	70
Saloman-Russell Primary Market Index	1572	24	60
Euromoney-First Boston Global Stock	1300	17	n/a

Source: The Stock Exchange, *Quality of Markets Quarterly*, Summer 1987

1986 by Morgan Stanley, a New York based investment bank, a branding problem which had already been evident with national indices began to emerge. The result was that other investment banks announced plans to introduce their own world indices. Three new 'international equity' indices have been launched by various institutions in association with different American investment banks in 1987, namely the FT-Actuaries World Index – a joint venture of the Financial Times, Goldman Sachs and Wood MacKenzie, the Saloman-Russell Primary Market Index, and the Euromoney-First Boston Global Stock Index. Moreover, at least two more series are thought to be being developed, by Shearson Lehman and Paine Webber respectively. In general, each index is calculated in a very similar way, all being weighted by the market capitalisation of their individual constituents. The major difference occurs in the selection of stocks. Table 3.8 gives a comparison of the four international equity indices.

The Saloman-Russell and Euromoney-First Boston indices tend to apply more stringent criteria to the selection of a stock with regard to the availability to foreign ownership and the degree of liquidity in foreign markets. Such differences will usually present minor deviations in the comparison between indices. The usefulness of one index as compared with another will depend on how one is trying to evaluate one's portfolio.

The instruments

Stock exchanges trade in two fundamental types of capital, equity (or risk) and debt (or fixed income) securities. The borrowers of the former are confined to the corporate sector, while the borrowers of the latter are more often government or similar public institutions, although corporate borrowers are rapidly increasing in debt markets generally. This is a manifestation of the process of securitisation of borrowing, which has been discussed previously. Because debt capital is the subject of a later chapter, little more will be discussed about debt capital at this stage, except to bring out comparisons between debt and equity.

Equity capital and debt capital

The nature of equities is probably best explained by discussing the fundamental distinction between the ownership of a company and that company's creditors, how their different interests are treated in a company's balance sheet, and the rights and protections afforded to each by the law.

The shareholder is legally an owner of the company, and will take a risk upon whether the company's profitability is sufficiently healthy for a dividend to be declared, i.e. when the company distributes its profits. He may also participate in certain other activities of the company, such as attending and voting at the general meetings of the company when, in particular, the board of directors is elected. It is that board of directors, not the shareholders, which has the responsibility for the company's managerial decisions and any ensuing actions between general meetings. Similarly, the shareholder of a company is not held responsible for that company's debt, save to the extent of any uncalled portion of his shareholding. This is the familiar concept of limited liability.

The creditor, on the other hand, who may be a bond or note holder, lends money over a period of time in return for a definite payment of interest, which may be at a fixed or variable rate. Apart from that he is only entitled to the return of his principal upon redemption or maturity of the loan.

Furthermore, in the event of liquidation of the company, equity is subordinate to debt. This means that creditors will be repaid first, on the assumption that net assets are adequate. It should be emphasised, however, that even creditors may enjoy differing levels of preference. This is usually determined by company laws in various countries. At the end of the day, it is only when all the creditors have been fully satisfied that outstanding liabilities to shareholders will be addressed.

Share equity enables a company to accomplish two objectives. By selling shares it is able to expand its capital base, and this, in turn, spreads the risks of doing business. The appeal of equity as an investment is as follows:

1. The investor must believe that the particular company will return a rate that is better than he could receive from other forms of asset.
2. The stock market and economic climate must be conducive to appreciation in share prices.

The term 'share' is usually used to refer to ordinary shares or, as the Americans call them, common stock. Ordinary shares under UK law must be issued with a par value, i.e. the minimum amount which must be paid in respect of their issue. This is usually 25p, but may be any amount. However, there is another category of share which is, in many ways, more akin to fixed income securities in that the amount of dividend is pre-stated, normally in percentage terms. These are called preference shares (or preferred shares in the United States), and usually rank just above ordinary shares in the scale of redress upon liquidation. In other respects they are not dissimilar to ordinary shares. Sometimes they have additional features, such as being convertible into ordinary shares at a later date. Or they may also be cumulative, meaning that if a dividend is omitted, it will be made good when the financial health of the company improves. They generally represent less than one per cent of the outstanding value of ordinary shares in the United Kingdom.

ADRs and trust certificates of beneficial interest

Two further categories of share issue peculiar to the United States are American Depository Receipts (ADRs) and trust certificates of beneficial interest. ADRs are designated as a convenient form in which US investors may hold and trade in foreign securities. They are registered negotiable documents, issued in the United States, which certify that a specific number of foreign shares have been deposited with an overseas branch of a US bank (or other financial institution), which acts as custodian in the country of origin. ADRs usually only represent shares which are traded on a recognised foreign stock exchange, but the holder will receive dividends and may exercise voting rights in the normal way, and can at any time request delivery of the relevant share certificates. Traditionally, the shares most traded in ADR form have been resource-based, such as South African gold mines and speculative Australian oil and mining companies, but the range of shares covered by these instruments is widening quite significantly.

Trust certificates of beneficial interest represent equity interests in assets of a trust which holds debt securities or other interests. They represent a pro rata ownership in the assets of that trust, and the holders are entitled to receive dividends based on their pro rata ownership. Voting power may, however, be limited to the election of trustees.

Registered and bearer shares

Whereas shares in the United Kingdom, the United States and Japan are generally in registered form, which makes the levy of stamp duty and capital gains tax far easier, the practice in many countries in continental Europe has been to issue most shares in bearer form. These can be readily transferred to another holder by hand. Dividends are payable to the actual bearer, or physical holder of the security, and the securities will carry coupons which are detached and exchanged for dividends when due.

Gearing

The debt/equity ratio, or gearing, of companies can vary quite considerably between countries. The average in the United States and the United Kingdom has traditionally been 1:1 or 50 per cent of each, whereas the gearing of Japanese corporations has usually been much higher, of the order of 4:1, which means that they have 20 per cent equity capital and 80 per cent debt capital, predominantly short-term borrowings from commercial banks. This gearing often depends upon the nature of the investment banking function in a particular country. The acceptance which shares have gained in historic terms with the investing public will often hinge on returns that equities have yielded against bonds and other investment assets.

An outstanding example of an area where equity capital has not usually been so popular as debt capital is continental Europe. This preference of continental European investors for bonds was probably created and nurtured for the most part by the role that commercial, all-service banks played. In this respect the large German banks such as Deutsche Bank, Commerzbank and Dresdner Bank were always at the forefront. Traditionally, the majority of shares in many German companies have tended to be held by banks, insurance companies and individual families. This meant that those available for trading was often limited to less than 50 per cent and sometimes as little as

Table 3.9 Share/debenture turnover of domestic and foreign companies on German
exchanges

DM million		Securities of domestic issuers		Securities of foreign issuers	
	Total	Bonds	Shares	Bonds	Shares
1982	128,784	74,203	35,161	14,268	5,152
1983	185,586	68,903	84,128	17,413	15,144
1984	234,347	110,380	84,705	22,441	16,828
1985	436,002	168,011	210,708	31,099	26,186
1986	602,545	237,612	294,693	37,230	33,032

Source: Deutsche Bundesbank

10 per cent of a company's equity capital, and additional corporate finance was raised through bank borrowing. In any case, bonds were perceived as much safer instruments than shares, a factor which proved attractive to investors who were more accustomed to political instability than British or US contemporaries.

Table 3.9 demonstrates this tradition and shows the clear recent tendency towards placing of shares.

The French concentration on debt rather than equity capital is an indicator of the traditionally controlled nature of the French economy, where much of industry received capital from state institutions or banks, often at very favourable rates of interest. Two factors which have contributed to change have been the expansion of the unit trust industry, following special tax concessions granted in the late 1970s, and the more recent privatisation programme of the government of Jacques Chirac. This was launched in November 1986, with the issue of shares in St Gobain SA, and since then 65 companies and banks, valued at about $US 35 billion, have attracted much interest. Table 3.10 demonstrates the effects of these trends.

The issuance of equities

A big consideration for a company contemplating a new equity share issue will be its ability to maintain its dividend to cover the number of new shares. This cost will usually be compared with the interest that would have to be paid on a new bond issue.

It has previously been stated that preference shares are sometimes issued with the right to convert. Loan stocks are also marketed in this

Table 3.10 Market capitalisation of French securities, PSE, official and second
markets

FF billions	Total	Shares	Bonds
1982	978.3	199.4	778.9
1983	1305.8	327.8	987.0
1984	1645.4	413.9	1231.5
1985	2162.6	649.6	1513.0
1986	2977.6	1104.2	1873.4

Source: Crédit Commercial de France, Paris Stock Exchange

way. Less common, but still affording the investor the potential of
capital gain, is the issuance of debentures or bonds with warrants
attached. These are certificates which give the holder the right to
convert the original securities into shares at a stipulated market price
within a determined period or, in some cases, even without time
limit.

Another method is the scrip or capitalisation issue (in UK terms)
or the stock dividend (in US terms) which offers existing shareholders
a dividend payment in the form of new stock rather than for cash.
Similar to this is the rights issue, whereby existing shareholders may
subscribe to new shares at a specified offering price, in proportion to
the number of shares already held. The offer will usually take the
form of a prospectus, which will detail the purpose of the issue and
the number of shares for sale to each shareholder. Yet another
method is a stock split, whereby companies may split their shares into
smaller denominations.

For a private company going public for the first time, the most
common method employed is an 'offer for sale', whereby the company
offers its shares to a specialist issuing house which, in turn, will offer
them to the public. Issuers sometimes arrange to offer shares for sale
by tender. This will usually entail allocating all the shares to higher
ranked offers at the 'striking price', that is the price of the lowest
acceptable application which, taken with higher bids, will clear all the
stocks on offer. A third method is to issue shares through a placing,
whereby the issuing institution sells shares to a number of other
institutional (and sometimes to individual) investors besides supplying
some to stock exchange market-makers to ensure a market.

Initially, stock may be subscribed to on a partly-paid basis, with
the balance due at the end of the period. An example of this was the

British Gas offer of early 1987, payable 50p on application, 45p on 9 June 1987 and 40p on 19 April 1988. This enables many investors, called 'stags', to purchase new offerings on a partly-paid basis and sell them before final payment is due, hoping for a highly-leveraged profit.

The players

The structures of operation vary widely over the various stock exchanges. New York and, since 'Big Bang' (see Appendix A), London operate what are known as dual-capacity systems, where the functions of broking and market-making can be fulfilled by the same firms. Others, such as Tokyo, still operate a single-capacity system, the basis of which is a separation of the different functions of broker and market-maker.

The brokers

Brokers are the agents who trade in stocks and shares on behalf of investors, and make their living on the commissions charged on deals. Under the rules of the International Stock Exchange in London they are bound to buy and sell shares in listed companies, Government stocks and other forms of traded securities at the best possible prices to the investor. They also process the transaction, and will sometimes provide research and investment advice and offer other services such as fund management.

As has previously been explained, there are several categories of brokers who fulfil this role in New York, such as commission brokers, floor brokers, and occasionally the specialist, while in Tokyo it is the regular member who buys and sells on the floor of the exchange.

The market-makers

These are the wholesalers who compete with each other to supply brokers with stocks and shares, and who also buy shares from brokers who are acting on behalf of investors wishing to sell. Unlike brokers, they charge no commission, but make their living on the spread, i.e. the difference between bid and offer prices. It is the specialists who perform this task in New York, and *saitori* members in Tokyo.

The institutional investors

It is the institutions, the big professional investors such as pension funds and insurance companies, who are generally the principal owners of shares or stocks. Millions of people all over the world who buy life insurance, invest in unit trusts or participate in a pension fund have a stake in stock markets, often without being aware of it, through providing the funds which institutions invest.

Pension funds own nearly one-third of UK quoted shares, probably worth around £150 billion. Nearly all the largest are nationalised industry funds such as the British Coal, the Post Office and the Electricity Supply pension funds, each valued at between £4 billion and £5 billion. Private pension funds and local authority funds are also major investors.

Insurance companies account for another quarter of UK share ownership by investing policyholders' money to provide benefits in the case of the life assurance groups or by investing the premiums paid for household, motor and other forms of insurance. Investment Trusts and Unit Trusts are also important institutional investors, who have a powerful presence in the stock market. The size of their funds means that they can influence Stock Exchange performance and the values of individual companies quite substantially. Table 3.11 gives a breakdown of UK shareholdings by category.

Figures for turnover by volume on stock exchanges very often yield a different story. For example, a recent survey revealed that, on the New York Stock Exchange, institutions account for approximately 46 per cent, private individuals account for approximately 30 per cent, and member firms who deal as principals 24 per cent, whereas the institutions on Amex only accounted for 33 per cent, while individuals were responsible for 49 per cent and member firms for 20 per cent of turnover. Similar surveys in Tokyo in recent years have shown that institutions account for 31.5 per cent, individuals for 41.6 per cent and member firms for 26.9 per cent of turnover. This situation was turned around in 1986 when, for the first time in history, domestic institutions' share of purchasing at 45.4 per cent surpassed the individual investors' share at 38.7 per cent.

It may be worth making two points here. Firstly, a high level of trading in relation to ownership by individuals and member firms may be an illustration of the speculative character of a market. Secondly, many countries are now positively encouraging the private ownership of shares, hence there is a change in these proportions.

Table 3.11   Shareholder breakdown

Pension funds	27 per cent
Insurance companies	21
Investment trusts	7
Unit trusts	4
Other institutions	13
Individuals	28
	100

Source: The London Stock Exchange, *Shareholder Study*, 1981

The individual investors

In the United Kingdom until 1984 there had been a steady decline in the number of private shareholders. The tide has now turned. The growth of employee share schemes, coupled with the privatisation of a string of previously public corporations, such as British Telecom, British Gas, British Airways, TSB and Rolls Royce, has substantially increased the number of shareholders, which are now estimated to account for at least 12 per cent of the UK adult population – some five million people.

Some market concepts and techniques

Long and short positions

The long position implies ownership, whereas the short position relates the opposite, a lack of ownership. It follows that the term 'going long', otherwise known as taking a long position, is no more than the market patois for the purchase of securities. And that position will remain 'open' until 'closed' by an ultimate sale.

'Short selling', however, occurs when an investor contracts to sell a security which he does not actually own. By doing so he 'opens a short position', which has to be closed, in order that delivery can ultimately be effected, through the purchasing or borrowing of the same security, known as 'short covering'. The only way that this practice will make money is if the sale is covered at a lower price than the original short sale.

Arbitrage

Short selling is often used as a tool in the process of arbitrage, which may be classically defined as that practice where an investor will simultaneously buy in one market and sell in a second, whenever legally able to do so. Although the effect of technology on information flows has reduced the opportunities for exploitation of traditional methods, and its nature has changed more towards the simultaneous buying and selling of substitutable securities in the same market, arbitrage still occurs in virtually all of the financial markets. However, since it is usually based on the smallest of price differentials, it has a tendency to create transactions of very large value, often highly leveraged in futures and options.

Program trading

Program trading, which has been a subject of constant discussion since the stock market crash of October 1987, embraces two main investment strategies – one of which is aggressive in character, known as index arbitrage, while the other, known as portfolio insurance, is defensive. Program trading was originally so-called on account of its involvement with a large 'program' or basket of stocks. Nowadays the term is more often applied in the context of contemporary arbitrage practice, which makes great use of sophisticated electronic computer technology in continuously monitoring the prices of baskets of stock, such as the Standard and Poor's 500 index, and comparing them with prices of dependent futures contracts, such as S & P 500 equivalent available on the Chicago Mercantile Exchange. When a disparity of adequate size emerges, and a market opportunity is indicated by the computer, then large portfolio trades may be automatically implemented.

Index arbitrage is designed to exploit these occasional price differences which emerge between such a basket of stock market investments and a highly leveraged dependent stock index future. And it is, indeed, transactions between the S & P 500 and its dependent future which are most popularly practised, the former on the New York Stock Exchange's Superdot 250 electronic order-routeing system, and the latter on the Chicago Mercantile Exchange or some other exchange offering a comparable futures contract. They now account for 75 per cent of all trading in stock index futures.

Such profitable trading opportunities for arbitrageurs will exist whenever that margin known as the 'basis' deviates substantially from its equilibrium (or its theoretical) value. This basis is no more than the difference between the index and any futures contract, which can be measured either in dollar value or index points. The equilibrium difference between the two, which is related to the equilibrium differences between the spot and futures prices of each stock within the index and futures baskets, is determined by the so-called 'Cost of Carry' which is an opportunity cost for holding the stock or 'carrying it forward' from the present to the future date.

Mathematicians (colloquially known as 'rocket scientists') at various large Wall Street houses, such a Salomon Brothers and Morgan Stanley, devised the computer programs which would spot these occasional anomalies and shift funds from one market to another to generate a risk-free gain. Since arbitrage trading, by its nature, drives stock and future prices together, however, heavy competition has now reduced these anomalies or spreads almost to nothing, and huge sums have had to be invested for any worthwhile profit to be generated. In consequence, the underlying dollar volume in the futures market has vastly exceeded that of the stock market itself.

Portfolio insurance, first devised by Professor Hayne Leland of the University of Berkeley, California, and marketed principally through a firm known as Leland O'Brien Rubenstein and Associates, but not introduced until 1985, has rapidly gained in popularity. It was argued that if fund managers were to hedge their positions in falling stock markets through a so-called 'dynamic adjustment process' – which involved selling futures at mathematically-devised trigger points reached with the aid of computers – this would be a far cheaper form of hedging, in terms of brokers' commissions, than if they merely sold the stocks; indeed it would be cheaper by a factor of ten. The futures involved do not need to be dependent futures, however. They may well be treasury bills or bonds. The point is that if the original stocks fall further, the loss is then offset by compensating profits on the expiration of the alternative contract, which is usually at 60 or 90 days. The ultimate danger is, of course, that this practice may stimulate a cascade effect.

Serious technical problems were formerly created four times each year, as the index futures, index options and individual stock options contracts all expired concurrently at the close of trading on the New York Stock Exchange. The term used to describe this phenomenon, which generated a large surge in trading volume at the closing bell, was 'triple-witching'. This was eventually overcome by a bilateral agreement between the New York Stock Exchange and the Chicago Mercantile Exchange to settlement-at-open.

Margin trading

One of the least understood market techniques is 'margin trading'. It involves buying securities on the back of credit extended by a bank or brokerage house involved in a transaction. This method is mainly used in the United States, but also to a much lesser extent on the continent of Europe. It allows the investor to gear up or leverage himself in order to buy shares, usually for a fraction of the purchase or selling price involved. For instance, if there is a margin requirement of 50 per cent, then the investor will merely pay interest on the margin at what is known in the United States as the 'broker loan rate', usually 1–1.5 per cent below the US prime rate. Any rise in interest rates, which makes the cost of holding such a position more expensive, will often provoke what is called a 'margin shake-out'.

Although 'margin trading' does not currently take place in Britain, there is a process which enables traders to leverage themselves quite highly, albeit for quite short periods. Shares trade in what are called account periods, or in market patois 'dealt for the account'. These periods normally run for two weeks, and an investor may deal in shares but not have to settle for ten days after the account has officially ended. In addition, if the investor wants to extend this leveraged period, he may arrange a 'contango' with a broker. By this method, the shares are carried over into a new account period. Interest, or contango, is paid on the money involved.

Corporate performance – the profile of a share

Prices and earnings

The minute-to-minute performance of a quoted share is reflected on stock markets by movements in that particular stock's price, and quoted in terms of pence in London, dollars in New York and so on. Prices may be quoted in newspapers and on screens as so many pence up or so many dollars, or even cents, off on the day. The basis of that judgement is the previous day's closing price. It should be made clear also that such a price is neither the actual price paid on purchase of that share at the previous day's close nor the price received when selling. It is the middle price, which is usually mid-way between the bid and offer prices, and therefore only an indication of a traded price. Moreover, the indicator of price movements, which will usually appear in newspaper listings in a column headed '+/−' or something similar, should be viewed as no more than a short-term indicator of whether a share price is on the way up or down.

In relation to the basis for that judgement of price movement, either the previous day's closing price, or the outright middle price at any moment of time, it must also be stressed that it is most unwise to use that price in any other way than as a point on a time series for that particular share or stock. The reason for this is that not only are different shares likely to have different base prices, or prices at the previous day's close, but even more fundamentally they may represent shares which had a different price denomination at issue. To take an example from the London Stock Exchange, if ICI and BAT shares had both risen by 14 pence during part of a day's trading this would tell us nothing more about the short term if the previous day's closing prices had been £11⁷⁄₁₆ and 420p respectively. Neither would it be helpful from the comparative long-term standpoint, since ICI shares have a face value of £1 while BAT's are denominated at 25p. The point is that, if a comparison had to be made between the performance of the two shares, it would be necessary to take the base prices, perhaps the previous day's close in the short term and the face value in the long term, and then project the two price movements from them, expressing the result in percentage change terms.

There are other uses, some more important than others, to which share prices and movements can be put as indicators of performance. The first, which is a fairly straightforward one, is as a snapshot measure of the capitalisation of companies. This always presupposes that one has available figures for the number of shares outstanding, which is then multiplied by the quoted price of a share. While the *Financial Times* does not publish these calculations for shares quoted on the London Stock Exchange, they can be found each Monday within the financial pages of *The Times*. A more important series of measures has to do with relating quoted prices to various other indicators, such as earnings and dividends, to give price/earnings ratios, earnings yields and dividend yields.

A company's earnings – the sum of revenue less expenditure (including interest) less tax – are equally of little value unless related to the capitalisation of the company. After all, the investor is ultimately interested in the return on his investment or, in aggregate terms, the capital employed. But again, this does not reveal a particularly useful

Table 3.12 Price/earnings ratios of shares quoted on major stock exchanges

Year-end	1982	1983	1984	1985	1986	1987
New York	14.7	13.0	10.4	13.7	14.1	15.9
Tokyo	25.8	24.7	37.1	35.2	47.3	–
London	11.5	13.9	13.1	12.3	13.4	4.5
Frankfurt	11.2	15.0	13.5	16.7	14.7	
Paris	6.6	8.5	11.4	13.0	17.0	
Hong Kong	8.6	7.6	9.2	14.9	15.9	
Singapore	20.9	28.2	20.4	18.1	36.7	
Sydney	11.1	15.1	9.6	11.0	14.0	

comparative measure. However, if a figure for the most recent year's earnings is divided by the number of shares outstanding, this produces a figure for earnings per share, or the EPS.

By dividing the quoted price for a share by earnings per share, the P/E ratio, or price/earnings ratio, is derived. As a succinct measure of the price which an investor has to pay for a given income from his shares, this is probably the most important single comparative indicator to be watched by the stock markets, particularly within the same industry group. If, for example, the average P/E in an industry group is 10, then a company with a P/E of only 6 is undervalued. Conversely, a company with a P/E of 15 is overvalued. Table 3.12 give the P/E ratios of shares quoted on the major stock exchanges.

The reciprocal of the P/E ratio expressed in percentage terms is the earnings yield. It is worth noting, particularly at times such as we have recently experienced when prices are changing abruptly, that the P/E and the earnings yield will always move in opposite directions. This is a relationship which may be observed daily in the *Financial Times*, both in terms of the London Stock Exchange, which is analysed in great detail, and the New York stock exchanges, based on Standard and Poors Composite Index. And it follows from this relationship that a low earnings yield with a correspondingly high P/E usually indicates an expectation of steadily increasing future earnings, tempered only by the fact that different companies have varying reporting periods and, in consequence, even the value of P/E ratios and earnings yields has its limits as a comparative measure.

A company will usually, if not always, retain some share of its profits, which it will hope to employ even more profitably, to the ultimate benefit of its shareholders. Only the remainder will be distributed, usually in the form of dividends, and the measure which

Table 3.13   Average dividend yields on major stock exchanges

Year-end	1982	1983	1984	1985	1986	1987
New York	5.2	4.4	4.5	3.8	3.6	3.13
Tokyo	1.6	1.3	1.0	0.9	0.7	–
London	5.7	4.8	4.6	4.4	4.2	4.5

expresses the total profits as a ratio of that part which is distributed is known as the cover. The measure expressing the dividend paid as a percentage of the quoted price per share, but not the total profits, is the dividend yield. Dividends paid out vary according to industrial groups. Some groups, such as United States public utilities, for example, are noted for high dividend pay-outs, while others, such as the high technology companies, show a preference for reinvestment

Table 3.14   Classifications used by major US rating agencies

Standard & Poor's	Moody's	Description
A+	high grade	highest rating
A	investment grade	high rating
A–	upper medium grade	above average
B+	medium grade	average rating
B	lower medium grade	below average
B–	–	lower than average
C	speculative grade	–
D	–	reorganisation

of earnings. In the latter case, capital growth becomes the growth criterion to be followed. Thus, even the dividend yield is only a conditional indicator of the financial health of a company. Table 3.13 shows average dividend yields on major stock exchanges.

Quality ratings

Shares are also rated as to quality by various international rating services, of which the most famous are probably the American agencies. The two biggest, and those which give the most visible, widely-disseminated classifications of domestic and international issues, are Standard and Poors (S & P) and Moody's. While the two agencies employ different financial models in their rating processes, their classification lists show that they both essentially break down their quality categories in a similar manner, as shown in Table 3.14.

These ratings can have a profound impact upon investor attitudes and indeed the subsequent price behaviour of shares. For instance, a stock rating which falls from A to B+ will probably suffer a drop in market price to reflect the higher risk now attached since the rating fall suggests a declining financial position, in terms not necessarily of sales or revenues but of a deterioration in the company's overall financial health. This situation can also lead to an additional cost of capital if new equity is to be raised in the future.

Following shares in the newspapers

A pragmatic way of assessing shares is through daily newspapers. The following points describe the *Financial Times* share listings:

1. Groupings of share types
   Listed shares are divided, for convenience, into a number of sectors – for example, engineering or electricals, British Government securities or investment trusts. Some sectors – such as mines – are broken down still further into sub-groups such as tin, diamond and platinum, etc.

2. The stock name
   Within the industry groups we see the names under which the stocks are traded, e.g. under the 'electricals' industry group – AB Electronic, AMS Inds 5p etc.

3. Performance record
   The two columns on the far left – headed 'High/Low' – are the performance record. These show the highest and lowest prices at which the stock has been traded during the year to date, or in the present case for 1986 and 1987 to date.

4. Price
   It should be stressed that the price listed in this column is only an indication of the actual price paid when buying a share or received when selling at close of the previous day's business. It is the middle price, which is usually mid-way between the bid and offer prices. Unless otherwise indicated, prices are quoted in pence and in denominations of 25p.

5. Price movements
    The next column, headed '+/−', shows how much this middle
    price of a share has risen or fallen on the previous day's closing
    price. It is no more than a short-term indicator of whether a share
    price is on the way up or down.

6. Dividend (net)
    This shows how much profit a company returned to its investors
    for each share they owned at the last distribution. Dividends are
    listed either as gross figures (before deduction of tax at the
    standard rate) or net figures (after tax at the standard rate). As
    with prices, unless otherwise indicated, net dividends are quoted
    in pence and in denominations of 25p.

7. Cover
    The cover is the ratio between a company's total profit and the
    amount of profit which it distributes to shareholders in the form
    of dividends. Therefore, when a dividend is said to be 'twice
    covered', the total value represents half the profit of a company.

8. Gross yield
    The gross yield represents the dividend expressed as a percentage
    of the share price. It provides an accurate indication of how much
    a share is actually yielding in income terms. For example, if a
    company pays a dividend of 10p per share and its share price is
    £1.00, then its gross yield is 10 per cent.

9. Price/earnings ratio
    The final column, the P/E ratio, is a measure of the price which
    an investor has to pay for a given income from his shares. It
    represents the share price over the most recent year's earnings
    per share (the net return earned by a company divided by the
    number of shares issued). For example, a company with a quoted
    share price of £1 and earnings of 10p per share would have a P/E
    ratio of 10:1, whereas a company with a share price of £1 and
    earnings of 20p per share would have a P/E ratio of 5:1.

CHAPTER FOUR

Money markets

The function of money markets

The term 'money markets' collectively defines a grouping of large banks and other financial institutions in a country, or group of countries, which facilitates the channelling of short-term wholesale funds from lenders to borrowers. The interpretation of 'short-term' in this sense varies from country to country. Generally it may be assumed to apply to funds with a final maturity of less than one year. Canada, where the money market embraces securities of up to three years' maturity, is an exception however. This is because the Bank of Canada is prepared to advance credit against certain securities with a maturity of three years or less.

Among the most important money markets are those for bills, interbank deposits and certificates of deposit, all of which involve the movement of very large quantities of institutional or wholesale funds – often individually amounting to many millions of dollars or pounds – agreed verbally between dealers over the telephone, with quick speed of reaction and at a low transaction cost. This is not to say that they do not influence the life of the individual, however. They do, in the sense that they are a source of immediate reaction to government economic policies through the medium of interest rates.

In common with bond markets but unlike the equities markets, money markets are markets in debt finance. That is to say, they loan specific amounts of money for specific periods to borrowers who will promise to pay a specified rate of interest. On maturity of the obligation, this is paid to the lender along with repayment of the principal amount. Unlike other debt markets, such as bond markets and fixed interest (or gilts) sections of stock markets, both of which normally trade in instruments of longer maturity, money markets are not strictly capital markets. Their primary concern is with the provision of liquidity, a sufficiency of which is maintained through advance and rediscounting facilities provided by the central banks, and the redistribution of that liquidity from lenders (i.e. those economic units within the short-term financial system which possess surpluses, often households operating through financial intermediaries which aggregate their savings, such as banks, building societies, pension funds and insurance companies), to those which experience shortages, usually government or business enterprises, which by nature of their social and commercial mandates are the net spenders in an economy.

It is for the reasons outlined above that these markets are also highly relevant to the conduct of monetary policy by governments through central banks. Just as the Bank of England influences British short-term interest rates by intervening in the money markets, in particular the discount market, so the Federal Reserve System in the United States, the Deutsche Bundesbank in Frankfurt, the Banque de France in Paris and others throughout the world do likewise. Central banks commonly use two major policy instruments, or strategies, for this purpose. They can, for example, impose a reserve requirement upon their banking system. This means that a variable proportion of funds has to be retained in a liquid form rather than lent. Such increased reserves, other things being equal, put upward pressure on interest rates until the desired effect is reached. Conversely, a reduction in reserves will have the opposite stimulant effect. The other instrument or strategy which is commonly employed is that of open market operations. This is when cash is either absorbed or freed into the financial system at any point in time, usually through the sale or purchase of treasury bills. Such transactions can be varied many times over through a period until monetary targets are temporarily reached.

An ideal money market could be said to demand three fundamental conditions. The first of these is a central bank, capable and willing to act as a lender of last resort. This facility enables the banking system to operate to lower levels of liquidity, making full use of available resources. From the standpoint of the central bank, there is the advantage of greater influence over the banking sector when the banks work to these finer margins. This means that, every time it chooses to influence the amount of cash and other liquid assets available through open market activities, its effects are not only felt much more rapidly, but a given intervention also has larger repercussions. A second condition, if the market is not to be limited in scope, is the need for an integrated structure of financial institutions holding a variety of assets with differing liquidity and profitability to be grouped around the central banks, each with a desire to switch their assets, whether they be in cash or other liquid or near liquid form, to meet the public demand for the supply of money or near money. A final condition, to inspire confidence, is the formulation and implementation of a system of prudential regulation to control and classify market assets. Having defined an ideal market mechanism, however, it must immediately be conceded that many advanced countries operate in an entirely satisfactory way without having such sophisticated markets in short-term money and short-dated securities.

Indeed, the United Kingdom is unique in the way in which the London money market carries out the function of equalising surpluses and deficits within the system. British commercial banks hardly ever deal directly with the Bank of England; instead they deal through the intermediation of discount houses. This policy has been followed since 1825. Only in times of national emergency, such as the two World Wars or a monetary crisis, has the Bank of England given direct assistance to the banking system, bypassing the money market.

Until comparatively recently, this job was done solely through the intermediation of the 'traditional' discount market. Only in the early 1960s did it begin to be shared with the 'parallel' markets in sterling interbank deposits, certificates of deposit and other instruments. That new role expanded further following the publication of the Bank of England's document, *Competition and Credit Control* in September 1971, in which it was stipulated that all banks should maintain a reserve ratio of 12.5 per cent to comprise certain specified reserve assets. Both the discount market and the banks chose to keep about 50 per cent of this requirement in call money.

The discount houses, in borrowing excess reserves from the commercial banks and then redeploying them into slightly less liquid instruments, perform several vital functions:

1. They make the call money market.
2. They cover the treasury bill market.
3. They assist merchant banks by providing an independent market for the discounting of bankers acceptances and non-government paper.
4. They indirectly assist the Bank of England in the re-financing of the public debt by dealing in short-bonds and other gilts nearing maturity.

Money markets

Table 4.1   Yield spread: US treasury bill v. US commercial paper (three month)

End of year	1981	1982	1983	1984	1985	1986	1987
Treasury bills	11.90	8.15	9.28	7.99	7.25	5.73	5.50
Commercial paper	12.78	8.81	9.89	8.34	8.01	8.04	7.80
Spread in favour of bills	0.88	0.66	0.61	0.35	0.76	2.31	2.30

Source: Morgan Guaranty Trust of New York, *World Financial Markets*

5.   They provide an alternative source of short-term funds for trade and industry.
6.   They make the secondary market in sterling and dollar Certificates of Deposit.
7.   They provide a source of reserve assets for banks.

In America and elsewhere this is done through commercial banks being required simply to maintain specific cash reserve ratios with their respective central banks, and then to rely upon rediscount facilities through the so-called discount window of the central bank when they need to replenish cash supplies. That is, they complete the equalisation function either by receiving direct assistance from the central bank or by passing on surplus funds to that central bank.

Short-term interest rates

The fundamental price on money markets is the interest rate, which will usually vary according to three criteria – the type of borrower, the length of maturity, and the difference between free market rates and manipulated rates. This means that it should never be assumed that there is only one rate for, say, three or six months' funds, in any particular money market. A government instrument will, for instance, always bear a lower rate of return than corporate paper, simply because the former is considered less vulnerable to default than are corporate obligations. Indeed, it may be assumed that it will always be the lowest for that particular point in any maturity spectrum. Table 4.1, showing yield spreads between three month US treasury bills and commercial paper, illustrates this.

Six month paper, for example, will usually yield slightly higher than three month, and similarly three month paper slightly higher than one month. This is merely because they are longer in maturity and will carry at least a marginally higher risk. This is the concept of the 'yield curve'. Finally, the rates of many instruments, such as treasury bills, are susceptible to the actions of central banks and treasuries and are by no means regulated entirely by supply and demand. The most common directly controlled short-term rate is the discount rate, by which central banks loan reserves to commercial institutions.

The calculation of discount yield

Most money market instruments are generally sold on what is known as a discount basis. This means that they are sold at a price lower than par, with principal to be paid back at redemption. It should immediately be stressed that a yield calculation on this basis is somewhat different to that for a traditional bond. That is, instead of being stated in coupon terms, the price reflects the present yield level in the market for an instrument of a particular yield level, term of maturity, and quality. The discount yield is, therefore, a composite expression of both price and yield.

Example
Assume that an investor purchases a treasury bill of one year maturity returning 10 per cent. The price he will pay will be 'about' 90 per cent of par, or in bond market terms, simply 90, with 100 per cent being paid back at redemption. The annual rate of return is thus 10 per cent. It follows that if the investor buys a six month bill with 10 per cent indicated level he will receive 5 per cent after six months, and that a three month bill with a 10 per cent level will return 2.5 per cent.

It should be emphasised that unlike bond yields, money market or discount yields are calculated on a different basis in the British and American markets. There is a difference between the British convention, where the year is assumed to have 365 days, and that of the United States, where discounts are stated on a 360 day basis. The term 'one year bill' still means the same thing, or it would if the longest current treasury bill in Britain did not mature in 91 days while those in the United States are rather longer, but the 360 day basis means that an investor will receive a slightly higher yield than on a 365 day basis.

The 360 day method is calculated as follows for a 10 per cent bill, with the 364 day numerator representative of 52 weeks times seven days:

$$\text{principal} \times \frac{\text{interest}}{100} \times \frac{364}{360} = \text{discount}$$

or $\$US\ 10,000 \times 0.10 \times \dfrac{364}{360} = \$1,011$

and

$$\frac{\$US\ 1,011}{\$US\ 10,000} \times 100 = 10.11 \text{ per cent}$$

The result is that this US method actually yields 10.11 per cent, which is more than the indicated interest rate level.

By comparison, although British practice follows the first two steps, it is then operated on an actual day basis. The calculation for a full one year bill will, therefore, be:

$$£10,000 \times 0.10 \times \frac{365}{365} = £1,000 \quad \text{and} \quad \frac{£1,000}{£10,000} = 10 \text{ per cent}$$

Moreover, if a bill maturing in 363 days is actually purchased, the yield will fall below 10 per cent.

The same procedure is followed for calculating yields for bills purchased after issuance date. For example, the yield for a bill with eight months to run would be calculated as follows in the United States:

$$\$US\ 10,000 \times 0.10 \times \frac{240}{360} = \$US\ 666.67$$

and $\dfrac{\$US\ 666.67}{\$US\ 10,000} = 6.67 \text{ per cent}$

In Britain the yield would be calculated thus:

$$£10,000 \times 0.10 \times \frac{240}{365} = £657.53$$

and $\dfrac{£657.53}{£10,000} = 6.67 \text{ per cent}$

To sum up, the discount basis succinctly states price and yield in a convenient market price. In the example immediately above, the investor will pay principal or the nominal amount of 10,000 minus the appropriate rate of $US 666.67 or £657.53. Thus the dollar value of a 10 per cent treasury bill with 8 months left to maturity is $9333 in the

United States and $9433 in the United Kingdom. The amount of interest can be ascertained at a glance by determining the discounted amount and dividing it by the nominal amount:

$$\frac{\$667}{10,000} = 6.67 \text{ per cent} \qquad \frac{£657}{10,000} = 6.57 \text{ per cent}$$

When comparing returns on money market instruments with those on longer dated bonds which have coupons attached, discount yields are often stated in what is known as 'coupon yield equivalent' or 'bond equivalent'. This may be arrived at by converting the discount yield into a bond yield, itself compounded over the life of the bond, as follows:

$$\frac{\text{quoted rate} \times 365 \times 100}{360 - (\text{quoted rate} \times \text{days to maturity})}$$

It should be noted that this calculation is based on United States conventions, where discount yields are based on a 360 day regime, but bond yields on a 365 day civil year. For the United Kingdom, the 360 on the denominator line would need to be replaced by 365.

The London money market

The discount market

Apart from a fundamental role in the overall financial system, London's discount market provides a distinct commercial and financial service in its own right, which has great significance. Its origins lie in commercial bill discounting and broking in the early nineteenth century. It was only later in that century that it began dealing in treasury bills and then eventually began buying and selling short-dated government bonds.

The discount houses and other financial institutions which operate in this part of the money market will typically borrow sterling from intermediaries on an overnight basis or 'on call', and invest in treasury bills, commercial bills and short-dated government bonds.

Commercial bills
We have noted that the commercial bill, or bill of exchange, is the traditional method by which industrial and commercial firms obtain

their short-term finance, especially those engaged in international trade. There are two distinct ways in which such documents can originate. The conventional 'bank bill' is drawn by a creditor company on a debtor, with the liability being subsequently 'accepted' by a bank or discount house for a fee. This means that the latter guarantees to pay for the goods being supplied by the creditor upon maturity of the bill. 'Acceptance credits', in contrast, are drawn by a debtor company and 'accepted' by a bank or discount house, which will guarantee to pay the amount owing in the event of the debtor defaulting. Once any bill has been accepted by a bank it is known as a 'bankers acceptance'.

This leads to a further classification of commercial bills as 'eligible' and 'ineligible'. In view of the increased importance of operations in bills, the Bank of England included, in its document *Monetary Control – Provisions* published in August 1981, two related steps to promote the discount markets. Firstly, it increased the number of banks whose acceptances it was willing to buy. These banks are known as 'eligible' banks, and this status makes the bills more marketable and secure than their ineligible counterparts. Traditionally, only a limited number of banks (such as the clearing banks and the acceptance houses) had this eligible status. However, in order to ensure an adequate supply of bills through which to conduct its operations, the Bank of England indicated a willingness to extend eligibility to a wider range of banks; in mid-1983 there were over 100 eligible banks. Secondly, to ensure that the discount houses, the main market-makers in bills, had sufficient funds at their disposal, the Bank obliged eligible banks to hold a proportion of their deposits (currently 5 per cent) in secured loans to the discount houses (and certain other specialised institutions).

Treasury bills

Although Treasury bills were the traditional way in which the Government, through the Bank of England, influenced monetary policy, their importance is now on the decline relative to commercial bills and other short-term instruments. This is the result of the present Government's policy of controlling and restricting the supply of money in the UK economy. 'Over-funding', through sales on the market of large quantities of longer-term gild edged securities, created the paradox of a chronic shortage of cash in the money markets. Limited stocks of outstanding Treasury bills precluded the option of buying back this instrument, resulting in a decision by the

Table 4.2   Bank of England treasury bill tender (4 December 1987)

Bills on offer	£100m	Top accepted rate of discount	8.1022%
Total of applications	£930m	Average rate of discount	8.0872%
Total allocated	£100m	Average yield	8.25%
Minimum accepted bid	97.98	Amount on offer at next tender	£100m
Allotment at minimum level	65%		

Source: Financial Times, 7 December 1987

Bank of England to offer through the discount market to buy or lend cash on eligible commercial bills.

Notwithstanding this, the Bank of England announces each Friday the value of Treasury bills which will be offered for sale by tender on the following Friday. These will normally be for a 91 day term. Table 4.2 gives an example of such a tender. Bids are made in amounts ranging from £5000 to £1 million, with the discount houses acting as market-makers, agreeing collectively to apply for all the bills on offer. Such purchases would be largely funded by the 'overnight' or other short-term loans from commercial banks. In the event of these banks then failing to renew their loans, discount houses can either sell any unfunded treasury bills back to the Bank of England or, if it is thought that the cash shortage is only temporary, borrow cash from the Bank.

In practice, the Bank of England can use this process to adjust interest rates through inducing either shortages or surpluses in cash. It can do this by adjusting the flow of cash to commercial banks, maybe by causing them to suffer a shortage through the issue of more treasury bills than the commercial banks can cover, then exacerbating that shortage by only assisting discount houses to cope with it at higher rates of interest.

Local authority bills and short-bonds

We have mentioned that discount houses have, over a number of years, also sought to extend the range of investments in which they have traded in various other directions. Among these have been local authority bills and government bonds of up to five years from maturity (short-bonds). Dealings in various local authority instruments takes place on the discount markets, including negotiable bonds (which are also quoted on the Stock Exchange), and bills, which are traded in the market and classified by the Bank of England on the same basis as are treasury bills. In addition, local authorities raise market loans, mainly from banks and other financial institutions. Short-term loans (up to one year) are sometimes known as local authority deposits. Involvement in government bonds began in the 1930s, during which period there had been a decline in the number of bills of exchange due to the world recession. The discount houses still hold these short-term bonds, especially when they believe that interest rates are likely to fall. Short-bonds are also traded by other institutions such as banks and building societies.

The Bank of England's operations in the discount markets

Until 20 August 1981, the Bank of England had lent to the discount houses at whatever rate of interest it chose to impose, usually for a seven day period. Since then, although it has still reserved the right 'to announce in advance the minimum rate which, for a short period ahead, would apply in lending to the discount markets', it has only exercised this on one occasion. In practice, the market discovers by trial and error at what rate the Bank is prepared to conduct open-market operations in bills with the discount market. And to understand how this works, it is necessary to be clear about the banking system's need to hold balances (or deposits) at the Bank of England.

Importance of Bank of England balances
In fact, because of their major role in providing cheque book and other payments services, it is mainly the London clearing banks that need to hold transactions, or working, balances at the Bank of England. The banks need working balances for three main reasons:

1. To make payments between themselves. When a customer of Bank A gives a cheque for £10 to a customer of Bank B the deposits of Bank A fall by £10 and the deposits of Bank B rise by £10. To complete the transaction Bank A must pay £10 to Bank B. This is done by A transferring £10 of its Bank of England balances to B. Each day there are huge amounts of transactions between the customers of the different clearing banks and the banks have to settle the net flows between them by transferring Bank of England balances amongst themselves. The clearing banks have to hold working balances at the Bank of England to ensure that they can meet their obligations.
2. To make payments to the government. The government banks

with the Bank of England rather than with the clearing banks. Because of this, payments between the government and the rest of the economy have a direct effect on the Bank of England balances of the clearing banks as a whole. When the government is receiving more payments than it is making, the clearing banks, in effect, have to transfer balances from their own accounts at the Bank of England to the government.

3. To obtain more cash (notes and coins). It is by drawing on their balances at the Bank of England that the banks obtain more cash.

Offsetting shortages and surpluses
Each day payments between the government and the rest of economy – resulting from government spending, the payment of taxes and a host of other transactions – usually amount to hundreds of millions of pounds. As indicated above, if the government is receiving more funds than it pays out, the banks will lose Bank of England balances and they may well face a shortage of these balances. If the government is paying out more than it receives there is likely to be a surplus of balances. The Bank of England generally offsets a shortage by buying bills from the discount houses and offsets a surplus by selling more treasury bills to the houses and banks. The rates at which the Bank is prepared to deal in bills have an important influence on the general level of short-term interest rates in the economy.

While the Bank of England has long been active in the bill markets, it formerly placed more emphasis on direct lending to the discount houses as a method of money market intervention. These new arrangements which placed more emphasis on intervening in the bill markets were only introduced in the latter part of 1980 and in 1981.

Procedures for intervention
In its money market operations, the Bank of England is prepared to buy treasury bills, local authority bills and banker's acceptances.

When introducing its new arrangements the Bank of England explained that it would seek to deal in bills with as short a maturity as possible. The Bank has defined a number of 'maturity bands' which refer to the periods remaining before bills mature.

Band 1: 1–14 days   Band 2: 15–33 days
Band 3: 34–63 days   Band 4: 64–91 days

The idea of concentrating operations in the shorter bands was to allow market forces more scope in determining the rates for longer maturities and hence the structure of money market rates. However, operations in bands 3 and 4 are by no means uncommon. As well as outright purchases of bills, the Bank provides funds to the discount houses by buying bills from them with an agreement that the houses will buy the bills back on an agreed day.

Under the new arrangements the clearing banks inform the Bank of England of the target level of daily balances they are aiming at. On the basis of this, and the Bank's own estimate of flows between the banks and the public sector, the Bank estimates the size of the likely shortage or surplus of central bank balances each day. The estimate is announced to the money markets in the morning and, if necessary, a revised estimate is announced at noon.

If there is a shortage, the Bank informs the discount houses that it is prepared to buy bills from them and the houses offer bills to the Bank at prices of their own choosing. If the Bank of England considers that the interest rates implied by the offers are appropriate for monetary policy then it will accept the offers and the shortage will be relieved. However, if the interest rates are considered too low the Bank will decline to buy the bills, forcing the houses to make further offers at higher rates.

When the Bank of England wishes to engineer a significant rise in short-term interest rates, it may decline to buy bills at all, or relieve only a part of the shortage through purchases of bills. Instead the Bank sometimes forces the houses to borrow directly from it and charges a rate of interest consistent with the higher level of rates that it wishes to see. The Bank of England adopted this approach when pushing up short-term interest rates in the autumn of 1981. The Bank of England sometimes also does this when it wishes to prevent (or limit) a fall in interest rates, in conditions where the discount houses and other market operators are expecting a significant decline in rates; this happened in August 1982.

The 'parallel' market

The 'parallel' sterling money markets operate alongside the discount market. Of these, the most important constituent markets are those for interbank deposits, certificates of deposit and local authority deposits – all essentially unsecured instruments which are unique to the professional end of the market. The interest rate levels of these instruments are not available to the average investor, but are set or controlled by central banks or monetary agencies, and they usually move closely together. By definition, the participation of banks is fundamental to the activity in these markets.

Interbank deposits

The interbank market is the largest of all the sterling money markets. As its name suggests, it is largely concerned with the borrowing and lending between banks of sterling funds, although discount houses, finance houses and local authorities also play a large part. Money brokers will often act as intermediaries.

Money may be lent on an overnight basis, for repayment on the morning of the following business day; on a day-to-day basis; at call, for periods of two to seven days notice; and for longer periods (time deposits) as high as five years, although the majority of deposits placed are for maturities of less than three months. Call deposits will normally be in sums of £250,000 or more, more probably in the case of overnight funds over £1 million. Time deposits are usually somewhat smaller, particularly at the longer end.

The operations carried out by the Bank of England in the discount market will usually affect the volatility of interest rates negotiated in this market, not least on the overnight market. For example, if the Bank injects more cash into the discount market, discount houses may find that they no longer require cash from clearing banks, which in turn will place cash on the interbank market. If the amount is sufficiently large, the market rates will fall. Rates can also be exacerbated in the case of lesser known banks, often because their names may not be acceptable to some market participants. And even when acceptable, they may be so only in limited amounts to those market participants who are risk averse. All participants operate on this system of limits, but rates quoted will also depend on the status of the bank bidding for funds.

Certificates of deposit

Domestic clearing banks, major commercial banks, branches of foreign banks in London and London accepting houses can also raise funds by issuing large value Certificates of Deposit (CDs). These normally have a minimum value of £50,000 rising in multiples of £10,000 up to £500,000. The maximum denomination is £1 million. Maturities range from one month up to five years, although most are issued for either three or six months.

A CD is basically a negotiable receipt certifying that a time deposit has been placed with a bank and will be repayable gross at a fixed rate of interest on a specified date. It is a bearer instrument, and its negotiable nature enables the original depositor to either hold the CD until it matures or realise his cash if required before maturity at a rate which will take into account the time-value of the money on deposit. Depositors will pay a small price for this liquidity but the value of the facility obviously depends to a great extent on the liquidity of the secondary market for CDs and on the rates of return that can be earned from placing funds in alternative markets. The CD market is to a large extent an extension of the interbank market, since more than half the sterling CDs issued are held by banks themselves. More recently, a number of building societies have issued sterling CDs. From the standpoint of an issuer, they represent an additional and slightly cheaper method of acquiring funds for a fixed term at fixed interest rates. In ensuring a strong secondary market, the discount houses have played an active role in promoting their use; CDs are currently very important in their portfolios.

The development of the interbank and certificates of deposit markets in the early 1970s had an important effect on how the banking system works. Before these markets existed, while a bank could increase its deposits to some extent by offering higher interest rates, it was not possible for a bank to increase the deposits that its customers chose to place with it. Nowadays, however, banks have much more flexibility since they can readily increase the funds at their disposal either by issuing certificates of deposit or by borrowing from other banks on the interbank market.

Effectively, the rates of interest on interbank deposits and CDs represent the marginal cost of funds to banks. Because of this, the interest rates charged on much of the banks' lending are linked directly to these key money market rates.

Finally, finance houses bid for deposits on an overnight basis and for fixed periods, generally up to one year. Many of these deposits are placed by banks and other institutions. There is also a company deposit market on which large non-financial companies bid for, and offer, funds. To a large extent the finance house and company markets are an extension of the interbank market.

Local authority deposits
Bills issued by local authorities and traded in the discount market are small in relation to the general deposits business carried out for periods varying from overnight to several years. There is, however,

no secondary market on these instruments. They only come within the orbit of parallel money markets because lenders are likely to consider the rates offered in the local authority market as an alternative to the interbank market.

Sterling commercial paper

A market in sterling commercial paper was first launched in the spring of 1986. The total outstanding is estimated to have reached about £500,000 by the end of that year, to have passed £1 billion by April 1987, one year after the launch, and to have reached £1.37 billion by the end of May 1987 with about 80 programmes in place. This may seem like quite modest progress, but there could be several reasons; firstly, the ability of this market to compete with the large existing market for bankers acceptances, secondly, legal uncertainties preceding the enactment of the Financial Services Act and thirdly, the fairly tight regulations imposed by the Bank of England as to the credentials of issuers. Borrowers must have a listing on the London Stock Exchange and net assets of £50 million, which immediately excludes a lot of potential foreign issuers together with state sector entities. Moreover, banks are not permitted to issue commercial paper in their own name. On the other hand, many of the companies which have come to this market have been those in service sectors, such as property and insurance, who are not permitted to issue bankers acceptances since they are not engaged in physical trade. Most commercial paper sells at rates around LIMEAN (the mean of the bid and offered rate for sterling deposits in the money market). Although this has sometimes been lower than the bill rates, especially with the shortest-dated maturities, it is still not low enough to attract the type of blue chip companies who could expect to issue at rates below the bid rate. Many can do that by issuing in the Euro commercial paper market and then swapping back into sterling. A healthy sign is that so far relatively little sterling commercial paper – some £70 million – has been left in the hands of banks, implying a healthy demand for funds.

The role of money brokers

A significant amount of business in the money markets, particularly in the interbank and local authority loan markets, is transacted through money broking firms. Brokers have access to a wide range of participants in the money markets and perform a useful function in bringing borrowers and lenders together. While broking firms operate in a range of markets, each has its own specialisation linked largely to its client base. However, for large banks with well-developed dealing departments, and extensive contacts in the financial markets, the use of a broker is often unnecessary.

Prudential regulation of the money markets

Prudential regulation is designed to ensure that financial institutions are soundly and honestly run and that they are able to meet their commitments at all times. Few would dispute that some sort of prudential control over financial institutions is necessary. Regulation is required for two main reasons:

1. If there were no regulation customers would have to judge for themselves the riskiness of doing business (in particular of placing funds) with the different institutions. Not only would this be quite costly in terms of the time and effort involved, but many customers would simply lack the information and expertise to reach informed judgements.
2. When a financial institution gets into difficulties, this may have serious adverse effects not only on its own customers but on the financial system and the economy more generally. The financial system is based on trust, and the inability of one institution to meet its obligations may reduce confidence in others.

However, though some regulation is necessary, excessive regulation can be positively harmful. The more the regulator limits the commercial freedom of action of financial institutions, the greater is the likelihood that efficiency and innovation within the financial system will be stifled. Competition between institutions is also likely to be impeded by the imposition of detailed controls. It is necessary to strike a balance between ensuring that the financial system is reasonably sound and the need to maintain efficiency and competition.

Supervision of the money markets is the responsibility of the Bank of England. To some extent this is an extension of the Bank's role in supervising the banking system, since the banks (including the discount houses) are major participants in the markets. The Bank maintains regular contact with the discount houses and there are weekly meetings between the Governor of the Bank of England and senior officials of the London Discount Market Association. The Bank is well placed to monitor the quality of commercial bills trades since it frequently buys such bills in the course of its money market intervention.

Many transactions in the markets are channelled through money brokers. The Foreign Exchange and Currency Deposit Brokers Association and the Sterling Brokers Association both follow codes of conduct drawn up between themselves and the Bank of England.

The United States money market

Whereas British commercial banks rarely use the Bank of England's discount window, United States banks will regularly use that of the Federal Reserve. They borrow through this source either by lodging eligible bills, which are then rediscounted at the discount rate, or else through direct advances against promissory notes.

This is one of the advantages of membership of the Federal Reserve system, which is not mandatory for US commercial banks. However, there are also some disadvantages. One is that members are required to contribute 3 per cent of their capital and free reserves to the capital of their local federal reserve bank – there are twelve of these, in what are known as federal reserve districts – and hold a further 3 per cent subject to call by the Federal Reserve. Another disadvantage is that, unlike reserves in the United Kingdom, which may be held as cash, in treasury bills and in other money market instruments, US bank reserves are restricted to cash held in the banks' own vaults or held interest-free at the Federal Reserve. This can have far-reaching effects on the banking system and monetary policy as a whole.

United States money market instruments are issued by the federal government, by state and local governments, and by corporate entities. As Table 4.3 shows, the obligations of federal government far outweigh those of the corporate, state and local sectors.

US treasury bills

Treasury bills have traditionally represented about 80 per cent of short-term US Treasury debt and accounted for approximately 40 per cent of total market debt. Widely utilised by the Federal Reserve in its open market operations, and the subject of a large secondary market, they directly influence the rate of all other money market instruments. Since they are issued by the highest quality credit risk in the United States, the Federal government, and their capital and

Table 4.3　US money market instruments outstanding ($US billions)

	1984	1985	1986	1987
Treasury bills	374.4	399.9	426.7	389.5
Commercial paper	237.6	298.8	330.0	357.1
Banker's acceptances	78.4	68.4	65.0	70.6

Source: Federal Reserve *Bulletin*

Table 4.4 US money market rates (%)

	29 January 1988	Previous 12 months High	Previous 12 months Low
Federal funds (weekly average)	6.66	7.78	5.98
Three month treasury bills	5.65	7.17	5.03
Six month treasury bills	6.02	7.65	5.39
Three month prime CDs	6.73	8.28	5.88
30 day commercial paper	6.63	7.62	5.93
90 day commercial paper	6.70	8.05	5.80

Source: Salomon Brothers (estimates)

interest is fully guaranteed by the US Treasury, they stand at the shortest and lowest end of the yield spectrum.

US treasury bills are sold at auction, in bearer form and in units of $10,000 to $1 million, through the Federal Reserve Bank of New York, at rates reflecting the conditions of the short-term money market. The majority are of three months' maturity (91 days) although, unlike in the United Kingdom, they are also issued with six-month and one-year maturities.

Discount rates on US treasury bills are different from yields on interest-bearing bonds. This is because they are based on the par value of the security rather than the purchase price, and also because discounts issued are based on a 360-day year, and not the 365-day year which applies to bonds and notes. Some of these points become more apparent in the context of Table 4.4 which is an example of rates which are published each Monday in the *Financial Times*.

Table 4.5   Commercial paper: worldwide issues outstanding in late 1986

	$bn
United States	322.7
(of which foreign issues	37.8)
Canada	11.4
Sweden	7.4
Spain	5.4
Australia	4.3
France	4.0
Hong Kong	1.2
United Kingdom	1.0
Norway	0.9
Singapore	0.3
Netherlands	0.3
Total (domestic markets)	358.9
Euronotes and commercial paper	35.0
Total	393.9

Source: Bank of England *Quarterly Bulletin*, February 1987

Commercial paper

The second most common instrument on US money markets is commercial paper. The US has the oldest and by far the biggest market in this particular instrument in the world. Indeed, the market has doubled in size in the three years between 1983 and 1986, the greater part of the increase coming from issues for foreign borrowers. In late 1986, this market represented some 82 per cent of the total worldwide issues outstanding, as shown in Table 4.5.

It is now some one hundred years since the first US commercial paper was issued, and commercial paper remains one of the simplest and quickest ways to raise money in the credit markets. As in the United Kingdom, it is represented by short-term promissory notes issued both in discount and coupon bearing form in minimum denominations of $25,000 by corporations in need of working capital and offering to pay full face value at the redemption. These notes are similar to CDs, except that they are issued either by finance or commercial and industrial companies rather than banks. This is demonstrated in Table 4.6, which shows that some 80 per cent of US commercial paper outstanding at January 1988 was that of financial companies, while only 12 per cent had been issued for banks.

Table 4.6 Commercial paper outstanding

$US millions	All issuers	Total financial companies	Total non-financial companies	Total bank related papers
January 1985	241,813	171,335	70,478	45,183
July	265,863	187,473	78,390	43,310
January 1986	297,704	212,097	85,607	38,828
July	313,976	232,718	81,258	40,839
January 1987	333,719	257,734	75,985	47,370
July	348,247	269,894	78,353	48,665
January 1988	380,339	296,397	83,942	47,119

Source: Federal Reserve *Bulletin*

US commercial paper comes in a variety of maturity dates, closely paralleling treasury bills. Most runs for 30 days, although legally it can extend to 270 days, and an innovation in the form of interest rate swaps is now allowing issuers to lock in interest rates for up to five years. Commercial paper of even the most highly rated US corporations will pay a premium over comparable treasury bill rates. In the yield spectrum it rates second only to banker's acceptances. This quality spread, or margin, can be seen in Table 4.4. Moreover, so long as proceeds are used to fund working capital, issues are exempt from registration with the Securities and Exchange Commission.

There are two methods through which US commercial paper is distributed. Directly placed commercial paper is sold directly to the public by the issuing corporations themselves. It was as long ago as the early 1920s that General Motors Acceptance Corporation became the first major company to place commercial paper directly, rather than through dealers, and directly placed paper now accounts for roughly 10 per cent of a figure of about $US 350 billion for all US commercial paper outstanding in mid-1987. While the largest and most frequent high quality borrowers are able to mount their own sales efforts in this way, others must rely upon the dealer network. Dealer-placed paper is sold by a small group of about a dozen well established speciality dealers, normally at a lower price (and higher yield) than directly placed issues. The trend in recent years has, nonetheless, been away from direct placement, falling from 52 per cent in 1983 to 46 per cent in 1986.

The US commercial paper market has, of course, experienced peaks and troughs in recent years. An example was when the Penn

Central Transportation Company filed for bankruptcy in 1970, leaving $83 million of commercial paper outstanding, a situation worsened by the subsequent collapse of the Franklin National Bank and various real estate investment companies. Open market trading of commercial paper began in New York in the early years of this century, and by 1920 some 4500 companies were actually issuing regularly through about 36 houses. Now there are around 1000 American and foreign corporations issuing commercial paper in the US domestic market, with foreign borrowers normally being required to maintain compensating balances held in the Eurodollar market by a commercial bank. One of the newer trends is towards broadening the scope of issuers. Sovereign borrowers such as Canada, Sweden and New Zealand have now been in the market for a couple of years, and US municipal borrowers too, including the New England Education Loan Marketing Corporation ('Nellie Mae') which launched a $100m issue through Chemical Bank in 1986.

Commercial paper has always been a bone of contention for bankers in the United States, as it has just become for their counterparts in Japan. During the 1960s commercial banks supplied nearly 90 per cent of short-term credit to non-financial companies. Their share is now well below 70 per cent. Their efforts at responding to this trend have always been constrained by the implications of the Glass-Steagall Act, which lays down laws separating commercial banks from investment banks. The abolition of this Act is, of course, an intention of the Banking Bill to modernise and reform financial services (S.1186), which was introduced by Senator Proxmire in November 1987, approved by the US Senate and passed on to the House of Representatives in March 1988. But a suit by the Securities Industry Association against Bankers Trust still languishes in the US Supreme Court some eight years after first being lodged. In the meantime, Bankers Trust has accumulated a clientele of about 70 issuers, which still puts it well behind Merrill Lynch and Goldman Sachs whose clients number about 400 and 350 issuers respectively.

Secondary markets in commercial paper, unlike those in treasury bills, are not well established. Although a patchy market does exist, this is usually confined to the paper of prime borrowers, with the majority of other paper being held to maturity.

Commercial paper is rated as to quality by the two major rating agencies, and their classifications are shown in Table 4.7.

The rating a company receives for its short-term debts helps underscore the basic law of all financial markets – investors demand a

Table 4.7 US commercial paper ratings

Standard & Poor's	Moody's	Description
A1	prime 1	highest grade
A2	prime 2	high grade
A3	prime 3	medium grade
B	–	lower medium
C	–	speculative
D	–	anticipated default

higher rate of return on risky investments than they do on high-quality, low-risk instruments.

Banker's acceptances

Banker's acceptances, time drafts drawn on and accepted by banks, are very much akin to the British 'eligible bill'. They are typically created to finance payments originating from letters of credit on import shipments or the storage of goods and most commonly bear maturities ranging from 30 to 180 days, although they can go up to 270 days. Interest is paid at maturity and calculated on the usual US 360-day discount basis. In the primary market, they are largely purchased by banks, commercial companies and other financial institutions as high-grade short term debt instruments. The Federal Reserve also purchases them in the course of its open market operations. Because of the liability of the banks for payment at maturity, these drafts are readily marketable instruments. And as in London, this is demonstrated by a very active secondary market of specialised dealers trading in extremely large denominations.

Federal funds and repurchase agreements

While US bank reserve requirements must be met on a daily basis, this system is such that it gives rise to overnight excesses and deficiencies. These are traded between banks in amounts of £1 million or more and are known as federal funds. The federal funds rate of interest is basically the market equilibrium rate at which such funds are cleared, although the market has been expanded since 1964 as a result of member banks being given permission to purchase balances from non-member banks and other institutions.

A market in repurchase agreements (called 'repos' or 'RPs') is also closely related to the federal funds market. This market also constitutes a channel through which banks can acquire temporarily idle funds from a customer in return for US government or other securities with a contractual agreement to repurchase on a future date. An additional premium is payable, representing the interest payment. Most RPs are issued for one day only, being used as a substitute for call money, although maturities of up to six months are not uncommon and they have been negotiated for up to one year. In the way in which commercial banks lend to each other, these markets are not entirely dissimilar to London's sterling interbank market.

Certificates of deposit (CDs)

There is no call or overnight money market in the United States, and banks may not accept term deposits for less than fourteen days. The alternative is for investors to place such money either in the repurchase agreements (RPs) previously mentioned, or on the secondary CD market.

Negotiable certificates of deposit (CDs) in the United States have very much the same characteristics in relation to time deposits as do their United Kingdom equivalents. That is to say, because they are evidenced by a certificate, they are of a much more marketable nature. By contrast, in accordance with Federal Reserve rules, an investor who, having placed a term deposit, then withdraws it prematurely, will suffer a penalty levelled at the amount of interest paid. CDs are also unlike other money instruments in that they have a stated amount of interest attached in coupon form and are not quoted on a discount basis. The best rates of interest are only normally available on amounts of $1 million or more, however, although the minimum denomination is $100,000. While maturities can range from fourteen days up to more than one year – there being no legally enforced upper limit – most are issued with a three months' maturity. Yields are often lower than the commercial banks' prime rates. The United States CD market is attractive to those institutional and corporate investors who require short-term liquidity and security.

Japan's money markets

The United States, as occupying power, first imposed regulatory restrictions on Japanese financial institutions immediately following the Second World War and, until the mid-1970s, Japan's financial system was rigidly compartmentalised and centrally controlled. The Bank of Japan exercised monetary control largely by regulating the discount rate (to which some interest rates are still linked) under the Temporary Interest Rates Adjustment Law, and also through open market intervention, usually in the *Gensaki* market for repurchase agreements since, even to this day, there are no well-developed short-term paper markets. These measures were sometimes supplemented through the administration of 'window-guidance', whereby the central bank would grant credit facilities at the discount window to commercial banks, long-term credit banks and other financial institutions in return for the imposition of ceilings on the lending plans of those banks. In addition there was Article 65 of the Securities and Exchange Law, which separates banking and securities business, in the same way as the Glass-Steagall Act operates in the United States.

The purpose of this strategy was twofold. In the positive sense, it was designed to maximise personal savings so that the investment needs of private industry and the rebuilding of public-sector infrastructure could be financed at low interest rates. High savings by households were fostered by minimal social security provision, tax-exempt savings, limited availability of mortgates and other consumer credit, and by the sheer depletion of financial assets in the aftermath of war. For the population at large, the fruits of savings were to be enjoyed mainly through fast growth in real wages rather than from interest or dividend earnings.

The negative purpose was to prevent the re-emergence of the enormous financial-industrial conglomerates which had previously wielded excessive power. The postal savings system offered low-interest, substantially tax-exempt deposit instruments, with maturities generally longer than those of private depository institutions and, in fact, at the beginning of 1988 it still accounted for one-third of Japanese personal savings. And the proceeds financed the investment requirements of the public sector, as well as such capital-intensive industries as steel and shipbuilding. This was largely due to a tax-free privilege that such deposits had enjoyed since as far back as 1875, but was discontinued in April 1988. Similar but less tax-advantaged deposit instruments were offered by 63 regional banks. A portion of these deposits financed local needs, but the greater part was on-lent to the 13 city banks (Dai-Ichi Kangyo, Fuji, Sumitomo, Mitsubishi, Sanwa, Tokai, Mitsui, Bank of Tokyo, Daiwa, Taiyo Kobe, Kyowa, Saitama, and Hokkaido Takushoku) and the 3 long-term credit banks

(Industrial Bank of Japan, Long-Term Credit Bank of Japan and Nippon Credit Bank). Whilst the long-term credit banks were allowed to issue three- and five-year debentures to fund the bulk of long-term industrial credit, the city banks were restricted to offering deposits with maturities of two years or less, providing working capital and medium-term loans to industry. Although the third big group of Japanese institutions, the securities houses (of which the big four – Nomura, Daiwa, Nikko and Yamaichi – represent nearly half the market in share trading and about two-thirds of all convertible bond trading) engaged in equity trading, their underwriting and distribution activities were modest and equity issuance was not a significant source of finance for industry. The scale of trust banks and insurance companies was similarly small during reconstruction. Besides the secondary trading of debt instruments was severely restricted both in scale and in terms of institutional eligibility to participate.

Reforms prior to 1979 were only applicable to the longer-term capital market, and it was not until May 1979 that deregulation of interest rates in the call-loan and bill-discount interbank markets commenced, restrictions on the banks' participation in the repo market were abolished, and markets for negotiable CDs without interest rate ceilings were established. These measures all immediately went some way to restore bank competitiveness. And as soon as the restrictions on size and maturity of negotiable Certificates of Deposit (CDs) were relaxed, so market pressures built up to decontrol rates on regular savings and time deposits, not least those on small postal deposits administered by the Ministry of Posts.

A whole series of events followed in quick succession. The Foreign Exchange and Foreign Trade Control Law was amended in December 1980, to bring an end to the effective separation of domestic and overseas markets which had prevented the outflow of funds. The Banking Law was revised in April 1982, to further promote the expansion and liberalisation of financial markets. And the United States then intervened to bring into being a joint Japan-US *ad hoc* group on yen-dollar exchange rate, financial and capital issues. The process of deregulation of Japan's money markets since that group reported in May 1984 has been rapid and substantial. Regulations on the conversion of foreign funds into yen were abolished, and the restrictions on Euroyen transactions by domestic banks lifted. The floor on the large time deposits which could seek market interest rates, which had stood at one billion yen in October 1985, was progressively lowered in 1986 to 300 million yen and then again down to 100 million yen in the Spring of 1987.

The volume of transactions in the interbank and other short-term markets grew rapidly between 1984 and 1986 and the aggregate average balances in the call, discount, CD and *Gensaki* markets grew from less than 24 trillion yen in 1984 to 40 trillion yen in October 1986. Yet these and other short-term money markets were still the preserve of sophisticated investors, and activity was slight compared with that in the United States. The value of treasury bills in circulation in Spring 1987, for example, although a recent innovation, was only two trillion yen ($US 13 billion) compared with nearly $400 billion in the US. Moreover, even now about 70 to 80 per cent of Japanese deposits are still being covered by fixed interest rates, most particularly at the short end of the market. And there is still much potential for a wider selection of products.

It is easy to understand the rationale behind the delays in the deregulation process, for it brings with it higher interest rates than those fixed by the Government. Since the Government is itself a large borrower, it would suffer considerably if it had to pay more for its money. Perhaps even more important, the control on small denomination deposits had been the lifeline of the commercial, regional and savings banks.

The market for call money

In so far as it is a market in which short-term liquid funds may be exchanged between financial institutions, Japan's call money market is very similar to the United States federal funds market. Both resident and non-resident non-bank entities may also participate. And although call money may be placed with a wide range of banks and institutions, more than three-quarters is absorbed by the thirteen city banks.

Since it has long been a tradition in Japan for industry to borrow heavily from the commercial banks, it is commonplace for the latter to operate substantial short-term deficits, known as 'overloan'. Positions are then balanced through the use of short-term call money. And this is why call money has represented up to about 20 per cent of total deposits and savings outstanding of all banks in recent years.

There are six specialised call money dealers in Tokyo, all of whom make two-way quotes and act as intermediaries in the interbank market in addition to dealing on their own account. But it was only after the Foreign Exchange Control Act of 1980 that this market was able to deal in foreign exchange and to bid for any deposits other than in yen. And, as has already been mentioned, it was only in the previous year that interest rates in the call money market had begun to be deregulated, relaxing the correlation with the discount rate. Otherwise it may be said that call markets are sensitive to liquidity conditions.

Japanese call money is always secured against specified collateral, which might take the form of Government securities, local authority bonds or eligible bills. This has recently been the cause of friction with some foreign banks and their governments, who say that, because of a shortage of suitable collateral, which has caused a reduction in the importance of this market, they have been prevented from lending to Japanese customers.

Finally, although the normal transaction size in call money has usually been in the range from 500 million to a trillion yen, small local savings banks may often accept deposits as small as 10 million yen. At the other extreme, the large city banks, may expect minimum deposits of some 3000 million yen.

Commercial bills

An alternative to the call money market, and one which attracts much the same participants and has similar interest rate levels, is the market for commercial bills. Originally issued to finance trade and commerce, these are similar to US banker's acceptances, being time drafts drawn on a bank by its customers and accepted by a bank, or drawn by banks themselves on customers' bills that have already been accepted. They are issued in varying sums, from about 250 million yen upwards with maturies up to six months. A secondary market has existed since 1971.

The Bank of Japan uses this market in the conduct of its open market operations, and will rediscount domestic non-finance paper of commercial banks and discount houses, provided it relates to specific trade transactions and has a maturity of between two and three months.

The Gensaki *Market (Repurchase Agreements)*

An increasing number of Japanese call loans are now also negotiated through the *Gensaki* market in the form of repurchase agreements

(RPs). In common with the practice in the United States, idle funds are temporarily exchanged for some form of security, such as government bonds or short-term paper, on the condition that they will be repurchased at predetermined terms at some future specified date. The prices will normally be set according to the median of the highest and lowest call money or time-deposit rates quoted on the day of a transaction, and the repurchase price is usually based on that of the original transaction plus interest rates on time deposits of comparable maturity. Although the Bank of Japan regularly undertakes one-month repo contracts with commercial banks, a typical obligation between the usual suppliers and borrowers of funds can range from overnight up to six months.

Yields on repurchase agreements along with a *Gensaki* index are published by the Japanese Securities Dealers Association based on an identical formula to that used for quotes on representative issues in the over-the-counter market.

Time deposits

Time deposits may be placed with a wide range of Japanese commercial banks, as well as with an even broader spread of financial institutions, including savings banks and long-term credit banks. While the commercial banks will accept four types, for terms of three or six months and one or two years, they are still constrained from taking deposits of a longer maturity. These longer terms are, however, accepted by other institutions, such as the trust banks and long-term credit banks, who nonetheless do most of their business at over six-month and one-year terms, and the city banks who, whilst expressing a preference for amounts over 100,000 yen, will also accept any size of time deposit.

Japanese time deposits are generally secured against specific assets, and rates of interest are calculated on a 365-day year basis, similar to that which rules in the United Kingdom, rather than following the US 360-day convention. These rates have tended to be two or three points higher than the official discount rate, although inclined to move below call market rates when banks are bidding competitively in short-term markets of limited liquidity. Interest rates on time deposits were first liberalised in October 1985, but only on deposits of one billion yen or more. Thereafter the floor was progressively lowered until, by April 1988, interest rates were only regulated on deposits of less than a mere 50 million yen.

Certificates of Deposit (CDs)

The first CD issue in Japan was only made by the city banks in May 1979, after the government's authorisation of issues of large-scale negotiable CDs of 500 million yen or more up to a ceiling of 25 per cent of capital, in an attempt both to help the banks offer more attractive interest rates and to provide corporations with a useful additional instrument in which to invest their short-term surplus funds. By the Spring of 1988 the minimum issue unit level had been progressively reduced to 50 million yen and the ceiling had been expanded to 300 per cent of capital and then abolished altogether. The maturity range had also been widened by extending the shorter end to two weeks and the ceiling to two years.

Money market certificates (MMCs)

Banks were first permitted to issue money market certificates in April 1985, in minimum denominations of 50 million yen, with maturities ranging from one to six months, at interest rates of about 0.75 per cent below CD rates, and up to a ceiling of 150 per cent of their net worth. The net worth restraint has now been reduced to 350 per cent, the minimum denomination has progressively been lowered to 20 million yen and the maturity term may now be up to two years. Moreover, since the differential on those longest maturities is now down to 0.5 per cent below the CD rate, this market is now beginning to actually compete with banks and postal savings accounts.

Banker's acceptances

A yen denominated banker's acceptances market was introduced in June 1985, only two months after that for money market certificates, as a first attempt to create that short-term paper market which would widen the Bank of Japan's monetary control options. So far, however, this market has not been a success. First, because the potential borrowers can obtain finance more cheaply from banks, and second, on account of the liability of these banker's acceptances to stamp duty.

Treasury bills

Yet another attempt to broaden the short-term paper markets was the introduction by the Japanese government in 1986 of short-term government bond or treasury bill issues as a development exercise in short-term government funding. By the beginning of 1987 the amount in circulation amounted to just 2000 billion yen ($US 13.3 billion) compared with nearly $400 billion in the United States. It should be stressed, however, that such issues are only used by the Ministry of Finance for cash management purposes. Moreover, there is no regular issuance, and the only purchaser is the Bank of Japan at below the discount rate. This means that a loss is incurred if they are sold on. Another impediment to the development of this market is that, since they are subject to withholding tax, treasury bills are not much favoured by foreign investors.

Commercial paper

Since 1984, the Ministry of Finance had allowed Japanese banks and brokers to deal in foreign commercial paper, and some Japanese companies had become issuers both in the United States and Europe. Deregulation went a stage further in November 1986, when Japanese banks were authorised to underwrite and make markets in Euroyen commercial paper. The real breakthrough came in January 1987, when the Bank of Japan published its views on how the eventual Tokyo commercial paper market should be structured. The most important of these was that, so as to overcome the legal restriction against banks dealing in securities, and in order to facilitate issuing procedures and enable banks to participate with equal rights in underwriting of and dealing in commercial paper, the CP certificates should be defined as promissory notes. This was a landmark in that it was the first time, since the erection of a segregated financial system after the Second World War, that securities dealers and banks were enabled to circumvent Article 65 of the Securities and Exchange Law and compete directly with each other. Whereas the securities dealers had been enthusiastic, the banks had always been wary of yet another market which would draw customers away from bank lending and this was certain to provoke an intensification of pressure on the authorities from the banks, intent on entering other securities markets. The central bank also proclaimed that the issuing companies should be required to pass credit ratings. Growth was to be slowed initially through a number of restrictions. Only the 180 companies with AA or AAA ratings and net assets of at least 300 billion yen would be allowed to issue CP and, of those, only 53 would be allowed to issue the paper without a bank guarantee. Even then, unlike US issuers, the Japanese companies were not allowed to issue direct to buyers. Issues had to be underwritten by institutions. And, for the time being, maturities were to be limited to between one and six months and the minimum denomination to 100 million yen.

The market for yen commercial paper was duly inaugurated on 20 November 1987, with banks and brokers contesting with each other to underwrite 790 billion of paper. Simultaneously, the Ministry of Finance also sanctioned the issue of Euroyen CP overseas by certain non-resident companies, including subsidiaries of Japanese companies. It also subsequently allowed non-residents to issue yen CP in Japan. Overseas subsidiaries of Japanese companies will not, however, be allowed to repatriate the proceeds of their Euroyen CP. This is linked to the fact that foreign companies and Japanese overseas subsidiaries issuing Euroyen CP do not have to pay stamp duty, whereas domestic issuers in Tokyo do, from 20,000 yen or 0.02 per cent on the minimum 100 million size of issue to 150,000 yen or 0.015 per cent on a 1 billion yen issue. But, right from the start, the pressure was on the Diet to liberalise these rates.

Notwithstanding the differences between securities houses, the yen CP market got under way with goodwill on all sides. Industry, banks and securities houses all saw CP as an ideal means of filling a short-term funding gap, as did the Finance Ministry, following its less than successful attempt to build up a new market in banker's acceptances.

International money markets

The international markets for short-term financial instruments possess similar characteristics to the domestic money markets. Those which will be discussed here are the markets for Eurocurrency deposits, which are concerned with lodgements of currency at a bank outside the country of origin, and related interbank and certificate of deposit markets; the extension of international bank credit, which has traditionally taken the form of syndicated loans, and whose market characteristics are therefore in some doubt (in common with the longer-term markets for international bonds these fall into two distinct categories, namely Eurocurrency credits and foreign credits); a relatively recent development, the securitisation of such credits through markets in note issuance facilities; and finally, Euro commercial paper.

London has, from the outset, been the centre of the world's Euromarket activity, and continues to account for some 30 per cent of gross Eurocurrency liabilities. Roughly another third of the market takes place in other European centres, most notably in Paris and Luxembourg, while a further substantial proportion has been accounted for by offshore banking centres, such as the Bahamas, Singapore, Hong Kong and Bahrain. Increasingly, since 1981, New York has been a major trading centre, with US banks accepting deposits on behalf of their own offshore branches and arbitraging between the Eurodollar and the domestic dollar markets. Eurodollar transactions are also settled via New York. Japan and Canada also have sizeable markets.

Historically, of course, the market was solely in Eurodollars. The dollar remains by far the largest traded currency, accounting for about three-quarters of all outstanding liabilities. Nowadays, however, Eurocurrency trading takes place in a whole range of other currencies, such as the Japanese yen, the Deutschmark, the Swiss franc, sterling, and the French franc. Gross liabilities at the end of June 1987 stood at the equivalent of $US 4,000 billion, of which three quarters were interbank liabilities, some 20 per cent were outstanding to non-bank entities, and about 3.5 per cent to official monetary institutions.

The international money markets came into existence for a number of reasons, and in particular the desire of international investors and multinational corporations to find ways around controls on international capital movements imposed by domestic governments (particularly the US government) and to circumvent various restrictions on the issuance of securities. The international markets are essentially unregulated markets. (As in other financial markets, distinctions over maturity are important, but what the Euromoney and Eurobond markets have in common is the way they operate outside national frontiers and are therefore largely free of national regulation.) There is little doubt that these markets will continue to adapt and change, to develop new techniques and instruments in response to changes in the financial, the trading and (especially) the regulatory environments.

Eurocurrency deposits
Call deposits may be made overnight, at two days' or seven days' notice for Eurodollars, Canadian dollars, sterling and the Japanese yen, and at a minimum call of two days' notice for other currencies. Time deposits for periods of one, three, six and twelve months may be placed for all currencies, while for some, such as the dollar and

sterling, terms of up to five years are available. In common with domestic money markets, however, these are essentially wholesale, interbank markets and transactions would usually be of the equivalent of $US 1 million or more, with perhaps a minimum of $US 50,000 to a private lender, although at less favourable rates. All transactions are on an unsecured basis, and banks will usually set limits on how much they will be prepared to lend to any other bank in any other country.

Deposits traded in the interbank Euromarket are essentially for fixed terms and at rates inversely related to the bank's size and status. The rate charged may be fixed relative to LIBOR (London Interbank Offer Rate) with large banks paying rates below LIBOR and lending their borrowed funds to smaller banks at a profit of $\frac{1}{32}$ per cent or more. Alternatively, the rate may be fixed in absolute terms. Smaller banks may also pass the funds on to other Euro banks, or may lend the money to corporate customers paying 1 per cent or more above LIBOR. Reports of the interbank activity (and in fact of most other Euro market lending) will usually refer to LIBOR, which is merely the arithmetic mean of the rates on £10m three month deposits offered at 11 a.m. by 'reference' banks (typically National Westminster, Bank of Tokyo, Deutsche Bank, Banque Nationale de Paris, and Morgan Guaranty Trust of New York). Since almost all short- to medium-term loans in the Eurocurrency market are determined on the basis of floating or pre-specified rates (in relation to LIBOR), a widely accepted and reported rate has obvious market advantages. The Eurocurrency interbank rate is generally the one money market rate for a currency which can actually be described as the true market rate. This is because, unlike the US federal funds or prime lending rate, for example, it is not susceptible to domestic regulations or other wholesale rates, which may be manipulated by a central bank or by commercial banks.

In many respects, certificates of deposit are now the most important negotiable instrument traded on the Eurocurency deposit markets. These may be issued by many US and other banks, clearing banks and branches of banks located in a number of countries including Canada, Britain and Japan. Small banks will sometimes buy Eurocurrency CDs from other banks on the understanding that the CD will not be traded. The effect of this agreement is that the liquidity of the small bank will appear, from inspection of the balance sheet of the bank, to be more liquid than it truly is. During times in which borrowing rates fluctuate considerably, the appearance of liquidity

Table 4.8   International bank credits

	1983	1984	1985	1986	1987
Eurocurrency credits	74222	112605	110317	84208	112104
Foreign credits	7852	13317	6647	9061	11012
Total	82074	125922	116964	93269	123115

Source: Morgan Guaranty of New York, *World Financial Markets*

may substantially affect the credit rating of the small banks. A second effect of this type of agreement is that the secondary market for Eurodollar certificates of deposit may be thinner in proportion to the volume of CDs outstanding than its domestic counterpart.

International bank credits (syndicated loans)

Apart from the interbank borrowing, which has already been described, borrowing on international markets has traditionally been in two forms, securitised over the medium- to long-term through the issue of Eurobonds or foreign bonds (see page 162), and in the form of international credits. The latter take the form of short- to medium-term borrowing, directly from banks, and generally through the medium of syndicated loans. The difference between Eurocurrency credits and foreign credits is that the former represent credits raised offshore or outside the country of the currency's denomination (hence Eurosterling credits would be raised outside the United Kingdom and Eurodollars outside the United States), while foreign credits are raised by foreign borrowers within the country of the currency's denomination. In common with foreign bonds, the principal market for foreign credits is the Swiss franc market. Table 4.8 shows Eurocurrency credit and foreign credit activity.

Since their inception, in the early 1960s, publicly announced credits, excluding those to US borrowers, expanded steadily. This was particularly the case during the oil crisis years of the 1970s, when the annual rate of expansion was between 20 and 30 per cent to a peak of around $80 billion in 1979. Borrowings by the developing countries, which had begun around 1970, had been accounting for just over a half of the total, rising to a peak of $US 48 billion in 1979. In turn, by far the largest component of that had been Latin American countries, notably Argentina, Brazil and Mexico, which had borrowed

Table 4.9   Gross international borrowing
(£ billions at annual rates)

	1983	1984	1985	1986 Jan–Sep
Securitised financing	87	151	215	258
Bond issues	77	112	168	232
NIFs and similar backups	10	29	47	26
Syndicated bank loans	67	57	42	40
Other backups	3	11	11	7
Total borrowing	157	219	268	305
Securitised financing as % of total	55	65	80	84

Source: OECD

both to finance development and their growing balance of payments deficits. Non-US borrowing tended to remain at around the $80 billion plateau up until 1983 when, apart from a sharp general decline, attributable to reduced balance of payments deficits, almost half of the loans to Latin American borrowers were actually granted in the context of special new money arrangements in conjunction with debt reschedulings and IMF-supported adjustment programmes.

Borrowing by industrialised countries had, meanwhile, generally been more for liquidity than development purposes, with the United Kingdom, Italy, Spain and Belgium all being borrowers at times of balance of payments deficit. In many respects 1981 was a watershed, as US borrowers entered into some $US 54 billion of borrowings.

But, by this time, another evolution was already under way. If, instead of US borrowings, 'non-spontaneous' lending to larger Latin American debtor countries had been deducted from the 1981 total, this would have left over $US 100 billion in new syndicated loans. By 1984 and 1985, the comparable figure was down to $30 billion and $19 billion respectively. Because such figures must include loans issued to replace outstanding or maturing credits, they will always tend to understate the true extent to which net new borrowing from banks is contracting.

In fact, if one goes a stage further, and excludes refinancings from the data on lending by banks in the Bank for International Settlements reporting area, and then deducts estimates for the acquisition by banks of short-term paper issued under NIFs (Note Issuance Facilities) and RUFs (Revolving Underwriting Facilities), and in some cases investments in long term securities, as suggested in the BIF's paper *Recent Innovations in International Banking* (The Cross Report) in April 1986, it is clear that the total of outstanding loans to non-bank entities actually contracted by $US 5–10 billion in both years. There were also similar falls in both lending by banks to resident non-bank borrowers and in cross-border international bank lending to non-bank entities outside the Bank for International Settlements reporting area, offset only by increases in international bank lending to US residents. But as syndicated bank loans fell, so the predominantly securitised assets, such as note issuance facilities in the short term and bonds and FRNs in the longer term, were on the increase. In short, the composition of new international credit was shifting. These trends are shown in Table 4.9.

Euro commercial paper and note issuance facilities

A third stage in the development of Eurocurrency markets, following syndicated loans and Eurobonds, was the introduction in June 1970 of a market in Euro commercial paper, following a joint issue by Schroders and a US investment bank of short-term promissory notes issued by major industrial companies. Of course, there was nothing new conceptually about such instruments, which had previously been widely used in Canada and the United States. The real innovation, however, was the development of the concept and mechanics to the special characteristics of the international Eurodollar market, for Euro commercial paper programmes, which in certain cases could also be issued by sovereign governments and their agencies and bought directly by investors in the money markets, seemed to have two ready advantages. They had shorter maturities than were offered by Eurobonds, which originally caused investors to opt for them as the rate of inflation increased, and they offered a higher yield when compared with CDs.

It seems quite natural that their eventual take-off should have followed upon the onset of the developing country debt crisis of 1982, when banks were seeking to make the assets on their balance sheets more liquid and the better quality borrowers were simultaneously realising that banks may no longer be the cheapest source of credit. The chosen instruments in these earlier stages were mainly note issuance facilities (NIFs). This is commercial paper auctioned through the tender panel system, which ties issuance to a line of credit from commercial banks.

The value of commercial paper outstanding has grown from virtually nothing at the start of the decade to an amount recently estimated (in the Bank of England's *Quarterly Bulletin* of 12 November 1987) at $53.8 billion at the end of September 1987. This means that if it had doubled within a year from the end of September 1986, which was marked by a further relative decline in the popularity of the NIF structure from $14.5 billion in September 1986 to $18.3 billion in September 1987. This had first been noted in 1986 as the standard of borrowers on the Euro commercial paper market improved – not least to include General Motors Acceptance Corporation, the largest single borrower on the US market. Meanwhile issuing concentrated in programmes not linked to underwritten facilities almost tripled from $12.4 billion to $33.6 billion. This same study also provided the first official view of the paper actually issued in the market. US borrowers had been the most prominent, with $8.7 billion of issues at the end of June, followed by Australia with $7.2 billion and Sweden with $3.8 billion. In sheer size, Chrysler Financial appears to have been the largest active issuer, with over $US 700m outstanding, followed by General Motors Acceptance Corporation and PepsiCo. Elsewhere French institutions have become more active.

This market is still very much in tune with the trend towards securitisation. Just as international bond issues have replaced syndicated credits as the longer end of the debt markets, so commercial paper is now gradually ousting short-term bank borrowing at the short end of the maturity spectrum. Indeed it is changing the fundamental role of the banking system. The corporate treasurer no longer turns to his bank for a loan each time he finds himself temporarily short of cash. Instead he turns to the commercial paper market. Similarly, if he has a surplus, he will buy commercial paper instead of placing the funds on deposit. The bank's function changes from being custodian of money to that of dealer or broker. Hence the other side of the same coin is the process of disintermediation.

As the range of borrowers has broadened, with programmes arranged now exceeding 500, a core of active and successful dealers of an extremely high calibre, well able to distribute and place the paper they have to offer, has emerged. Among the leaders are Citicorp Investment Bank, Swiss Bank Corporation International and Shearson Lehman Brothers International. The success of these dealers has to some extent been dependent upon the view that they took on the future structure of the market. Table 4.10 shows the top dealers in Euro commercial paper.

Table 4.10   The top dealers in Euro commercial paper
Based on programmes publicised between January 1985 and mid-February 1986

	No of programmes
Citicorp	33
Merrill Lynch	31
Crédit Suisse First Boston	30
Swiss Bank Corporation International	22
Morgan Guaranty	13
Morgan Stanley	13
Salomon Brothers	13
Shearson Lehman	12
Enskilda Securities	11
Chase Manhattan	9
S G Warburg	7
UBS (Securities)	7
Bank of America	6
Bankers Trust	6
First Chicago	6

Source: International Financing Review

Although Euro commercial paper is negotiable and may be traded in a secondary market, the current situation is not characterised by a great deal of such trading. This is because many borrowers appear to expect their dealers to place paper firmly with end-investors, whom experience has shown will usually hold on to it until maturity. In the sense that one of the great concerns of would-be investors in commercial paper could be liquidity, this creates something of a paradox. But many dealers would argue that this misunderstands the type of liquidity that investors really want. After all, so long as the dealer himself is always prepared to buy back paper, an investor is assured of the ability to convert his investment into cash at any time. Since the experience of the GMAC programme of 1986, borrowers have been quick to consider the expertise of their dealers by examining how much, if any, of their paper has been circulating in the secondary market. Any dealer who dumps paper with professional traders is now regarded as suspect, on account of the risk that in the process the price of the paper may get distorted. That would also mean that a fundamental objective of Euro commercial paper programmes – that of attracting a new range of investors – was not being fulfilled.

Another recently reported development, arising from the October 1987 collapse in share prices, was an accentuation of the Euro commercial market's segregation between paper in top-rated sovereign credits, which are trading at ever deeper discounts to interbank rates, and that in notes issued by lesser corporate and bank names, where banks have tended to be the only buyers. This is thought to be a by-product of recent attempts by central banks to prop up the US dollar which have resulted in them being very liquid in that currency. As interest rates on the US treasury bill market have fallen so steeply, so those for Euro commercial paper, which are still pegged to the Interbank market, have looked more attractive. Central banks only invest in top-rated sovereign names, such as the French and Swedish governments. This same effect has also provoked a revival in the secondary market.

This latest development raises two important points. The attraction of Euro commercial paper, being cheaper than comparable paper in domestic markets, has in turn had an enormous general impact upon the efficiency of currency and other domestic money markets, where arbitrage questions are often of bewildering complexity. Secondly, ratings of issuers, whose number, as has previously been reported, rose to more than 500 during 1987, are likely to gain in importance.

CHAPTER FIVE

Bond markets

A bond is technically a medium- or long-term debt instrument. That is to say, unlike many money market instruments, which normally mature within one year of their issuance, bonds usually have maturities of from one year upwards. Both are debt instruments, that is to say no ownership is conferred as a consideration of the originating financial transaction, as it is with equities. Instead, it is only the possession of financial resources which is exchanged, usually over a predetermined period, in return for a reward which is known as interest. This is also fixed in advance, often in absolute terms, but sometimes against an acceptable variable, such as rates of inflation or rates of interest used in other transactions, maybe an interbank deposit rate.

The issuers and the investors

Bond issuers, whether governments, municipalities, banks or other corporations, or a whole host of supra-national agencies, such as the World Bank, the European Investment Bank, the African Development Bank and the Asian Development Bank, will issue securities with different terms in order to finance specific capital needs. The word capital should be emphasised here, since this is distinct from the fundamental function of money markets, which is to satisfy the needs of liquidity.

An industrial corporation might choose to structure its borrowing in the form of bonds, for instance, in order to finance a project from which repayments of the principal do not accrue until the project has been assumed profitable, perhaps in ten or twelve years. Governments and municipalities, both of whom indulge in massive capital projects, from defence to hospitals and from schools to public housing programmes, may either gear their borrowings to the amortisation of the projects or else simply borrow for, say, twelve years because they may have less debt to repay in that year than in fifteen years' time. Alternatively, borrowing may be done simply to take advantage of what the borrower perceives to be favourable interest rates at the time. There are several reasons which can be used to justify these last two criteria, such as the replacement of stock maturing shortly, the financing of a budget deficit if not otherwise satisfied, control of the money supply and interest rate structure (although this would normally be a function of the money markets) and the nationalisation of industries (although this goes against recent international trends).

Just as each financial market and each sub-segment of it attracts a special type of issuer, so, almost simultaneously, it attracts investors who utilise it for very specific reasons. In the case of bonds, most are purchased by those risk-averse institutions or individuals who wish to mitigate risk by matching their assets against liabilities of a similar nature (and for a similar period of time). Having said that, it is probably the shorter-term bonds which least satisfy the description. This is because they are much closer to money market instruments, and have always been heavily traded by the banking sector, and, in the United Kingdom in particular, by the discount houses and building societies. They are also attractive to general insurance companies as a repository of funds for maybe three or four years.

The medium- and longer-dated instruments are basically investment vehicles which are held by institutions such as pension funds, life insurance companies, investment or unit trusts and others involved in fiduciary activities, all of whom will require a guaranteed annual return from a significant portion of their portfolios. An insurance company, for example, may determine that it needs an annual return of a minimum percentage in order to offset actuarially projected payments on its claims. By purchasing a quality bond of that coupon level, it can ensure that these projections will be met. Similar considerations would apply to a pension fund, which is entrusted with retirement monies. It would invest a certain percentage of its port-folio in long-term instruments, which would guarantee a rate of return, in order to protect the employees contributing to it. At the same time, it should not be assumed that the pension fund will necessarily hold until maturity. After all, pension funds are often required to submit to quite severe performance criteria, and they may well be tempted to move investments, at times of steep yield curves, for example. Notwithstanding this, however, those who use bonds as

Bond markets

Table 5.1 Bonds issued as a percentage of gross domestic product

	1972	1973	1974	1975	1976	1977
Austria	3.27	2.30	1.98	4.87	5.85	4.66
Belgium	11.12	9.00	7.72	9.26	8.30	13.23
Canada	2.87	2.26	2.70	3.49	3.41	4.86
Denmark	8.59	9.43	8.29	12.67	10.53	10.30
France	2.16	2.64	1.16	2.37	1.96	2.06
Germany	4.31	2.93	2.63	4.86	4.41	4.41
Italy	8.61	2.70	5.11	11.10	5.99	12.17
Netherlands	1.86	1.02	1.37	2.48	1.54	2.68
Norway	3.03	4.35	4.19	4.82	3.07	3.36
Sweden	6.47	8.16	7.02	7.98	6.58	5.57
Switzerland	6.69	6.59	4.59	11.27	14.70	8.97
United Kingdom	0.81	2.46	1.30	5.80	4.89	7.23
United States	3.58	3.18	4.19	7.02	7.69	6.96

Source: OECD, *Financial Statistics*

a high-yielding conduit for their personal savings will be the ones who place security before risk.

Investment in long-term instruments is an important part of the savings function in most industrialised societies, but the actual proportion represented by bonds varies from country to country. An indicator of this phenomenon can be found in Table 5.1 which, although somewhat historic, still illustrates bond issuance (all types of bonds) as a proportion of the gross domestic product of the major industrial nations.

Bond issuance will obviously increase as GDP increases in each country, and it can be seen that certain investors in some European countries, such as Germany, Belgium and Denmark, favour bonds as investment vehicles more than others in the Netherlands or France.

Universally, bonds are classified according to the nature of the issuer. And, generally speaking, the highest credits in an economy are obligations of the government. Wide variations occur within the other categories mentioned above in terms of creditworthiness.

Maturity classification of bonds

While a bond is technically a debt instrument with a maturity of longer than one year, an exception being Canada (because of its central bank's willingness to accept paper of up to three years' maturity for rediscounting to the banking system), corporations in particular will rarely issue such instruments with a maturity of less than five years. Governments and their agencies do so, however, and, while bonds in the technical sense, these issues are more properly referred to as notes. But it should be stressed that notes refer to bonds issued with short maturities, and not to long-term bonds with only several years left to maturity.

Any mention of a medium term instrument will normally refer to bonds which fall within a five to eight year maturity range. Similarly, those with a maturity of ten years or more are usually considered long-term. But term structure classifications do vary from market to market. A long-term instrument in the Eurobond market, with a maturity of from nine to twelve years, for instance, is considered 'intermediate' in both American and British market parlance. This is no doubt because the maturities on United States bonds can reach up to forty years, while in the United Kingdom there is a category of bonds, known as undated stocks, which have no maturity dates attached to them at all. That is exceptional, since, as mentioned above, bonds generally carry an interest rate that is fixed in some way and also have a fixed repayment date. Sometimes they are also secured against the assets of a company.

The functions of a bond market

New issues

In most countries, the primary market for bonds is not an organised entity and does not have a central location. It is merely an expression that is applied to the process of marketing a new issue, once all the terms have been agreed. It is normally dominated by the commercial and investment banks who manage issues. In the case of government issues, an official government broker often carries the responsibility for setting the terms of an issue and then distributing the securities among banks, brokers and security dealers.

The new issues market in most domestic economies is regulated by the appropriate central bank, treasury or monetary authority. Oddly enough, the major exception to this rule is in the United States, where the credit conditions are the sole restricting influences upon the bond markets. Many European countries, notably Germany, the Netherlands, France and Belgium, operate what are known as queueing systems in their bond markets. These entail placing the potential issuers in a queue to the market according to their financial needs, creditworthiness, and various political considerations. They also enable the regulatory authority to avoid congestion in the markets; that is, the markets remain relatively stable and the supply of new issues can be timed to take advantage of perceived demand.

Queueing systems are most effective in economies desirous of protecting their internal interest rate structure from the damage that can be caused by either a flood of new issues on the market or by the leakage of currency created by foreign borrowers. In the case of the United States, however, the sheer size of the economy plus the fact that the dollar is the primary international reserve currency makes a queuing system somewhat impractical. The bond market in the United States has been restricted only once, in 1964, and then only to foreign issuers.

The secondary market

The function of secondary bond markets is distinct from that of the primary markets. In common with secondary markets in equities, they do not help to raise new capital for issuers, but rather confine themselves to trading existing issues between investors. Their major function is the establishment of price levels and, regardless of how short-lived this may be, this is the level at which demand and supply find an equilibrium.

An example of the actual bond trading process itself serves to illustrate the economic functions of the secondary market, and emphasises the problems that can arise when applying general theoretical ideas to the marketplace. When an investor with bonds to sell approaches his broker (or bank in the Continental markets) and indicates his desire to liquidate a position, that broker will quote him what is commonly known as the spread, the bid–ask quotation on the bonds. If we assume that the spread is 95–95½ he may sell bonds at 95, or conversely, buy them at 95½. The ½ point differential represents the dealer's profit margin on the transaction; that is, assuming that prices remain the same while he completes both sides of the transaction.

This simple process is at the very heart of the pricing mechanism the markets perform. Naturally, this spread on the bonds is quite volatile and should not be considered as static; it may change from hour to hour. The one factor which does affect it is interest rate movements. In Eurobond and foreign bond markets, which will be considered more thoroughly later, currency considerations also play a major role in investment risk. This is a risk which affects the major participants in the secondary market as well as investors, because bond dealers finance their own bond inventories in much the same way that margin traders do in the stock markets; that is, by borrowing money. The cost of these funds can have a major impact upon price levels in the secondary market.

A dealer will normally buy his bonds for his own account utilising overnight or other short-term funds in the same manner as money market traders. If a dealer were to take a position in 9 per cent bonds worth $1 million, he might borrow money (under normal interest rate conditions) at, say, 7½ per cent. Since the cost of funding would be less than the interest which he would receive on the principal amount, he could then afford to keep the bonds in his inventory until they were placed with a final purchaser. Under inverse yield conditions, where borrowed short-term money costs more than longer-term bond interest rates, the dealer would be losing money while he sought to place bonds with reluctant buyers. This condition – when a large quantity of bonds, and especially new issues, is held by dealers rather than final investors – it is commonly referred to as 'overhang', the point where supply exceeds demand.

A situation such as this will obviously indicate disequilibrium in the market place. In the case of bond markets, it has one additional effect. When many dealers are faced with such a condition, they will eventually be forced to sell off their inventories in order to reduce their liability rather than hold on for improved conditions, thereby depressing prices. This is referred to as 'professional selling'. Whether or not demand becomes elastic or inelastic thereafter will depend to a great extent upon how resources are allocated among dealers themselves plus the interest rate conditions which originally created the inverse yield curve situation. Such elementary market functions will quite naturally vary from market to market.

Types of bond

Although, as has already been mentioned, the traditional type of bond, known as a 'straight', carries a specified fixed rate of interest, known as the 'coupon', with a specified fixed repayment date, known as 'coupon date', bonds now come in a multiplicity of other types, which are listed and defined below.

Convertibles

Convertibles are typically debt obligations of a corporate borrower convertible into a specified number of ordinary shares (common shares in US) of the issuing corporation at a price and a date (or dates) which are predetermined. Although premiums are typically quite modest on an investment-length view, if underlying ordinary shares appreciate significantly, they do tend to become a quasi-equity usable in the practice of arbitrage. Bonds with warrants are really a variation on convertibles, since the attached warrants provide the bondholder with the option to purchase ordinary shares at a pre-determined price. An advantage is that the warrants may be detached and traded as securities in their own right.

Floating rate notes

Floating rate notes (FRNs) are bonds issued for a specified time period but with a variable interest rate. Normally this is fixed regularly at three or six monthly intervals above a money market rate, such as LIBOR or the treasury bill rate prevalent at the time, as was the case in the United States up to 1984. At that time the 'mismatch' formula was introduced, whereby an FRN would be priced at a spread over six month LIBOR which would be re-set monthly, enabling investors to earn a so-called yield pick-up. There have since been other variants, such as the 'issuer-set period' and 'variable spreads'. FRNs are especially popular in times of interest rate uncertainty since, being pegged to money market rates, they are the only bonds which can overcome the vagaries and lost opportunity costs which are inflicted by inverse yield curves. Since interest is payable semi-annually, and sometimes quarterly, the effective yield to the investor is greater than on a straight bond of identical coupon and maturity.

Droplock issues

This technique seeks to combine the benefits of bank loans and bond issues. The borrower arranges a variable-rate bank loan with the provision that if long-term interest rates fall to a certain level within the life of the loan, the bank loan is automatically refinanced by a placing of fixed-rate long-term bonds with a group of institutions. While companies have shown an interest in this technique, it has mainly been used by the local authorities and in the international markets.

Rising coupon issues

The annual rate of interest paid on these bonds increases over time according to a prearranged schedule. This technique reduces the cash flow pressure on the borrower in the early life of the bond.

Currency conversions or option bonds

With this technique (a feature of the Eurobond market) investors have the option of converting their holdings into bonds denominated in another currency at a predetermined rate of exchange, and similarly to receive the interest in a currency that is predetermined, perhaps at a rate ruling, a specified number of days before it becomes due. The main attraction for the investor is that the risk of capital loss on his investment due to exchange rate fluctuations is much reduced.

Tranche issues

Bonds are issued in a series of tranches at different rates which can be matched to the funding needs of the company. Quite a number of such issues have been made in the Eurobond market.

Zero coupon bonds

These are single-payment long-term securities which do not call for periodic interest payments. They are sold at discounts from par and the investor's entire return is realised at maturity. The United States used this formula in 1982 to repackage US Treasury Bonds into so-called 'STRIPS', 'CATS' and 'TIGERS', so that, at the bondholder's request, the Federal Reserve would separate designated securities into individual coupon components and corpus or principal payment. The term 'STRIPS' is short for 'Separate Trading of Registered Principal of Securities'.

The term structure of interest rates

Each individual bond maturity category in the term structure will usually have a different interest rate level attached. Ordinarily, money market instruments will pay the investor less than a fifteen year bond. The reasons for this are grounded both in the amount of risk associated with the debt instrument in question, and an element of investor expectation, which comes from opportunity costs and other factors which also enter into the analysis. There are two basic elements which fundamentally shape the framework of the overall interest rate term structure in terms of risk, and therefore determine the rates of interest which the borrower will pay over different terms. The lender will want to have some indication of the borrower's creditworthiness, to gauge the amount of time his money will be at risk.

The facile assumption is usually that, among borrowers of high credit standing, the amount of interest will increase for each year outstanding on a bond. This means, for example, that were a government to decide to launch several new bond issues with varying life spans simultaneously, let us say one for seven years and the others for ten and twelve years respectively, then the second and third would carry progressively higher interest rates than the first. The rationale supporting this is not so much that there is any greater risk of default from a first class borrower as time moves on, but rather that the longer he holds his government paper the greater is the chance of sharper increases in the prevailing interest rates.

Given that there are no inflationary or recessionary pressures in the economy, and no tight monetary policy, these are the considerations behind the positive yield curve, which like all such graphs indicates the secondary market yields of bonds already trading in the market place. It is the creditworthiness of the borrower which determines the basic yield along the vertical axis of the graph, and the perception of risk of those interest rate changes which determines the slope of the curve as one moves along the horizontal axis. In so far as such graphs are then used to price new issues of bonds, they perform one of the most useful functions in bond markets. Let us suppose that this particular curve represents yield on US government bonds and that the Treasury decides to float a new ten year issue. By examining it, the issuer can gauge the price and yield level to be attached to the new issue. In some cases, the level may be lower or higher than existing yields, depending on credit market conditions and investor interest.

The general trend of positive yield curves of United Kingdom bonds over the past fifty years has been an upward slope over the one-to-ten maturity range, but almost flat thereafter, although other shapes have been observed. In both July 1973 and July 1979, for example, the curve only sloped upwards for about four years before flattening out and, in August 1984, it sloped upwards for maturities of less than six years and downwards thereafter. This approach to the yield curve, known as the 'expectation hypothesis', has not infrequently given rise to some scepticism, based on the shortcoming that the forward rates which are derived from redemption yields often do not bear a close relationship to short-term rates subsequently observed in the market, although easy answers have never been forthcoming. Two other theories which have been advanced in an attempt to explain positive yield curves have been the 'segmentation hypothesis' which seeks to segment the shorter- and longer-term markets, and the 'liquidity preference' hypothesis, based on risk aversion on the part of investors. However, neither has given any more satisfactory answer than the expectations hypothesis.

A positively-sloped yield curve is, however, not the only type evidenced in the credit markets. There are many variations, depending upon the state of both the market and the economy. An extreme condition, which arises when the short-term rates are actually higher than the long-term, reversing the more normal order of events, is the inverse yield curve. This is usually brought about when short-term interest rate levels are raised to control the growth of the domestic money supply. This has the effect of providing investors with a disincentive to purchase long-term bonds, when funds can be placed in the money markets at less risk and a higher yield. The adjustment in money supply generated as more and more investors take this course eventually flattens out the curve.

The concept of yield

There are several other factors concerning yield calculations and interest rate fluctuations in the markets which should be taken into account when considering how bond markets operate.

Firstly, the connection between price and yield is important. A bond selling at below par (par equals 100 per cent of value) is said to stand at a discount, while one selling above par will be said to stand at a premium. In terms of price, these discounts and premiums are measured in points (1 per cent of par value). Thus a dollar bond with a par value of $1000 which falls a point loses $10 in value. Its yield will also have changed. In yield terms, bonds are measured in basis points, or units of 0.01 per cent, so that a bond which moves 10 basis points moves by 0.10 per cent in terms of yield, for example from 7.5 per cent to either 7.4 per cent or 7.6 per cent.

The second factor is concerned with the inverse relationship between price and yield. When prices fall yields will always rise and vice versa. This means that the bond which in falling one point in price lost $10 in value could only have gained basis points in yield and one that had gained a point in price could only have lost basis points in yield. The converse is of course that a yield gain indicates a weakening in price while a yield loss is indicative of a price gain. There are several different measures of yield – the interest yield, redemption yield, and yield to average life – all of which will be differently influenced by the change in price.

Interest (or current) yield

This is simply the current return on an investment in the form of its payments of interest only. In its crudest sense, this is calculated by expressing the coupon rate of a bond (in money and not percentage terms) as a percentage of its current market price.

$$\frac{\text{Coupon rate (in money terms)} \times 100}{\text{Current market price}}$$

Since bond prices are calculated as a percentage of par, and then translated in money terms, a bond paying interest at 6 per cent per annum and selling at 95 would have its current yield calculated as follows:

$$\frac{6 \times 100}{95} = 6.32 \text{ per cent}$$

While this form of calculation would be appropriate in the case of government and short-dated stocks, it would lead to the wrong result in other cases. This is because of the need to take account of accrued interest, or the total amount which would be due between the last dividend payment and settlement day, on the assumption that interest is paid on a day-to-day basis. This needs to be deducted from the quoted price before any yield calculation is attempted. The resulting price, net of accrued interest, is termed the clean price. A more precise way of expressing the interest yield calculation would be:

$$\frac{\text{Coupon rate (in money terms)} \times 100}{\text{Clean price}}$$

Even when adjusted in this way, however, the current yield is far from being a very useful definition. This is because, apart from ignoring the fundamental nature of bond risk, which is time, it also fails to incorporate the capital gain or loss on redemption. Moreover, there is an optional third consideration, which is the taxation effect.

Redemption yield (or yield to maturity)

The redemption yield is the tool most widely used by investors in the comparison of stocks. It indicates the return which an investor will earn from his investment if that bond is held until redemption. However, despite the exposure of the limitations of current yield in its crudest form, the result is still far away from this definition. Firstly, it ignores the fundamental nature of bond risk, which is time. It also fails to incorporate the capital gain or loss on redemption. Moreover, there is an optional third consideration, which is the taxation effect.

The calculation which addresses the second of these considerations, and is the tool most widely used by investors in the comparison of bonds, is the gross redemption yield. This indicates the return an investor will earn from his investment if that bond is held until redemption. It should still be stressed that this is only the notional return to an investor who pays no tax at all, and is the discounted value of the future capital gain or loss on a stock plus the present value of interest payments to be made until redemption. This can be expressed through the following formula, solving for i.

$$P = \sum_{t=1}^{n} \frac{C_t}{(1+i)^t} + \frac{1000}{(1+i)^n}$$

Where C = the capital received on redemption,
     P = the present value of the principal receivable at redemption, plus the present value of all future income, both discounted semi-annually at half the redemption yield rate;
     n = the number of years to final maturity;
     i = the redemption yield;
     g = the coupon rate.

For illustrative purposes, however, the redemption yield could be calculated by the following rule of thumb formula:

$$\frac{\text{coupon} +/- \dfrac{\text{discount or premium}}{\text{years to maturity}}}{\dfrac{\text{market price} = \text{redemption price}}{2}}$$

Assuming that there is no tax payable on capital gains, bonds are redeemed upon maturity at par. This means that, despite the fact that it is currently selling at 95, a bond valued at $950 today would be redeemed at £1000 in ten years time, providing a capital gain of $50. On the basis of the above formula, therefore, the redemption yield on that bond would be:

$$\frac{\$60 + \$(50/10)}{(\$950 + \$1000)/2} = 6.66 \text{ per cent}$$

The obvious point that emerges is the difference between the interest yield and redemption yield of 0.34 per cent or 34 basis points. This would be on account of the 5 per cent discount currently prevailing in the market. The greater that discount became, the larger would be the basis point differential caused by movement in the redemption yield component of the equation. Conversely, if the bond rose to a premium, the interest yield would then be greater, since the investor would be faced with a capital loss at redemption, such as when a bond bought at 105 was redeemed at 100. In fact, the only time when the two measures will be identical is when the bond is selling at par, thereby eliminating the possibility of any capital gain or loss.

The redemption yield is therefore the true yield on a bond, reflecting both its current and the future return. It should be noted, however, that a redemption yield must, at times, be adjusted for bonds whose average life is shorter than their stated redemption due to sinking fund retirements. For instance, a bond issued for a fifteen year period may have mandatory sinking fund redemptions attached which set aside bonds for retirement after the fourth year. Thus, the bond may have a life of only 11 or 12 years rather than the original 15 years. Redemption yield (in these cases yield to average life) must take account of the shortened lifespan.

Although the redemption yield is undoubtedly the most widely quoted measure of return, it is not entirely satisfactory. It has a fundamental weakness, not least for those who wish to accumulate guaranteed sums in the future. This hangs on the unpredictability of rates at which future interest payments can be reinvested. This is particularly true in the case of high coupon stocks, where the variable element, which is future income, represents the larger proportion of the return, while the fixed element, capital appreciation, is minimised.

Finally, the above calculations have all been made on the basis of bonds which only pay interest once per year, such as Eurobonds, regardless of the currency of denomination. The reality is that many bonds, not least most United States issues and all British gilts, pay interest twice a year and, in consequence, yield more than bonds of a similar coupon that pay only once a year. Although this is an opportunity cost calculation, it enters into investor behaviour just the same. For example, if an investor has a choice between two US dollar bonds of a similar coupon rate, one of which pays interest semi-annually while the other pays annually, then by choosing the semi-annual bond, the investor is free to invest his half year interest, thereby raising his total annual return for the year above the stated coupon on the bonds. This makes the point that yield calculations must always be adjusted to recognise the frequency of interest payments to the investor.

Bond elasticities and the coupon effect

Mention has already been made of the price and yield behaviour of bonds trading in the secondary market as the prime determinant in the pricing of new issues. In fact, they determine the cost of borrowing through all segments of the credit markets. But as with any financial instrument and also with commodity trading in the market place, bonds are not merely affected by supply and demand factors. They also have their own peculiarities which, if misunderstood, can lead to an entirely false view of interest rate movements.

To take an example, an investor who purchased bonds of fifteen year maturity in 1977, with a coupon of 9 per cent, would have found that short-term interest rates rose over the ensuing two years, and the new long-term bonds of similar maturity were issued with coupons of 10 per cent. As a result, the secondary market price of the 9 per cent issue fell to a discount, such that if the investor attempted to sell it he incurred a capital loss.

What would the market price of those 9 per cent bonds have been in the light of the new yield levels? If all other factors were equal, it could be assumed that they would have a yield similar to the new issues. This would mean that the investor seeking bonds at that particular point in time would be presented with two choices: either

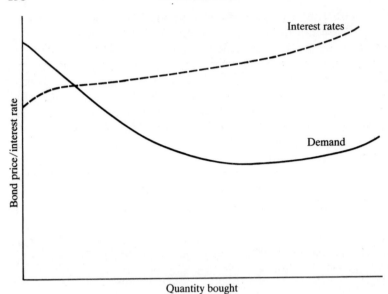

Fig. 5.1   Demand elasticity of secondary market issues
Source: Charles R. Geist, *A Guide to Financial Markets*

purchase the new issue with the higher coupon yield or purchase the existing issue with a similar yield to maturity. This market condition can be seen in Fig. 5.1, which shows the demand elasticity of secondary market issues. As interest rates rise, bond prices will fall; the fall will halt as secondary yields become comparable to new issue yields.

However, demand will not become elastic until prices have fallen sufficiently to attract investors. Eventually, the depressed prices on the secondary market will encourage arbitrage which will bring the yields into line.

This is not to imply that all yields in the market will be congruent. Certain bonds will have higher prices than other comparable issues due to scarcity value and the structural nature of trading, plus commissions. Tax considerations also play a large part in determining yield, especially when demand comes from foreign investors. There is also another factor, which is partly financial and partly psychological. This is the coupon effect, which would be evident in a case when, say, a 5 per cent or 6 per cent bond was compared with the new issue and the mechanics of demand elasticity no longer necessarily applied.

The coupon effect holds that bonds with low existing coupons will

Table 5.2 Bond coupon effect (annual yield – %)

price	7%	9%	11%	13%
100	7.00	9.00	11.00	13.00
98	7.29	9.32	11.34	13.37
96	7.59	9.64	11.70	13.76
94	7.89	9.98	12.06	14.16
92	8.20	10.32	12.44	14.57
90	8.53	10.67	12.83	14.99
% change in yield	21.8	18.5	16.6	15.3

Source: Charles R. Geist, *A guide to financial markets*, 1982
Note: This table assumes ten year maturities.
The percentage change in yield is that due to price change from 100 to 90.

be more volatile in periods of interest rate volatility than those with higher coupons. The low coupon issue will plummet in price more rapidly than the one with a higher coupon because the return to the investor becomes unrealistic as rates move higher. Table 5.2 illustrates this.

This effect is an example of the inelasticity of demand for such bonds; a price deterioration suggested by rising rates will engender little purchasing enthusiasm due to the fact that the low coupon issues are at the bottom of the range of investment choices outstanding. Implied in this concept is the notion that investors have a minimum threshold below which it becomes uneconomic to hold low-yielding bonds.

Although inelasticities are an excellent way of illustrating supply and demand within the markets, they do not always adequately describe the actual workings of bond markets, since both the concepts and the trading arenas are imperfect. Thus, despite hypothetical examples used for descriptive purposes, it should be remembered that price levels are determined by the availability or scarcity of the commodity involved. The assumption that instruments of similar character should trade at similar levels assumes perfect competition and/or perfect investor knowledge.

The assessment of risk

As the bond markets have become more international in scope, especially since the establishment of the Eurobond market in the mid-1960s, the creditworthiness of issuers and their debt has become

Table 5.3 US bond ratings by service

Standard & Poor's	Moody's	Classification
AAA	Aaa	highest quality, lowest risk
AA	Aa	high grade
A	A	high medium grade
BBB	Baa	medium grade, some speculative elements
BB	Ba	lower medium grade, speculative elements
B	B	speculative only

crucial in determining which instruments bear the most serious investment consideration. The assessment of risk on corporate bonds is a
complicated process, and it is not surprising that professional investors
and investment advisers have tried to find ways of simplifying the
problem. In the United States, where bonds are a more important
source of corporate finance than in Britain, there are a number of
specialist firms which produce 'ratings' of bond issues. The established
agencies, which also rate stocks, are the New York based Standard
and Poor's Corporation and Moody's Investor Services. In Britain,
meanwhile, similar services are performed by the Extel Group. A
somewhat less frequently used system was also designed in 1973 and
approved by the Society of Investment Analysts and the Institute of
Actuaries. In all cases, bonds are rated as to safety of principal and
timeliness of interest payments.

Ratings provide the common denominator that modern portfolio
theory requires in order to diversify both the risk and scope of bond
invetment. In order to determine the appropriate quality mix of
bonds which will yield the highest return while, at the same time,
remaining within legal or other parameters, portfolio and investment
managers rely heavily on bond ratings. Put another way, ratings help
investors determine their indifference level – that frontier on the
yield curve which they will not cross due to the risk of the bonds
involved.

The ratings provided by Standard and Poor's and Moody's are set
out in Table 5.3. Generally only the first three categories of each are
considered to be of high investment grade. This is true regardless of
the category of bond.

Secondary market yields on groups of bonds must always explicitly
state the rating category of the bonds being used. This is especially
important for comparison purposes and in economic analysis, since

rating category yield differentials are often made in order to gauge investor reaction to economic events. During recessions, the yield gap between high and low quality American corporate bonds often widens, reflecting investor concern over those companies in the lower category whose businesses will most likely feel the brunt of an economic slowdown. Comparative bond yields are quite important in financial market economics as indicators of economic trends and investor preferences.

Under the British system, the company is rated according to its size, the relative amount of debt it uses for financing its operations and the proportion of its profits required to pay interest. The issue is rated according to the security, its priority (in the event of default) and the borrowing limits which are fixed for other issues which might subsequently be made. The ratings are made available to investors by stockbrokers who specialise in analysing corporate bond markets. Unlike in the US, ratings are calculated simply by a mechanical application of well-defined criteria. The highest quality is rated as AA while the lowest is EE; note that a rating of EA is quite possible for a well-secured debenture issued by a very risky company.

In the international bond markets there is as yet no universally recognised rating service and the difficulty of estimating the complicated risks of international bonds is a factor inhibiting the participation of a wider range of investors in this type of market. Both Moody's and Standard and Poor's rank some bonds by the type of issuer, which in the case of 'official' bond issues includes an assessment of the political stability of the government. The coverage of the service is, however, more limited than that provided by their US domestic rating operation, though it is expanding.

Domestic bond markets

The United Kingdom

The gilts market
Gilt edged securities are loan stock isued by the British government, which is the principal issuer of sterling bonds. While it borrows from many different sources and uses a wide range of financial instruments, gilts are its largest source of finance. Gilts are thus named on account of being the debt instruments with the highest credit quality in the country; the term actually dates back to the nineteenth century, when

the actual bonds had a gilt edge around them. In more recent years, as consecutive governments have become increasingly monetarist in their views, gilts have been important instruments in the conduct of monetary policy, and have been used as an ideal channel for excess liquidity. Funds raised in this way may be used for very different purposes, such as expenditure on roads or building and for lending to nationalised industries or local authorities. Bonds issued by nationalised industries but guaranteed by the government have, in the past, also come under the heading of gilts, since the effective security for lenders is the same as for 'pure' government issues. The last outstanding example of these was the 3pc British Transport issue, redeemable between 1978 and 1988.

Unlike in the United States and Japan, where the majority of bonds trade over-the-counter, gilts are listed and trade primarily on The London Stock Exchange in a similar way to equities. Interest is paid semi-annually and at interest payment date, with stocks subsequently trading ex interest (similar to ex dividend shares). Until the 'Big Bang' of October 1986, London's gilt market was a single capacity market in which two jobbers were dominant and 12 brokers probably did 90 per cent of the business. There were minimum commissions for all gilts with a maturity of over five years and price spreads were relatively wide. There are now 26 gilt market-makers (GEMMS), including the former jobbers and brokers and a number of new entrants, and six inter-dealer brokers (IDBs). There is no strong demand for a centralised price display service, although a mid-price service is provided on TOPIC (which is the Stock Exchange's viewdata system). It has been mentioned elsewhere that each market will usually have an indicator or benchmark bond, which is usually the most heavily traded on the market. Known as the Long Bond, this changes from time to time. At the beginning of 1988 this accolade was held by the 8¾ per cent Treasury 2003/2007. Table 5.4 gives an analysis of gilt edged securities traded on The London Stock Exchange.

It will be seen that, as at 30 September 1987, there were 130 different gilt edged securities outstanding with a total nominal value of over £140 billion. Of these, 44 had maturities of less than seven years, 36 had maturities of between 7 and 15 years, and 35 had maturities of more than 15 years. Six of the latter group may actually be classified as undated. But this range and variety is not fortuitous. The shorter-dated gilts are very close to money market instruments and have always been heavily traded in the stock exchange and over-the-counter by the banking sector, particularly discount houses and

Table 5.4 Gilt-edged securities of The London Stock Exchange

30 September 1987	No. of securities	Nominal value £m	Market value £m
Short (under 7 years)	44	50877	55937
Medium (7–15 years)	36	47064	49054
Others (over 15 years)	35	30771	28883
Index-linked	15	11802	11786
Total	130	140514	145660

Source: The Stock Exchange, *Quality of Markets Quarterly*

building societies. The longer-dated gilts, meanwhile, may be regarded as pure investment vehicles which are traded by long term institutions, such as Pension Funds and Life Assurance Companies and the like.

Although the gilt share of the total market value of London's Stock Exchange has fluctuated quite sharply in recent years, with the prolonged bull market which culminated in the October 1987 crash, gilts have continued to dominate turnover, as shown in Table 5.5.

This was despite the sharp falls in gilt yields in recent years, often to below the UK inflation rate. Such negative net returns had not dissuaded the domestic investors overmuch, largely because of a lack of suitable high-yielding alternatives. In consequence, net sales of government securities still accounted for over 80 per cent of the central government borrowing requirement in the 1983–4 fiscal year. This lack of suitable high-yielding alternatives was also very much the case when exchange controls prevented the free purchase of foreign securities by domestic investors, as it was in the mid-1970s, when the investment premium added a surcharge to the price of purchasing foreign securities.

New issues of gilts are offered to the public by the Government broker on behalf of the Treasury, normally at the beginning of a specified subscription period, and in many cases to replace loans that are to be redeemed. And although at one time they were only issued in the form of straight bonds, with fixed coupon and redemption date, several variations in both issue and redemption conditions have been introduced in recent years. Some years back, gilts with variable rates of interest linked to the average Treasury bill rate were offered, although none of these remain outstanding. The aforementioned 3 pc British Transport 1978–1988 was an example, on the other hand, of a

Table 5.5 Turnover of gilts on The London Stock Exchange

	£ million December 1979	%	£ million September 1987	%
Total market value, all securities	280325	100	1848831	100
of which gilts	57765	21	145660	8
The year to:	December 1979		December 1986	
Total turnover, all securities	168936	100	646265	100
of which gilts	128948	76	424415	66

bond which was redeemable at the option of the borrower over a period of time. This was one more way of providing the Bank of England and the Treasury, who act as investment managers on behalf of the public sector, with some extra flexibility.

In 1981, index-linked gilts were introduced, on which both the interest and the maturity value depend upon the level of the retail price index eight months before the payment. If these bonds are held until they are redeemed, investors can be sure of receiving a return which will more than compensate them for any changes in retail prices. They are therefore especially popular with long-term investors, such as insurance companies and pension funds, who may wish to secure real returns with the minimum of risk. There were 16 of these still outstanding at 30 September 1987, with a nominal value of nearly £12 billion.

Because of the upward trend in the number and value of gilt edged stocks issued, the redemption of one issue will usually imply a replacement issue of stock at terms which will reflect the market conditions at the time of issue. Such an ability to delay or advance the redemption and issue of bonds can be very useful to the government. This is, after all, the rationale behind allocations on the 'tap' basis, where the total amount of new money can be acquired bit-by-bit as fractions of the total amount are placed in the market at periods conducive to subscription at the specified coupon level and maturity term, rather than generating a sudden influx. If demand is poor, the tap may be turned off temporarily and vice versa. Such a method also enables the authorities to maintain control over secondary market yields. Cash flows can be phased to help investors too, through a requirement for less than full payment at time of issue. For example, in September 1982 the government issued a stock called 'Exchequer

10pc 1988' for which investors had to pay only £20 on application, a further £40 at the start of November, and a final £37 in December. This stock was issued by tender, that is investors had to specify in advance the price at which they would be willing to buy the bonds. In the event the issue was successful, and because there were applications for more than the amount of stock offered, those investors who had offered prices at the minimum issue price of £97 did not receive the full amount of bonds for which they had applied.

A further experiment in gilt issues was first tried on 13 May 1987, when £1 billion of Treasury 8 per cent 1992 stock was issued in £50 partly paid form through an auction procedure loosely modelled on that used for United States Treasury Bond auctions. This was followed on 23 September by a similar issue, this time an £800m issue of partly-paid Treasury 9 per cent 2008 'A' stock and again, on 13 January 1988, by a £1 billion partly-paid issue of Treasury 8¾ per cent 1997 'C' stock. Only the first of these auctions was for a new issue, however, where prices had to be determined by primary dealers. The others were for additional lots of existing issues. These three issues were respectively covered 2.34, 1.54 and 1.07 times, with spreads between the accepted bids of 50, 80 and 160 basis points over the three issues. While the general assumption immediately after the third auction had been one of great doubt about the continuation of such issue methods, this view was quickly countered, by both the Bank of England and a decent majority of the market's primary dealers.

Apart from the prudential reason that they represent the best credit quality in the country, gilts have become increasingly important as investor favourites in the past twenty years for tax reasons. Because they trade on the Stock Exchange, and benefit from London's reputation as an international financial centre, they have attracted a great deal of international investment interest too. This is, of course, linked to the foreign investor's perception of the future of sterling. Provided he does not perceive a depreciation during his holding period, the gilt yield may still be better than the overall return available in his home country. Coupled with the domestic demand from pension funds and other institutional investors, it is this which has made the traditionally high yielding gilts perhaps the best known of all British investment vehicles. An increasing need for debt financing by the British treasury has, until recently continued to dominate the domestic bond market as such, in many cases to the detriment of domestic corporate borrowers.

Local authority and public board loans

Local authorities and public boards (such as the Clyde Port Authority and the Water Boards) also issue bonds which are traded in London. The local authority instruments are divided into two types – yearling bonds, which normally have maturities of one year, and the longer term variety with maturities in excess of five years. Coupon rates depend upon the quality of the municipality issuing the paper plus the term involved. Local authorities have the option to borrow specified quotas of funds from the government's Public Works Loan Board, but do from time to time decide to make direct issues on the market. During the late 1970s a large part of the local authority net borrowings were at variable interest rates, but in 1981 both Leeds and Swansea issued fixed interest bonds (offering interest payments of 13.5 per cent and 13.75 per cent respectively) redeemable in the year 2006. A variation in the type of bond issued by local authorities was the 'droplock' stock of which one example listed on the Stock Exchange was issued in 1981 by Birmingham. In this case, the droplock feature only existed for a year since the stock was automatically converted in 1982 into a 13.5 per cent fixed interest bond redeemable in 1989, which can still be seen at the top of the 'Corporation Loans' list in the *Financial Times*.

Corporate debt

Although bonds have traditionally been an important source of funds for British industrial and commercial companies, there was a period of more than a decade in the late 1970s and early 1980s when relatively little money was raised in this way. With persistent high levels of inflation, which had led to similarly high long-term interest rates, many companies were reluctant to commit themselves to paying for long periods of time. Instead, many corporate borrowers turned to a traditional source of funds, the clearing banks, for medium- and long-term funds. This was often even done through an overdraft facility, rolling over the principal on the due date. More recently, as inflation and long-term interest rates have fallen, there has been a limited revival in the corporate bond market. This was encouraged to some extent by the authorities, partly for monetary control considerations – borrowing from the banking system increases the money stock whereas borrowing on the bond market does not. Thus the Bank of England has tended to place rather less emphasis on selling long-dated stock in its funding programme. This is intended to ease the pressure on long-term interest rates and so encourage companies to issue more bonds. Despite this, very little fixed interest debt has been issued, although there have been some limited issues of convertible debt.

Convertible debt appears attractive to companies who expect profits to increase in the short or medium term. The argument advanced is that interest payments offered on convertible debt are lower than for fixed interest debt and that market conditions would not currently support an issue of more ordinary shares. For investors, convertible debt is a compromise between the high-yield of fixed interest payments and the uncertainty involved in holding risky ordinary shares.

In addition, the government has decided on changes in corporate tax provisions designed to make it more attractive for companies to issue two particular types of bonds:

1. Index linked bonds – with these bonds either the capital or the interest is adjusted in line with changes in the retail price index.
2. Deep discount bonds – these bonds pay little or no annual interest but instead are sold by the company at a large discount to their value on redemption (or maturity). They reduce the cash flow pressure on a company (since little or no interest is actually paid) and could be useful, for example, as a way of financing investment projects that take a long time before generating profits for a company.

Companies may issue bonds either in the form of loan stock or debentures. Both types of bond involve the appointment of a trustee who checks that the borrowing company is carrying out the terms of the contract. Often in the case of debentures, the loan is 'secured' by specific assets such as land or buildings so investors may be reasonably confident, in the event of default, that they will be compensated for losses. Debentures are therefore more secure than loan stock because the debenture holders have the right to enforce their security (by the use of a receiver seizing and selling the specified assets).

It will be remembered that, in the event of liquidation of a company, holders of loan stock and ordinary creditors are repaid after debenture holders but before ordinary shareholders. If companies have issued more than one loan stock, then the priority of payment between loan stock investors is made known at the time of issue.

While investors are accustomed to hearing of large profits (and losses) being made from investment in shares, investment in bonds is generally regarded as being safer. This is not, in fact, a true picture of fixed-rate bonds, especially in periods during which interest rates shift rapidly. In 1982, for example, bond prices for some British government securities rose by more than 30 per cent. With corporate and foreign bonds there is also the possibility of loss from the borrower's failure to pay interest or to repay the loan when due.

Bulldog bonds

Since 1981 foreign companies and institutions have again issued 'bulldog' bonds. These are sterling bonds issued in Britain by foreign borrowers, such as the Danish, Swedish and Australian governments, companies such as Inco Limited, and institutions such as the World Bank and the European Investment Bank. Reasons for such issues can vary; in the case of a company, the proceeds might be used for building and buying equipment for a factory in the United Kingdom. In other cases the issuer believes that sterling is going to decline in value and that therefore the 'high' nominal interest rate will be much less important to borrowers making profits in foreign currency, since the loan repayments will be cheaper in real terms. Bulldog bonds have traditionally been issued at fixed rates of interest though, as with Eurobonds, there have been some floating rate issues. Typically these bonds are issued through an offer for sale; the other method of issue is by way of a placing.

The United States

Although it is rarely valued as a single entity, the United States debt market, now valued at around $2,500 billion, is the largest in the world. Its proliferation of issuers can be conveniently categorised into three distinct groups, namely federal government issues (which include those issued directly, such as treasury notes and bonds, as well as those securities issued by federal agencies), issues by state and local governments (known as municipals), and corporate and foreign issues. Table 5.6 is an example of figures which are published each Monday in the *Financial Times*.

Treasury notes and bonds

The borrower in this case is the Federal government, itself the largest single borrower in the United States, together with its various agencies. The Federal government borrows through treasury notes, which are coupon bearing securities with a maturity of two to ten years, and also through treasury bonds, which have maturities of

Table 5.6 US bond prices and yields

	25 December 1987	Average % yield
7 year treasury bonds	104.25	8.66
20 year treasury	103.62	8.96
30 year treasury	99.62	8.92
New 10 year A financial		10.05
New AA long utility		10.00
New AA long industrial		9.90

Source: Salomon Brothers

between 10 and 30 years but are subject to statutory limitation of 4¼ per cent on the coupon. At the present moment, however, the US treasury is authorised to issue up to a level of $24 billion per annum in bonds without regard to the interest rate limit. New issues are announced by the Treasury about one or two weeks before the issue date, and the price is determined at auction by competitive bidding. In its primary form, the market comprises banks, dealers and institutions, although it is permissible for individuals to bid. Subscriptions may be made directly to the Federal Reserve Bank or indirectly through a bank or brokerage house. The minimum denominations for treasury notes are from $1000 to $10000, while those for bonds are usually from $5000 up to $10000, and very occasionally up to $50000. The most common minimum denomination for both types, however, is $5000. There is a large and active secondary market through banks and dealers. Minimum trading denominations are either $500 or $1000. They are traded at a price quoted to fractions of ¹⁄₃₂ dictated by prevailing market yields, plus interest accrued on the bond or note; interest is calculated semi-annually on the basis of a civil year of 365 days.

Federal agency securities
The federal agencies, being legally authorised to administer selected lending programmes on behalf of the Federal government, aim to attract private capital into specific social and economic areas. Traditionally these were the housing and agricultural sectors, but more recently they have included community development, small businesses, trade financing and universities.

These agencies can issue a wide range of securities, including notes, bonds, debenture participation certificates and 'pass thru' securities, although any agency will usually specialise rather than generalise over the whole group. Agencies separate into two sub-groups – government owned, which issue securities fully guaranteed by the full faith and credit of the US Treasury, and privately owned by government sponsored, whose securities are secured only by the full faith and credit of the issuing agency. There is a moral obligation on the US treasury, however, to assure that the principal and interest of all federal agency securities are protected and honoured.

Most of the growth in the market is accounted for by five main agencies. On the government owned side is the National Mortgage Corporation, which issues mortgage backed 'pass thru' certificates, colloquially known as 'ginnie maes'. On the private side, meanwhile, are the Federal Home Loan Banks (FHLB), the Federal Home Loan Mortgage Corporation (FHLMC), which issues participation certificates colloquially known as 'freddie macs', the Federal National Mortgage Association, which sells debentures and short-term notes colloquially known as 'fannie maes', and the Consolidated Farm Credit System. Other government owned agencies still issuing to the public are the Farmers' Home Administration and the Maritime Administration. There is also the Federal Finance Bank (FFB), but this does not now issue securities direct to the public. As borrowers, all of these agencies represent a good credit risk, but they fall into two groups – government owned and government sponsored – and the former group represents slightly better security for invested funds.

Municipals
The second group comprises state and local governments, which are generically referred to as municipal borrowers. These also issue notes and bonds, with special tax exempt coupons.

Corporate and foreign issues
The third group consists of corporations and foreign issuers (see Table 5.7).

The rate of interest paid on these various instruments varies according to the issuer. Coupon rates on municipal bonds are lower than those of the other two varieties. This situation has been created because interest paid on municipal issues is exempt from federal income tax. This stems from an early nineteenth century Supreme Court ruling which held that the federal government did not have the power to tax the states and, concomitantly, municipal entities within

Table 5.7   Domestic bond issues in the United States ($ billions)

	Municipals	Corporate	US Government*
1977	46.8	42.0	47.0
1978	48.6	36.9	60.0
1979	43.5	36.7	74.7
1980	48.4	41.3	
1981	47.7	40.5	
1982	78.3	43.9	
1983	85.7	52.2	
1984	128.8	69.4	
1985	214.2	119.6	
1986	147.0	231.9	
1987	102.4	209.3	

*Amount of total bonds outstanding, excludes bills and notes
Source: Federal Reserve *Bulletin*

the states. Therefore, municipal bond interest is free from federal tax. Conversely, interest on Federal government obligations is free from individual taxation. As a result, coupon rates on municipal paper can be as much as 200 basis points (2 per cent) lower than on similarly rated corporation paper. Municipal issues have their own interest rate structure but are, nevertheless, affected by general interest rate movements in the capital markets.

Among the other two categories, the rates on United States government paper are lower than those on corporate paper, reflecting the high credit rating assigned to government issues. For this safety, the investor gives up yield when he invests in such bonds. The yields on corporate bonds are the highest of these groups although substantial discrepancies exist within this general category.

Due to the size of the New York Stock Exchange, convertible bonds are popular instruments since they offer a fixed rate of interest (although normally lower than that on straight bonds) plus the potential for capital appreciation via the shares.

Government securities and municipal issues trade over-the-counter in the United States. Corporate issues may be traded on the New York Stock Exchange (if they are listed) but most orders are, in fact, filled over-the-counter. Despite this seemingly diverse market, the reporting procedures for dealings established by the various regulatory authorities has created a standard and relatively efficient market within each compartment.

Medium-term notes

This market is really no more than an extension of the domestic commercial paper market to maturities exceeding one year. Effectively launched in 1984, it had expanded to some $40 billion within two years. Like commercial paper, MTNs are offered continuously through dealers, and maturities range upwards from one year to five years, with slightly less than a third having a maturity of between two and three years. The active benchmark issuers are very similar to those in the commercial paper market, led by GMAC. The argument is that MTNs offer borrowers great flexibility, since they can spread maturity profiles, issue small amounts of debt to meet specific needs, reduce the fees and other costs of a bond issue, and capture exactly investors' requirements.

There is practically no secondary market for MTNs, however. Instead, they are placed with institutional investors who identify needs for specific maturities, often because of matched-funding techniques which aim to match the cash flows from investment holdings exactly to the payments which a pension fund, for example, must make to its beneficiaries. About a third of the purchasers tend to be banks; bank trusts and thrifts both account for about 30 per cent, insurance companies about 13 per cent, corporations a mere 10 per ent and pension funds and individuals the remaining 15 per cent.

Yankee bonds

Yankee bonds are the United States version of a foreign bond. As such they are the equivalent of the British 'bulldog' bond and the Japanese *samurai* bond, in that they are issued by foreign governments, corporations and municipalities but are denominated in US dollars. As such, they pay interest and trade in normal United States fashion, and, in almost all cases, are highly rated instruments comparable in the eyes of the market to highly rated US corporations.

Yankee bonds are floated by borrowers desirous of US dollars, for whatever reason. Traditionally, they yield more than comparable US issues due to their foreign nature. A yield differential must therefore be attached in order to market these instruments effectively. At year end 1978, the Yankee bond market was capitalised at about $20 billion nominal value. More recent issuing activity is recorded in Table 5.8.

The foreign sector of the American market was the only compartment ever subject to any sort of capital controls. In the mid-1960s, the United States suffered a balance of payments disequilibrium caused in part by a large net outflow of long-term investment funds.

Table 5.8   Yankee bond issues ($US millions)

	1977	1980	1984	1985	1986	1987
Total	7428	5795	5487	4655	6782	5911
of which:						
Canadian entities	3022	2136				
international organs	1917	550				
others	2489	743				

Source: Morgan Guaranty Trust of New York, *World Financial Markets*

In order to redress part of this problem, limitations were placed upon domestic investors purchasing foreign securities. This was accomplished through the Interest Equalisation Tax of 1964 (IET). Effectively, this measure closed the American capital market to foreign borrowers for ten years by taxing the yield premium foreign securities paid over their comparable American counterparts. The market became again active in 1974–75 when the IET was lifted, but the yield premium on these foreign securities re-emerged for many of the same reasons.

High yield bonds (junk bonds)
These are high-yielding bonds of below investment grade, that is at below Baa by Moodys and below BBB by Standard and Poors, which yield a minimum of 200 to 250 basis points (2 to 2.5 per cent) above the yield on Treasury bonds.

They constitute a revival of a form of instrument which was popular in the 1920s and 1930s which, when joined by so-called 'fallen angels' bonds from the Great Depression, constituted some 40 per cent of all corporate bonds outstanding in 1940. However, the default rate during that time, about 10 per cent per year, created such an aversion to this type of instrument that by 1970 only some 4 per cent of bonds outstanding were junk.

Prior to the revival of this market, by Drexel Burnham Lambert in 1977, at a time when equities were depressed, banks and life insurance companies had held a monopoly over the provision of longer-term money to the small and medium-sized companies. But once investors had gained a taste for high-yielding and high-risk paper, junk bonds could be issued for takeovers and buyouts, allowing newcomers to compete for the control of corporations. Whole industries, such as cable television, have grown on a diet of junk, and the market still has about $125bn outstanding as shown on Table 5.9.

Table 5.9 Junk bond issues

	New issues	Total value $US millions
1980	46	1379.6
1981	37	1279.6
1982	56	2499.0
1983	98	7534.4
1984	133	14111.3
1985	182	14754.1
1986	228	32399.6
1987	191	31132.6
to 6 July 1988	42	6702.5

Source: IDD Information Services

The turnaround in new issues in 1987 was a manifestation of the bankruptcy of the steel company, LTV, in 1986, which refocused attention on the high default risk of these instruments compared with investment grade bonds. This is the highest rate since the 11.4 per cent of 1970, when Penn Central went down. This has, in turn, excited the Federal Reserve to the prospect of new regulatory measures. An awareness of this earlier in 1987 in turn prompted many companies to convert junk bonds into equity, and new issues during 1988 were only a fraction of those in the previous three years.

Japan

In terms of new issue volume, the Japanese bond market is second only to that of the United States. The majority of bonds are issued by the government, local governments (semi-governmental organisations), municipalities and banks, which together account for about 92 per cent of new bond issues in the Tokyo market. Until recent measures of a deregulatory nature, private placements comprised no more than about 30 per cent of the market, while corporate bonds took as little as 5 per cent. Table 5.10 is an example of figures which are published each Monday in the *Financial Times*.

The secondary market is active, but closely regulated by the authorities, which inhibits the free play of market forces. In common with the United States, it is almost all traded over-the-counter. About 50 per cent of turnover is represented by the market for repurchase agreements, known as the *Gensaki* markets.

Table 5.10 NRI Tokyo bond index
December 1983 = 100

	17/12/87	Average % yield
Overall	139.44	4.72
Government bonds	140.16	4.36
Municipal bonds	140.30	5.19
Government-guaranteed bonds	141.50	5.21
Bank debentures	134.57	4.46
Corporate bonds	138.83	5.61
Foreign bonds (*Samurai*)	139.99	6.54
Government 10 year – estimate par yield		5.16

Source: Nomura Research Institute

For non-residents, the attractiveness of the Japanese bond market is reduced by a 20 per cent withholding tax on interest for most types of bonds, except those issued at a discount from par.

Japanese yields are calculated on a different basis from that employed in most other financial markets. That is to say, interest is not compounded in the same way.

Government bonds

There was no Japanese government bond market until 1965. Since then, however, prompted by an increasingly pressing need to sell debt, this has become one of the most broadly-based markets in the Japanese financial system.

Apart from short-term government guaranteed bonds, which are issued by the same method and with the same terms as treasury bills, the Bank of Japan, on behalf of the Japanese government, issues three types of bond. These are the shorter-term two, three and four year so-called Japanese Government Bonds (JGBs), longer-term bonds with a maturity of 10 years, and 20-year 'super-longs'. The number of bonds issued each year will depend on public works requirements, public capital investment and government loans. Usually they represent about 50 per cent of total new issues and of bonds outstanding. Individual issues, which may be for up to 1200 billion yen, are made monthly, in amounts determined in advance and announced in the government's annual budget, but currently in the order of from 700 billion to 800 billion yen per month. Table 5.11 shows the level of issues in recent years. These primary issues are

Bond markets

Table 5.11 Japanese government bond issues (trillion yen)

1981	1982	1983	1984	1985	1986	1987
14.03	18.29	19.21	18.82	23.36	26.39	26.84

made through a comprehensive underwriting syndicate, which includes various kinds of banks, the securities houses and certain other institutions, including life insurance companies, although there is increasing pressure for a more flexible auction system.

Government bonds are issued in minimum denominations of 100,000 yen (sometimes one million yen), and most carry semi-annual coupon dates with the remainder only paying interest annually. Although most are coupon-bearing, some of the medium term instruments – that is those with a maturity of less than five years – may be issued at a discount. Interest is calculated according to a 365 day year. Yields on government bonds are comparable with those obtainable on other bonds, including good quality corporate bonds.

Local government bonds
These are issued by prefectures, cities, towns and villages in amounts which are determined by their autonomous local budgets. They are, therefore, not issued on a regular basis, but only as requirements for funds arise and represent only about 4.3 per cent of bonds outstanding. If private placements are included, the proportion of outstanding bonds is over 15 per cent. Like government bonds, they are issued with maturities of between one and ten years, are normally coupon-bearing, mostly pay interest semi-annually, and redeem capital upon maturity. Minimum denominations are 100,000 yen. Principal and interest are fully guaranteed by the government, and yields are generally about 0.15 to 0.3 per cent above government bond yields.

Government guaranteed bonds
Bonds in this category are issued by the specialised long-term credit banks which grant loans of five to fifteen years to industry, commerce and agriculture. Such banks are the Industrial Bank of Japan, Nippon Credit Bank, Bank of Tokyo, Shoko Chukin Bank (Central Bank for Commerce and Industry) and the Norinchuki Bank (Central Bank for Agriculture and Forestry.

The principal and interest on these bonds is guaranteed by the government but requires the resolution of the local assembly and the approval of the Minister of Home Affairs prior to issue. They are issued on an irregular basis and constitute about 9.5 per cent of the market (or 21.8 per cent including private placements). These bonds are coupon bearing with maturities of up to ten years and in minimum denominations of 100,000 and upwards. Interest is paid both annually and semi-annually, and capital is redeemed in full at maturity. Yields are about 25 per cent greater than government bond yields.

Bonds issued by public corporations, semi-governmental corporations and special corporations are also government guaranteed to the amount specified annually in the government's budget. They are a sub-group of government-related organisation bonds.

Financial debentures
Financial debentures are issued by long-term credit banks and certain other banks. They are secured against the general assets of the issuing bank, which must additionally meet certain minimum requirements. Otherwise they are similar to corporate bonds. They have maturities of from one to ten years. The longer issues are coupon-bearing, while those of five years or less may be discount bearing. Most pay interest semi-annually and repay capital at maturity. Their denominations are in minimum amounts of 100,000 yen and upwards. They comprise about 25 per cent of the bond market and yield approximately 0.45 per cent more than government bonds.

Corporate bonds
The Japanese market in domestic corporate bonds, known as industrial bonds, languished until early in 1987, largely overlooked as a centre for fundraising and investment. The reasons for this were manifold, although two stood out more than others. The first was that in more recent years it had usually been cheaper to borrow yen outside Japan. The second was that the issuing rules for bonds, which had been circumscribed under Article 65 of the Securities Exchange Law, demanded that, in addition to an underwriter, which had to be a securities firm, an issuer also had to commission a bank to arrange collateral.

The turning point came early in 1987, when the Ministry of Finance introduced a package of deregulatory measures. The first concerned the number of companies allowed to issue straight bonds without collateral, which, since 1979, had been limited to only 70 of the largest highly creditworthy companies, while those allowed to issue similar convertibles had been limited to 180. This had the effect of both restricting the interaction of demand and supply necessary for an efficiently operating market, and increasing the costs charged to companies for bond issues. In consquence, it had been more usual for companies to raise capital through equity markets, bank borrowing, or the issue of bonds in foreign capital markets. Under the new arrangements, these limits were raised to 170 and 330 companies respectively, and there was also a relaxation of minimum net-worth requirements, with encouragements to seek formal credit ratings from recognised agencies.

Further restrictions concerning the birth and age of domestic bonds had also been an impediment to the issue of the shorter maturities. There had been long waiting periods preceding the filing of prospectuses and the setting of coupons. It is hoped that such problems will be overcome by a bill on shelf registration due to be placed before the Diet in March 1988.

A further restriction had surrounded private placements of corporate bonds, which had suffered under an issue ceiling of two billion yen and a so-called 'no return' rule. The latter meant that any issuer which had already launched a public bond was thereafter prevented from tapping the private market. Despite this, private placements had constituted around 30 per cent of the total bond market, although with a very restricted marketability since most were being held to maturity, which was normally less than five years. New rules published in November 1986 and adopted in April 1987 raised this issue ceiling to 10 billion yen and abolished the no return rule altogether.

The major corporate borrowers in the domestic bond market are the nine electric power companies, Japan Airlines and NTT (Nippon Telegraph and Telephone). The bonds issued by NTT in coupon bearing and discount form, and known as subscriber bonds, are the most actively traded of all bonds issued on the domestic capital market. Turnover is approximately 4000 billion yen per year, and almost all of this is transacted in the over-the-counter market rather than through the stock exchange. About 95 per cent is represented by coupon bearing rather than discount bonds, although the same volume of each type is issued each year.

For some corporate bonds, such as NTT, the amount of the issue need not be specified in advance. Instead it can depend upon the amount actually taken up or subscribed for. For the majority of issues it is more common that the amount to be issued is announced in advance. If subscriptions fall short of that amount, then the whole issue is invalidated, unless underwritten by a securities company.

Although corporate bonds are issued for up to twelve years, the general rule is that bonds with maturities of less than five years are issued on a discount basis and those of longer maturity on a coupon basis. The exception is for NTT, which issues discount securities with maturities of 11½ years.

Discount bonds have two special features. Firstly, they do not pay interest at regular intervals. Instead they are issued with very large discounts to principal to be redeemed at par. The size of this discount will depend, of course, on prevailing interest rate levels at the time of issue. Secondly, they are taxed at issue and are thereafter free from tax. This means that discount bonds bought in the secondary market are also free of the 20 per cent withholding tax normally payable on interest. Minimum denominations of corporate bonds, both coupon and discount, are 50,000 yen or 100,000 yen.

*Foreign bonds (*Samurai *and* Shogun *bonds)*
There are two distinct sections of the Japanese foreign bond market. The older is the conventional and larger market for yen-denominated bonds issued in Japan by foreign borrowers, known as the *Samurai* market. Inaugurated as long ago as 1970 by the Industrial Bank of Japan with a 6 billion yen issue for the Asian Development Bank, this market was twice closed completely for new issues in its formative years, in 1973 following the oil crisis and in 1978 during the foreign exchange crisis. Although there was a relaxation in 1979 for an issue by Sears Roebuck, it was not really until early 1982 that a limited number of the biggest corporate names began to appear, the market having previously been closed to all but the sovereign borrowers, government owned or government-guaranteed agencies and supra-national institutions. Table 5.12 shows the development of the *Samurai* bond market.

The *Shogun* market, for bonds denominated in foreign currencies but issued within Japan, is a much more recent creation. Its first launch was in 1985, when the Bank of Tokyo led an issue of $US 300m for the World Bank. Of the 15 issues up to the beginning of 1987, only two had been for pure corporate names – a $US 100m deal for Southern California Edison and a $US 50m deal for Sohio, a US subsidiary of British Petroleum.

The European markets

Bond financings and investment have traditionally played a larger

Bond markets

Table 5.12   The *Samurai* bond market

	1970	1977	1978	1979	1980	1981	1982	1983	1984	1985
Public issues	1	22	26	14	15	34	38	36	37	38
Value (billion yen)	6	450	650	270	260	600	660	600	1030	1150
Private placements	–	8	8	4	2	15	34	30	32	27
Value (billion yen)	–	260	300	170	75	550	750	700	750	850

Source: Industrial Bank of Japan

role in the major European countries than elsewhere for several reasons. The high savings ratios of European investors has meant that a high proportion of their incomes have been lodged with the commercial banks. These institutions in turn invest funds on behalf of their clients in bonds and also act as investment bankers for a large proportion of native industry. The result has been that banks have performed a twofold function: they both invest savings and raise capital, serving as efficient conduits of funds to industry.

This function has a long history in Europe. The banks have played a pivotal role in many economies for over one hundred years and have weathered numerous wars and political upheavals. They have proved much more resilient than the European stock markets in this respect and, as a result, share investment has normally taken a back seat to bond investment. Added to this is the fact that commercial banks are also able to perform investment banking functions (underwriting), unlike their American counterparts who are restricted under the Glass-Steagall Act. These combined functions have created a different sort of investment behaviour from that which exists in the United States and, to a lesser extent, in Britain.

After the Second World War, many European economies were protected by exchange controls in order to aid their recovery. Since then, many of the controls have been lifted, and today the bond markets in Holland, Switzerland and Germany enjoy international investor interest. Foreign bonds issued in these countries are included in Table 5.13. Issuing activity is largely due to the fact that these currencies have proved strong on foreign exchange markets, and, from the standpoint of borrowers, have relatively low coupons.

The Swiss franc foreign bond market continues to be highly favoured by international investors. In terms of size it has usually been second only to the Eurodollar market, comfortably surpassing

Table 5.13   Foreign bond issues ($US billions equivalent)

	1977	1979	1983	1984	1985	1986	1987 Jan–Oct
Total	16.21	22.27	27.83	27.95	31.02	39.36	36.81
% increase/decrease		+37.4	+25.0	+0.4	+11.0	+26.9	−6.5
United States	7.43	5.79	4.55	5.49	4.66	6.78	5.91
Germany	2.18	5.38	2.67	2.24	1.74	–	–
Switzerland	4.97	9.78	14.30	12.63	14.95	23.21	23.98
Netherlands	0.21	0.08	1.09				
United Kingdom	–	–	0.81	1.29	0.96	0.32	–
Japan	1.27	1.83	3.77	4.63	6.38	5.22	3.07
Others	0.15	0.68	1.73	1.68	2.34	3.82	3.86

Source: Morgan Guaranty Trust of New York, *World Financial Markets*

international markets in all other major currencies. Over 400 issues worth $24 billion were registered in 1987, virtually unchanged in US dollar terms from 1986. This was almost certainly on account of a dearth of equity-linked bonds issued subsequent to the October 1987 stock market crash, since it was reported that nine of such issues for Japanese borrowers were due for launch in December were cancelled. Otherwise, this trend was comparable with the greatly enhanced issues of Euroyen-dominated securities. This was certainly related to the fact that Japanese borrowers have for a long time headed the list of foreign issuers on the Swiss franc securities market, although other industrialised countries and also international agencies have been prominent.

Table 5.14 shows that Union Bank of Switzerland, Crédit Suisse and Swiss Bank Corporation, which jointly run the main bond issuing syndicate, increased their domination of the market with a share up fom 67.68 per cent in 1986 to 71.36 per cent in 1987.

Bond trading in Europe centres around the various stock exchanges, where many of the bonds are listed. This is not to imply that over-the-counter trading does not occur, but the exchanges do play a more central role.

A good deal of currency switching and bond investing between European currencies exists on the same basic lines as those mentioned in connection with British gilts. This cross-border investing is facilitated by the foreign exchange activities provided by the major banks, many of which operate sophisticated forward markets in the major

Bond markets

Table 5.14 Swiss franc foreign bond lead managers, 1987

Manager	SWF bn amount	Rank	Market share %	No. of issues
Union Bank of Switzerland	8.969	1	25.95	77
Crédit Suisse	8.493	2	24.58	94
Swiss Bank Corporation	7.200	3	20.83	70
S G Warburg Soditic	1.637	4	4.74	21
Banque Paribas (Suisse)	0.811	5	2.35	11
Wirtschafts-und-Privatbank	0.744	6	2.15	9
Citicorp Bank (Switzerland)	0.700	7	2.03	8
Handelsbank Natwest	0.695	8	2.01	12
Swiss Volksbank	0.620	9	1.79	8
Kredietbank (Suisse)	0.540	10	1.56	9
Industry total	34.560 (1986 – SWF 41.76 billion)			

Source: Euromoney Swissware

currencies. Thus, when interest rate differentials between continental bond markets occur, a certain amount of currency switching will also occur and some narrowing of these differentials may take place.

The major types of bonds previously mentioned also exist in Europe. But other variations also exist which have never become popular in the United States or in Britain. For instance, in France several types of bonds exist which are indexed to the price of gold or other commodities. Finland at one time experimented with public bonds indexed to the inflation rate. All of these varieties only accentuate a strong bond tradition; without it such variations would never have been possible.

In some countries, notably Holland and Belgium, debt instruments assume slightly different forms than the bonds we have examined previously. They are often referred to as debt certificates and their issuance and secondary market trading depend upon the commercial banks. These instruments can at times form a large part of overall bond issues in any given year.

International bond markets

There are two distinct forms of international bond issue – the foreign bonds which have already been discussed, which are largely denominated in Swiss francs, and which represented some 17 per cent of the new issues of three years or more during 1987, and Eurobonds, which accounted for the remaining 83 per cent. The essential characteristics of the latter are that they are offshore instruments, sold exclusively in markets other than those of their denominated currency and, therefore, not subject to the rules of that home market. That is to say, a Eurosterling bond would not be available within the shores of the United Kingdom and would not, therefore, be subject to UK legislation. This contrasts directly with foreign bonds, which, as has been described, are issued in markets other than those of their borrowers, but usually in the domestic market of the currency in which they are denominated, and are therefore subject to that market's rules, for example bulldog bonds in the United Kindom market, yankee bonds in the United States market, and *Samurai* bonds in Japan.

After surpassing the value in US dollar terms of international bank credits in 1985 at $168 billion, issues of all international bonds – Eurobonds and foreign bonds combined – increased by a further 36 per cent during 1986 to reach a peak of $US 228 billion representing some 71.0 per cent of all international borrowing. While issuers came overwhelmingly from industrialised countries, with borrowing by all other areas in the world still in decline, this was despite a continuing downward trend in United States' issues from their peaks of 1984 and 1985 (see Table 5.15).

This trend continued throughout 1987, contributing greatly to the 22 per cent fall in international bond borrowing as against 1986. Australia, Canada, France and Spain all borrowed less in overall terms in 1987, while Japan took over as the principal borrower and the Latin American countries came back into the markets. The latter contributed to the moderate recovery in international bank credits, since such borrowers have not normally had access to the bond markets. An exception was Colombia, which, unlike most of the others, has not had to reschedule its debts, and made a $US 50m issue in 1987. Otherwise, the only remotely comparable event was the $US 10m private placement in Japan in 1985 by Pemex, the Mexican state oil company. The first Latin American country to actually raise money on bond markets subsequent to the rescheduling of its debts was Venezuela, with a $US 100m issue in the first week in February 1988, although at markedly less favourable rates than for a typical European sovereign borrower, such as Sweden. This is probably the beginning of a new trend, with new devices which incorporate bonds and notes increasingly replacing loans as the usual way of extending credit to developing countries.

Bond markets

Table 5.15 International bond issues and bank credits – by country of borrower

$US millions	1983	1984	1985	1986	1987
International bond issues	76329	107411	167756	228106	177291
% increase/decrease		+40.7	+56.2	+36.0	−23.3
International bank credits	82074	125922	116964	93269	123115
% increase/decrease		+53.4	−7.1	−20.3	+32.0
Total	158403	233333	284720	321375	300406
% increase/decrease		+47.3	+22.0	+12.9	−6.5
Industrial countries	102652	177077	226711	273653	248758
% increase/decrease		+72.5	+28.0	+20.7	−9.1
United States	20276	65054	69194	55703	45412
Japan	14428	17526	21269	35283	45591
United Kingdom	2726	8899	25424	24109	33225
Canada	8571	13124	17184	23752	10161
France	8626	11298	18773	20027	16022
Australia	5737	5816	14407	19251	11349
Italy	4876	6933	11033	12723	13421
Germany	3197	2165	3452	12589	10922
Developing countries	38256	39725	32139	23884	28070
% increase/decrease		+3.8	−19.1	−25.7	+17.5
Latin America	15592	17464	8115	3395	10729
Asia	12978	15893	18410	14444	13219
Middle East/Africa	9686	6368	5614	6044	4122
Eastern Europe	1294	3244	5236	3941	3564
% increase/decrease		+50.7	+61.4	−24.7	−9.6
International organisations	16201	13287	20635	19896	20013
% increase/decrease		−18.0	+55.3	−3.6	+0.6

Source: Morgan Guaranty Trust Company of New York, *World Financial Markets*

The Eurobond markets

A prerequisite for the foundation of the Eurobond market was, of course, the rise of the Eurodollar as an international currency in the late 1950s and early 1960s, when the US dollar first supplanted sterling as the primary reserve currency used in international financial transactions. Great quantities of US dollars were finding their way into European and other offshore banks, partly on account of a large United States balance of payments deficit, and partly as a result of the absence of any US capital and exchange controls. Since Regulation Q of the Federal Reserve put a ceiling on the level of interest payable by

US domestic banks on time deposits, it became more attractive to hold these dollar deposits in foreign banks at higher rates of interest, which in turn made available an important and easily accessible source of funds, not subject to Federal Reserve requirements.

The birth of the Eurobond market really took place in the mid-1960s following on the imposition by the United States of capital controls. The domestic borrowers were prevented from exporting domestic funds, while foreign borrowers (with some exceptions) were being denied access to the US capital market on account of the Interest Equalisation Tax of 1964, and both turned to the Eurodollar market for their capital needs.

London remains one of the chief centres of the Eurobond market. For technical reasons, Eurobonds are normally quoted on a stock exchange, often London, but sometimes Luxembourg or the Netherlands. However, dealings rarely take place in the other locations. Even in London, the market's development has largely by-passed the Stock Exchange. This is because, although the total market has at times been capitalised at a US dollar equivalent of over 200 billion, making it the second largest bond market in the world behind the United States, the secondary market trading of Eurobonds has largely taken place off the floor of the exchange, mostly over the telephone with the banks and securities firms acting as market-makers in Europe, Asia and North America.

This market was originally attracted to London because it provided a centre with only very limited regulatory constraint. US companies were able to issue bonds in Europe without the rigorous Securities and Exchange Commission registration procedure, and this meant that limitations on the structure of issues were determined more by what investors would buy than by any official edict. As already mentioned, there are also no official rating requirements.

Some of these cherished freedoms now seem in jeopardy in the wake of the United Kingdom's Financial Services Act 1986, which imposed early in 1987 an entirely new set of costs and constraints which tested to the full the Eurobond market's ability to adapt to change while simultaneously fighting for its profitability. This has been a very controversial issue, particularly in the secondary market, mainly because operators feel that the style of regulation is at cross purposes with the way in which the Eurobond market works. Nevertheless, this development has brought about the market's own trade organisation, the Association of International Bond Dealers (AIBD), which expects to become a recognised investment exchange under the new regulatory structure, and it is now history that its International Securities Regulatory Organisation (ISRO) has merged with the Stock Exchange in a new self-regulatory organisation.

Early growth of the Eurobond market outside the reach of the national regulatory agencies was mainly attributed to European retail demand for dollar-denominated paper. These rich individual investors were further attracted to the bearer form of the Eurobond, which represented an anonymous investment. Some bonds are still distributed to the retail clients of Swiss banks and other wealthy European investors, not least those crudely categorised Belgian dentists. However, these individuals are vastly outnumbered by institutions, and the market's investor base is these days essentially a professional and wholesale one.

Two high-volume automated clearing systems have grown up alongside the Eurobond markets. These are Euroclear, which is based in Brussels and operated by Morgan Guaranty, and Cedel, based in Luxembourg, and owned by a group of international banks. No paper actually changes hands at these centres, however, for both are essentially giant book-keeping operations, with the actual instruments – usually high-denomination bearer documents – held under lock and key at sub-custodian banks around the world. Settlement in both cases is done by a batch process computer system on the basis of buy and sell instructions received from client institutions. Transactions are cleared overnight on the eve of value date at Euroclear and around midday on the value date at Cedel.

At the outset, of course, almost all Eurobond issues were US dollar denominated. Gradually, because of the imposition of similar capital controls by other countries, and then as the Bretton Woods system gave way to a floating currency regime in the 1970s, various other currencies began to be used, not least the Deutschmark, sterling and the Japanese yen. This range was extended even further around 1980 with issues of multi-currency bonds, which gave investors a choice of interest and redemption payments, and artificial 'packages' such as European currency units (ECUs). Table 5.16 shows recent trends in the currency composition of international fixed rate bond issues.

Eurobonds too were originally only issued at fixed rates of interest, but again the passage of time has seen evolution. There has been a wide variation in their terms of issue and in the determination of interest and repayment, with floating rate, convertible, droplock bonds and bonds with warrants all becoming commonplace. While governments and banks have tended to be the main issuers of FRNs,

Table 5.16 Currency composition of international fixed rate bond issues
(including convertible bonds, warrants and zero coupons)

in % terms	1981	1982	1983	1984	1985	1986
US dollar	49	54	44	50	47	48
Swiss franc	23	20	25	17	14	13
Deutschmark	7	10	11	9	7	
Japanese yen	9	7	7	8	12	13
Sterling	4	3	4	5	3	
Dutch guilder	3	3	3	3	2	
ECU	1	2	3	3	6	
Other	4	1	3	5	9	

Source: Bank of England and Bank for International Settlements

traditional fixed rate issues have continued to be favoured by industrial and commercial borrowers. Eurobond issues are normally handled by a syndicate of banks and/or international securities firms, led by one or more lead manager, with the syndicate either buying or underwriting the issue and then placing the bonds with the investors. Normally, they will pay a slight coupon premium over a comparable bond issued in a domestic market. This is on account of their expatriate nature. Because they are 'bearer' securities, their holders do not have to be registered. Table 5.17 shows the currency composition of FRN issues.

The compositional shift into non-straight Eurobond issues coincided largely with the decline in credit intermediation by banks. It is understandable, therefore, that the most rapid area of growth was in the issuance of floating rate notes (FRNs), which are a close substitute for syndicated bank lending. Their share of the new issue volume rose from 12 per cent in 1980 to more than one-third of a much larger market in 1985. In fact, in terms of Eurodollar bond issues alone, FRNs actually overtook straights in that year. The simultaneous spread of FRNs to non-US dollar sectors was, however, slower. This was in part a reflection of regulatory and other restraints placed on their usage, notably in the Deutschmark, Japanese yen and French franc sectors. Table 5.17 also illustrates that sterling was the only currency other than the dollar to account for a significant portion of the FRN market until 1985. It was then that borrowers were allowed to issue FRNs in the Deutschmark foreign bond and Euroyen sectors. Yet another element of innovation in this context has been

168   *Bond markets*

Table 5.17   Currency composition of floating rate note issues

in % terms	1980	1981	1982	1983	1984	1985
US dollar	93	94	98	94	92	86
Swiss franc	4	2	1	1	1	1
Sterling	3	–	–	5	6	5
Other	–	4	1	–	1	8

Source: Bank of England and Bank for International Settlements

the new types of interest formulae. These have included capped FRNs (which contain maximum interest rates either over the life of the instrument or beginning two or three years from the original issuance); mismatched notes (where the interest rate payment period is, for example, six months but the interest yield is adjusted more frequently); in 1985, the novel feature of perpetual FRNs (which were converted into equity in case of solvency problems); and in 1986, the collateralised mortgage obligation (CMO), directly linked to a pool of mortgages and guaranteed by one of the US government agencies.

Table 5.18 shows in more detail why, after reaching a peak of $188 billion in 1986, Eurobond issues fell by nearly 22 per cent in 1987 and the 48 per cent decline in Eurodollar issues alone underlined one important reason, namely the prolonged decline of the dollar. It had already become apparent in late 1986 that buyers with base currencies other than dollars were losing interest and looking for alternatives, and these were often yen and sterling-based instruments. Meanwhile, dollar-based investors had begun to prefer US treasury bonds, where investments could be more perfectly hedged.

A second set of problems surrounded the market for floating note rates. Already late in 1986 the entire perpetual sector, valued at $US 17 billion, had seized up on account of inadequacies in issuing procedures and an ultimate oversupply. There was also a problem of direct competition from the shorter-term commercial paper and interest swap markets. The latter, in particular, enables borrowers to achieve cheaper terms, simply by issuing fixed-rate bonds and then swapping them for floating-rate money. Later in the year, this market also suffered from uncertainty over the US–Netherlands Antilles tax treaty.

The third area of uncertainty derived, at least in the earlier part of

Table 5.18 Eurobond issues

$US millions	1976	1980	1983	1984	1985	1986	1987
Total	14479	23970	48501	79458	136731	187952	147227
% increase/decrease		+65.5	+102.3	+63.8	+72.1	+37.5	−21.7
US dollar	9276	16427	38428	63593	97782	118220	61691
% increase/decrease		+77.1	+133.9	+65.5	+53.8	+20.9	−47.8
Deutschmark	2713	3607	3817	4604	9491	16870	14687
% increase/decrease		+33.0	+5.8	+20.6	+106.1	+77.7	−12.9
Sterling	–	974	1947	3997	5766	10510	14863
% increase/decrease			+99.9	+105.3	+44.3	+82.3	+41.4
Japanese yen	–	304	212	1212	6539	18673	24226
% increase/decrease			−30.3	+472.7	+439.5	+200.9	+29.7
ECU	99	65	2019	3032	7038	6965	7676
% increase/decrease		−34.3	+3006.1	+50.2	+132.1	−1.0	+10.2
Other	2391	2593	2078	3020	10114	16713	24084
% increase/decrease		+8.4	−19.9	−152.7	+234.9	+65.2	+44.1

Source: Morgan Guaranty Trust of New York, *World Financial Markets*

the year, from heavy competition from a then raging bull market in equities. This was the root cause of the high incidence of issues of Japanese equity-linked bonds with warrants, which rose from 25 issues in 1985 to 120 issues in 1986, and American convertibles, which increased from 12 to 40 issues in 1986. Both were, however, rendered unfashionable overnight following the October 1987 stock market crash.

The cumulative result of all this was that by early in 1987 it was already quite clear that the volume of new issues was exceeding investor demand, and that the books of underwriters were awash with unsold issues Some sources would argue that this liquidity shortage could have been partially mitigated if the larger traders had given way to the introduction of an automated screen quotation system in pursuit of market transparency.

A second series of analyses, from a different source (see Table 5.19), corroborates some of these points. The total number of Eurobond issues decreased from 1621 in 1986 to 1377 in 1987, quote close to the 1985 level of 1366. This represented both a decline of $40 billion in value compared with the $48 billion rise registered in 1986, and a further decrease in the US dollar's share of the market, to 41.9 per cent compared with 70 per cent in 1985 and 63 per cent in 1986. The

Table 5.19 Eurobond issues in 1987 – by currency

1987 rank	Currency	Total raised $bn	Issues	1986 rank	Total raised $bn	Issues	1985 rank	Total raised $bn	Issues
1	$US	59.919	496	1	114.710	826	1	94.161	661
2	Yen	23.530	165	3	18.120	160	3	7.019	80
3	Sterling	14.436	117	4	10.605	79	5	5.493	60
4	D-mark	14.265	128	2	20.043	179	2	11.198	165
5	$ Austr.	9.180	192	7	3.561	91	6	3.134	92
6	Ecu	7.455	70	5	7.104	81	4	6.798	127
7	$ Can.	5.996	93	6	5.179	87	7	2.883	55
8	FF	2.074	19	8	3.476	46	8	1.111	21
9	$NZ	1.494	27	11	0.561	15	–	–	–
10	DKR	1.407	32	10	1.120	27	–	–	–
Total		142.997			182.552			134.510	

Source: IDD Information Services

market share of the Japanese yen, on the other hand, climbed to 16.5 per cent compared with 5 per cent in 1985 and 10 per cent in 1986. This may be viewed both as the result of successive Japanese deregulations in 1984 and 1985, which enabled home borrowers to raise funds outside of Japan, and at the same time an effect of the continuing regulation of other sectors of the Japanese financial system, namely higher coupons on Euroyen bonds than on comparable domestic issues.

This table also demonstrates how other so-called 'currency' sectors, especially the Eurosterling, Australian dollar and Deutschmark markets, fared in relation to the Eurodollar sector. The sterling market share increased for a second year running to 10.1 per cent against 5.8 per cent in 1986 and 4.1 per cent in 1985, while the Australian dollar share, which had fallen from 2.1 per cent in 1985 to 1.4 per cent in 1986, rose to 6.4 per cent. Meanwhile, the market share of the Deutschmark fell back to 10 per cent after the rise from 8.3 per cent to 11 per cent during 1986. But all were affected by the previously mentioned and various general pressures on the market. Some 34.5 per cent of total issues came in the first quarter of the year, falling to 25.3 per cent in the third quarter and to 14.3 per cent in the final quarter. Significantly, over half the German issues and only slightly less ECU issues came in that first quarter. Possibly controls

Table 5.20 Top twenty Eurobond lead managers

	1987			1986				1985		
1987 rank	$bn amount	Market share %	Issues	Rank	Issues	$bn amount	Market share %	Rank	$bn amount	Issues %
1 Nomura Securities	19.200	13.4	122	2	131	14.803	8.1	8	5.098	3.8
2 Crédit Suisse First Boston	9.400	6.6	75	1	102	19.812	10.8	1	19.208	14.3
3 Deutsche Bank	8.232	5.8	68	3	91	12.444	6.8	5	7.839	5.8
4 Nikko Securities	8.020	5.6	58	10	54	5.141	2.8	25	1.817	1.4
5 Yamaichi Securities	7.851	5.5	74	12	59	4.440	2.4	20	2.243	1.7
6 Daiwa Securities	7.552	5.3	70	5	86	8.963	4.9	11	2.988	2.2
7 Morgan Guaranty	5.342	3.7	46	4	65	9.897	5.4	3	7.866	5.8
8 Morgan Stanley	5.187	3.6	36	6	74	8.868	4.9	6	6.529	4.9
9 Salomon Brothers	4.461	3.1	36	7	54	8.235	4.5	4	7.843	5.8
10 Banque Paribas	4.453	3.1	42	8	66	7.002	3.8	10	3.377	2.5
11 Industrial Bank of Japan	4.169	2.9	41	16	25	3.034	1.7	34	0.870	0.6
12 S G Warburg	3.926	2.7	36	18	24	2.788	1.5	17	2.399	1.8
13 Union Bank of Switzerland	3.257	2.3	26	11	46	4.874	2.7	9	3.837	2.9
14 Commerzbank	2.754	1.9	28	19	39	2.713	1.5	13	2.548	1.9
15 Dresdner Bank	2.277	1.6	20	30	–	–	–			
16 Swiss Bank Corporation	2.149	1.5	24	17	23	2.886	1.6	14	2.547	1.9
17 Goldman Sachs	2.139	1.5	19	14	22	3.621	2.0	7	5.410	4.0
18 Baring Brothers	2.066	1.4	17	29	–	–	–			
19 LTCB of Japan	2.001	1.4	15	20	21	2.553	1.4	36	0.825	0.6
20 Bank of Tokyo	1.796	1.3	17	31	–	–	–			
Industry totals	142.997		1377		1621	182.651			134.512	

Source: IDD Information Services

Table 5.21   Euromarket turnover ($US million)

	Straights	Convertibles	FRNs	Others
Primary market				
$US	429.6	0.0	0.0	6234.2
Previous week	128.6	0.0	211.0	8271.2
Other	851.2	0.0	83.8	496.0
Previous week	1248.3	0.0	0.0	668.2
Secondary market				
$US	22514.7	2097.7	7793.7	7374.6
Previous week	18766.4	2109.8	9284.0	5746.3
Other	23335.3	750.5	5837.3	21226.5
Previous week	22605.2	933.8	2656.4	19996.4

	Cedel	Euroclear	Total
$US	12407.2	34037.3	46444.5
Previous week	12103.8	32414.2	44518.0
Other	21867.9	30712.7	52580.6
Previous week	21433.4	26645.8	48079.2

Source: AIBD   Week to 4 February 1988

still exercised by German capital markets authorities over the issue of Euro Deutschmark bonds, such as the imposition of a two week notification period, which is still an impediment to swap-related issues, and the failure of the federal government to abolish the Börsenumsatzsteuer (stock exchange turnover tax), have contributed to this.

It is interesting to see how the changes which took place in 1987 influenced the league table of Eurobond league managers, shown in Table 5.20. Japan's Big Four securities houses are all in the top six, undoubtedly a result of the growing volume of yen issues in the year. Nomura finally established itself as the premier house during the first quarter of 1987, and ended up with a share almost as large as the 14.3 per cent held by Crédit Suisse First Boston in 1985. Apart from Nikko, Yamaichi and Daiwa, two Japanese long-term credit banks, LTCB and the Bank of Tokyo, were also in the list. Three banks which had appeared in the table in 1986 were not among the top 20 lead managers in 1987. The most notable of these was Merrill Lynch, which narrowly failed to make the list after being second in 1985 and ninth in 1986. The others were Shearson Lehman, which dropped from thirteenth to twenty-eighth, and Société Générale. Meanwhile, two banks which had featured in the table in 1985, Orion Royal and Lloyds, have now left the Eurobond market altogether.

Week-to-week turnover in Euromarkets

The ongoing position in the Euromarket turnover is encapsulated in Table 5.21. This information is published in the *Financial Times* each Monday; this example is from early 1988. The lack of interest in convertibles and FRNs emerges strongly in the first section, which plots issues in the primary market. The second portion gives an overview of the secondary market, illustrating the strength of straights and others (largely the Japanese equity-linked issues). Finally, the third portion breaks down the market's turnover as handled by the two standard clearing mechanisms (Euroclear and CEDEL).

CHAPTER SIX

Foreign exchange markets

Definition

The foreign exchange market may be defined as one of the several markets in financial assets, the assets to be traded in this case being two or more currencies simultaneously. As a market in financial assets it is closely related to the money markets, where short-term money is traded; the capital markets, where long-term money is traded; and national stock exchanges, where finance-denominated stocks and securities are traded.

In common with other markets, trade in the foreign exchange market is determined by prices. The prices in this case are foreign exchange rates, which may be viewed as the relative price of two national currencies, or the price of a currency expressed in the terms of another.

As with prices in other markets, exchange rates are, in the final analysis, determined by the interplay of demand and supply for the respective currencies. In a world of reasonably free movement of capital between countries, equilibrium in foreign exchange markets requires that the demand by asset owners for stocks of different currencies and financial assets denominated in them be equal to the stocks of these currencies and financial assets which exist at that moment.

History and physical characteristics

Foreign exchange markets have existed for as long as international trade in goods and services has taken place, and their history goes back to the time when they acted as clearing houses for bills of exchange.

Nowadays, in addition to those traders who carry out the transactions in goods and services that influence a country's current account, the holders of financial assets in foreign currencies – including firms, pension funds, unit and investment trusts, commercial banks and private individuals – have a significant presence in the foreign exchange markets. In addition there are the mainly speculative participants, who will make their turn on buying and selling that which they do not necessarily need or do not even have, in the hope that they can subsquently sell or buy at a profit before the delivery date. Finally, there are the central banks, which intervene heavily in foreign exchange markets for a host of reasons, sometimes in their own name, sometimes through an intermediary, such as a commercial bank. This will often depend upon the extent to which they wish their presence to be detected, for instance in times of currency crisis when they aim to protect parities. This sort of intervention has been commonplace, certainly since the Bretton Woods system was set up in 1944. Of course, the European Monetary System demands that central banks intervene at predetermined limits.

Unlike many stock markets or commodity markets, but in common with money markets and capital markets, foreign exchange markets in English-speaking countries have not traditionally had any physically recognisable market place. The market transactions typically take the form of a communication between the head offices of two banks in recognised market centres, usually over the telephone, but sometimes by telex or other more sophisticated means of communication. A foreign exchange dealing room is usually characterised by traders sitting in front of a telephone switchboard with direct lines to hundreds of other banks, which can be activated at the press of a button. Also much in evidence in modern dealing rooms are masses of video screens giving details of prices traded throughout the world. Decibels of noise are usually directly related to the level of activity on the markets.

The tradition in many European countries has been for the foreign exchange dealers all to meet together at a predetermined time each day of trading in a room within the local stock exchange or bourse. This is usually known as the fixing. Because all dealing is done in public, the final price of the day will become immediately available as the basis of legal agreements or the rate for deals between banks and their customers.

Market operations

A deal will be agreed verbally, and invariably followed by a written note of confirmation of the transaction. Although there are exceptions, deals in the spot market are usually transacted for settlement on the second working day following, known as the value date.

While certain large corporations do have their own traders, it should be emphasised that foreign exchange is part of the payments mechanism. Therefore, it is quite natural that people should traditionally have turned to banks to act as their agents, or intermediaries, in such transactions. This should not, however, be interpreted as meaning that banks do not act as principals. Indeed, a great deal of business is now conducted on their own account, performing their function as 'market makers' in the professional interbank market. This is where overall supply and demand are consolidated and foreign exchange rates are determined.

It is important to emphasise two further points. Firstly, activities on the foreign markets are usually the prerogative of bank head offices, or their overseas representative offices. Secondly, banks tend to be selective in the currencies in which they are prepared to deal, often but not exclusively concentrating on deals where their own national currency forms one side of the transaction.

This leads us to a further corner of the market, namely foreign exchange brokers. A reducing number of international firms perform this important complementary function. Brokers, who are specifically prevented from trading as principals on their own account, play a crucial role in the arrangement of transactions in the interbank market, operating on the basis of a commission or brokerage. One typical situation where the intercession of a broker might be useful would be when two banks wishing to trade in the market vary too much in size for a full reciprocal basis to be established. Another would be when what is known as an 'exotic' currency is to be traded. Banks also use brokers to 'show prices', more often than not on just one side of the market. There is an established terminology here, known as 'hitting' and 'taking'. 'Hitting' refers to an agreement to match another bank's bid or offer. 'Taking' refers to the other bank's acceptance of the 'hit'. It is only after the deal has been closed that the broker will disclose the name of his client.

The global nature of markets

The foreign exchange market is truly worldwide, and continues throughout the full twenty-four hour span of a normal working day. Banks in the Far East and Australia, including branches of major US and European institutions, begin trading in Tokyo, Sydney, Hong Kong and Singapore at about the time that most traders in San Francisco are closing for the previous day. As the Far East closes, trading in the Middle East financial centres, such as Bahrain, has been going on for a couple of hours, and the long trading day in the big European centres like London, Frankfurt and Zurich is just about to begin. Although some of the large New York banks have an early shift to minimise the time differential with Europe of five to six hours, New York trading does not usually get going in full force until about 8 a.m. local time, by which time the London traders will already have had their lunch. To complete the full circle, banks on the West Coast of the United States also extend normal banking hours so that they can trade with New York or even Europe, on one side, and with Tokyo, Sydney, Hong Kong and Singapore on the other.

In general, the daily habits of foreign exchange dealers bear no relation to normal banking hours. They are often required to leave their beds in the middle of the night to deal in a market that is characterised by the sharpness of its movements. At the other end of the day, they may often be found at their desk well into the evening in an endeavour to square a position. This is perhaps the reason why foreign exchange dealers are nearly always markedly on the younger side of middle age.

The foreign exchange rate

The foreign exchange rate has already been defined as the relative price between two national currencies. Displays of such rates have become familiar to us when either passing a bank in a major city or reading the business columns of daily newspapers. And these might tell us, for example, that, for each pound sterling with which we wished to purchase US dollars, we would receive 1.80 US dollars (one dollar and eighty cents). Let it now be assumed that the purchaser of such dollars was a tourist or businessman, and that, at the termination of the visit, he had a surplus of dollars to convert back into sterling. Also that there had been absolutely no movement in exchange rates over the ensuing period. He would certainly not recover one pound sterling for each one dollar and eighty cents. Indeed he would be fortunate to recover one pound for each one dollar and eighty five cents. That is to say, there would be a loss of 5 cents on the original value of each pound sterling. This is the difference between the banks' buying and selling prices, or to use the technical terms, bid and offer prices. It is called the spread, or banker's turn, and is intended to cover their costs in the transaction. And we note that the bid price, at which the bank is prepared to buy the dollars back, is higher than the offer price, at which it will sell.

Spot rates

The market rates quoted in the morning edition of a newspaper, such as the *Financial Times*, would be different to those quoted to individuals by the banks. The sterling/dollar spot rate might, instead of 1.80 and 1.85, be 1.8245 and 1.8255, or 1.8245/55 as it will be displayed. This is because those spot rates are for very large transactions, probably of at least one million US dollars, where the bank is prepared to take a commission of only ¹⁄₁₀ cent per dollar or 0.1 per cent.

The term 'spot' rate emphasises the immediacy of the transaction (although the delivery will actually take place two days hence – on the value date), compared with the forward rate, which has to do with a pre-determined future date. Moreover, rates which represent the value of a currency in terms of another are also known by the general term of cross rates. It should be stressed, however, that it is not usual to use this term when dealing in one's own base currency. It is more appropriate in a cross deal between two foreign currencies. It may also be noted that the term 'the cross rate' is traditionally used when expressing the Canadian dollar price in terms of US dollars.

Quotations of most currencies are based on their value in terms of one US dollar unit, and are known as direct quotations. Those of some currencies, meanwhile, such as the pound sterling and the Irish punt, are more often expressed in terms of the number of US dollar units which they constitute, and known as indirect quotations. This phenomenon is largely based on convention, and has to do with the fact that one prime currency unit in UK and Ireland has traditionally been considerably more valuable than its US counterpart. And it is this convention which is followed by the daily quotations in the Financial Times. With direct quotations, the lower the number of units to the base currency, for example the US dollar, the stronger the currency in question. The Japanese yen, for example, is in a much stronger position when there are 135 yen to the dollar than when there are 200 yen to the dollar. And, of course, the yen would be much stronger still if there were only one yen to the dollar. The converse will apply in the case of indirect quotations, just as the rule previously advanced will be reversed for direct quotations, that is the bid price will be lower than the offer price.

American newspapers, notably the *Wall Street Journal*, have traditionally quoted all currencies by their equivalent in terms of US dollars, for example .5988 dollars to the Deutschemark or .007407 dollars to the yen. This is known as the North Atlantic convention. These are, of course, merely reciprocals of European quotations.

Forward rates

The difference between spot rates and forward rates has already been emphasised. A forward rate is the relative price between two currencies for delivery at some stipulated time in the future, which is generally one month, two months, three months, six months or one year later.

The forward rate is determined either by adding a premium to a prevailing spot rate between two currencies, thereby making it more expensive, or by subtracting a discount from a prevailing spot rate between the two currencies, and making it cheaper. Premiums and discounts can be expressed in two ways, either in terms of the actual currency, which is the more common method, often at the secondary level such as cents and pfennigs, or on what is known as a 'per cent per annum' basis. The latter expresses the premium as an annualised percentage of the spot rate, that is to say multiplying by twelve in the case of the one month rate and by four in the case of the three month rate. The new rate, adjusted for the premium or discount, is known as the outright rate, and it is at this rate that the forward trade is transacted.

A comparison of closing forward rates, as listed in the *Financial Times*, with the comparative rates in the Eurocurrency interest rates table immediately below it shows that, in most cases, currencies with a higher interest rate are quoted at a discount and those with a lower interest rate are quoted at a premium. Of course, from the United Kingdom standpoint, the premium will have to be deducted while the discount is added. This is the effect of the indirect quotation.

It must immediately be emphasised that the outright rate should never be interpreted as a forecast of a spot rate at some subsequent date. It is little more than the effect of the differential between the respective interest rates of financial assets of a comparable term in the two currencies in question. Those interest rates are determined on the money markets, simultaneously with the determination of spot exchange rates on the forward exchange markets, and, just as simultaneously, they may be integrated with the latter to construct a forward rate. This is a close relationship which is fundamental to a proper understanding of the foreign exchange and money markets, which is explained through a theoretical concept known as the interest rate parity theorem, or alternatively the theory of interest arbitrage.

The interest rate parity theorem

This theorem has four variables:

S   = the spot exchange rate;
F   = the outright forward exchange rate;
i(A) = the interest rate over a comparable period on financial assets in the currency to be sold;
i(B) = the interest rate over a comparable period on financial assets in the currency to be purchased.

The critical relationship is the differential between variables i(A) and i(B). Assume that currency A is the US dollar and currency B is the Swiss franc, and the three-month interbank interest rate on Eurodollars is 12 per cent and that on the Euroswiss franc is 5 per cent. Also that the spot exchange rate is 2.50 Swiss francs to the dollar. The intention is to purchase 2.5 million Swiss francs three months forward.

The bank will purchase 2.5 million Swiss francs immediately on the investor's behalf and invest them for three months at a deposit rate of 5 per cent p.a. The investor must presume that the bank will have paid one million US dollars in consideration of the purchase, and must forego the interest on those dollars for the three month period, which would be at the rate of 12 per cent p.a. Since interest will be received on the Swiss francs at 5 per cent p.a., the net interest foregone will be at 7 per cent p.a. or 1.75 per cent over three months. It is this 1.75 per cent which the bank will charge as a premium on the spot US dollar/Swiss franc exchange rate. Calculated on a spot rate of 2.5 it will be 0.0125 Swiss francs, the outright forward rate being 2.4875 Swiss francs to the US dollar.

This may be formalised as follows:

$$F = S\left(1 + \left[\frac{i(B) - i(A)}{100} \times \frac{x}{12}\right]\right)$$

where x = term of forward transaction in months

It follows that, had the Eurodollar interest rate been 5 per cent and the EuroSwiss rate 12 per cent, with the differential between i(A) and i(B) negative, that is, if the interest rates had been juxtapositioned, there would have been a discount of 1.75 per cent or 0.0125 Swiss francs on the spot rate, and the outright forward rate would have been 2.5125.

In particular, it should be observed that the larger the interest rate differential, the steeper will be the progression of premiums or discounts. Conversely, with a set of interest rates of close to nil differential, the progression of the premium or discount will be 'flat'. In such cases, it is not unusual for some periods to be in premium and others in discount.

Dealing in the market

The four basic deals

When considering the subject of foreign exchange, it is wise always to avoid the great deal of jargon that surrounds it and remember one simple truth. No matter how sophisticated they may seem all foreign exchange deals fall into one of four basic categories – buying, selling, borrowing or lending.

Buying and selling need no further consideration. They are merely a transfer of the ownership of one currency against the consideration of another. As has been explained, forward purchases or sales are much the same, an adjustment for the interest element having been included in the form of premium or discount.

Borrowing and lending of foreign currencies is more complex. Firstly, an interest payment will have to be made, at the market rate for the borrowed or lent currency. Secondly, when the loan matures, the principal will have to be repaid at the new exchange rate. This may imply a gain or loss.

Covering risk through the use of forward rates

Forward exchange rates may be used as a form of insurance, in covering the risk of a foreign exchange gain or loss. A UK importer, for example, in undertaking a contract to buy goods from Germany where the delivery date is at or around three months ahead, on the basis of recent and foreseen trends in exchange rates, will face the risk that the Deutschemark might appreciate against sterling in this period. He might decide to cover that risk by purchasing Deutsche-marks immediately for delivery in three months' time, and paying the necessary premium. Alternatively he could wait until payment is due and then to cover on a spot basis. The different sorts of enterprises which trade across national frontiers, from the small companies who do not have large reserves to the larger corporations who do, have different perceptions of risk, and it is these perceptions which will determine whether or to what extent they choose to cover that risk. The principal will, of course, be similar when the product traded is either a service or a financial claim.

Swaps and time options

Banks operating in the interbank market, some large corporate clients and, most particularly, central banks, trade frequently on the basis of a swap transaction. This may be defined as a pair of foreign exchange deals that amount to the simultaneous purchase and sale of a foreign currency for two separate value dates. The key aspect is that the bank arranges the swap as a single transaction with a single counterparty, which may be either another bank or a non-bank customer. However, both deals do not have to be entered into by the same two partners. Notwithstanding that, the result is still that, unlike outright spot or forward transactions, there is no foreign currency risk incurred, known as an 'open position', since the same bank contracts both to pay and receive the same amount of currency at specified rates. The virtue of a swap is that each party is enabled to use a currency for which he has an immediate use in exchange for one for which he has no immediate use. This is, therefore, a very useful investment facility for the temporarily idle currency balances of an international corporation or financial institution. The swap also provides a mechanism for a bank to accommodate the outright forward transactions executed with customers or to bridge gaps in the maturity structure of its outstanding spot and forward contracts, known as 'balancing the book'. That is to say, long and short positions which are identical in size but of different delivery dates can be matched.

In theory, it may appear that the two value dates in a swap transaction can be any pair of future dates. In practice, this is not so, and it will soon be discovered that markets exist for only a limited number of standard maturities, and if the precise date was unknown but within a particular period of time, then it might be necessary to take a so-called 'time option', which could prove to be quite expensive. Returning to standard transactions or swaps, one of these would be the 'spot against forward' swap, where the trader buys or sells a currency for the ordinary spot value date and sells or buys it back for a subsequent value date, perhaps six or twelve months forward. Another common transaction, particularly in the interbank market, is the 'tomorrow next' swap or 'rollover'. Here the dealer buys or sells a currency for value the next business day and simultaneously sells or buys it back for value the day after. More sophisticated and rarer, because of the limitations on forward maturities, is the 'forward-forward' swap, where the dealer will buy or sell for one forward value date, say one month, and then sell or buy back for value at another date, say three months. In a 1977 US turnover survey, 40 per cent of total turnover for the 44-bank sample reflected swap transactions, mostly for maturities of less than a week. Only 5 per cent represented outright forward transactions, mostly with non-bank customers.

The financial futures market

One further form of covering foreign exchange risk is through the futures markets. These are the subject of the final chapter of this book.

The evolution from fixed to floating exchange rates

The Bretton Woods system

During the term of the Bretton Woods system, which governed international monetary behaviour between 1944 and 1971, exchange rates were to a great extent centrally determined. Each currency had a predetermined parity with the US dollar, and was only permitted to fluctuate within narrow margins defined by intervention limits set at 1 per cent on either side of that parity. Member countries of the International Monetary Fund were required to intervene to keep their currencies within these parameters, often with the assistance of the IMF. Only occasionally, if a country was successful in demonstrating to its fellow members that its currency had reached a state of fundamental disequilibrium, was a one-off devaluation or revaluation sanctioned by the International Monetary Fund. The government of the United States effectively underwrote this system by undertaking to convert US dollars freely into gold at a fixed price of $35 per ounce. This form of convertibility was known as the Gold Exchange Standard, which differed from its predecessor, the Gold Standard, in that central banks were no longer obliged to convert their own currencies into gold on demand but would still undertake to exchange for a currency which could be converted, in this case the US dollar.

Although this system had been under fundamental pressures from time to time, it did not actually break down until August 1971, when the President of the United States, President Nixon, announced the end of convertibility. A short period followed when most major countries resorted temporarily to floating exchange rates, until the system was shored up by the Smithsonian Agreement in December of that year, which set new intervention margins at 2.25 per cent either side of the central rate against the dollar, without convertibility. Floating rates then became virtually universally adopted in 1973, when this amended regime broke down, and there followed some years of currency crises as the so-called Committee of Twenty attempted to devise some alternative disciplined scheme. Finally, in 1978, the statutes of the International Monetary Fund were formally amended to permit floating rates.

Attempts at foreign exchange stability continued, however, if initially only on a regional basis. In March 1979, for example, eight countries of the European Community came together within the exchange rate mechanism (ERM) of the European Monetary System. This was the culmination of some previous efforts at economic and monetary union (known as 'the snake in the tunnel') in the context of the Werner Plan, in order to give at least some additional stability to European exchange rates. The exchange rate mechanism of the EMS permits margins of 2.25 per cent either side of a central rate against each other country in the system, with the optional alternative available to facilitate the participation of countries such as Italy, liable to find their currencies almost persistently under pressure, of a 6 per cent margin. A central fund, the European Monetary Co-operation Fund, facilitates the settlement of payments resulting from intervention, rather as the IMF did under the Bretton Woods system.

Exchange rate volatility and misalignments

More and more observers have been alarmed by the violence of the swings in exchange rates under the contemporary floating regime. This concern culminated in the Plaza Agreement of September 1985 at which the Group of Five (G5) recognised that the pattern of current account balances arising from the prevailing configuration of policies and exchange rates in the largest countries was unsustainable. It was at this stage that, under concerted intervention, the US dollar commenced to weaken from its then unrealistically overvalued levels and started the slide which still continues.

The Louvre Accord of February 1987 created the impression that satisfactory progress could and would be made in addressing these problems. But the July and August US trade deficits combined with wider surpluses in Germany and the Asian NICSs and a restricted narrowing of Japan's trade surplus soon changed this perception. The result was rising inflation expectations and increases in interest rates, which resulted in Black Monday and the October stock market crash. So far there is little ground for hope. The Gramm-Rudman-Hollings mechanism (whereby the President is authorised to make cuts in 'controllable' government spending if the projected budget deficit exceeds that laid down in the Balanced Budget and Emergency Deficit Control Act of 1985) is clearly insufficient to satisfy the US budget issue. Without a satisfactory settlement to that problem, a meeting of G5 with subsequent compensating adjustments by the countries in surplus is unlikely. Currency volatility remains in the centre of the world's economic stage.

When discussing the general subject of volatility, it is always important to distinguish between two distinct phenomena, volatility and misalignment. Volatility, in this sense, means the short-run variability in the exchange rate from hour to hour, day to day, week to week, and month to month. And misalignment describes the persistent departure of the exchange rate from its long-run equilibrium level. Put another way, exchange rates can be volatile around an equilibrium level of competitiveness in the short-run or stable over long periods while still misaligned.

Exchange rate determination under a floating currency regime

Expectations

Foreign exchange rates under a floating regime are far more than a function of market supply and demand. Mention has already been made of the diversity of market participants, all of whom are brought to the market for different reasons, and each of whom may be influenced by different outside considerations, which may be economic or political in origin. At least 60 per cent of these are not concerned with the financing of trade, nor are they really concerned with financing the acquisition of tangible assets overseas. They are interested in something much more vital, namely highly liquid asset portfolios which are adjusted across national borders according to perceived expectations of what may or may not transpire in the future. Such asset holders, motivated by precisely the same desire for profit as governs actions of producing, exporting and importing firms, seek to arrange their portfolios so as to achieve an optimum return for a given level of risk. The contemporary deregulation and internationalisation of markets has greatly contributed to this new-found freedom.

The active anticipation of the future impact of current policy developments and changes in the key economic variables has become an important part of economic decision-making by all kinds of macroeconomic actors. It is a phenomenon born of the economic disorders of the 1970s, when the floating of exchange rates coupled with a general acceleration of inflation in industrial countries increased the level of risk attaching to asset portfolios. The economic environment of the mid-1950s to the late 1960s, which had been characterised by low rates of inflation, stable economic growth and relatively constant exchange rates, had enabled international economic actors to take a generally sanguine view of the future, with expectations being based simply on extrapolations of past trends. By comparison, they now take into consideration all available information which theory and experience suggest is relevant to the formulation of 'expectations' about future movements in exchange rates.

Expectations concerning exchange rates start with two different kinds of longer-term observation. The first is that exchange rates tend to adjust so as to offset inflation differentials between countries. That is to say, the countries with habitual low inflation such as Japan, Germany, Switzerland and the Netherlands, being the so-called strong currency countries, will tend towards revaluation, while countries such as Italy, Spain and Portugal, with habitual high inflation, will have a propensity to devalue. This process will, of course, follow a different pattern in controlled regimes, such as the European Monetary System – where it will result in periodic realignments – than it does in freely floating regimes, where it will be affected on a continuous basis through the process of appreciation or depreciation of a currency. In essence, this assumption follows Gustav Cassel's Purchasing Power Parity Theory (*Money and Foreign Exchange after 1914*, Constable, London, 1922) which was rejuvenated in at least five studies in 1978 (Frenkel, Genberg, Kouri and Braga de Macedo, Niehans, Artus and Crocket).

The second observation argues that, if a country has a current account deficit or surplus exceeding what may be considered the stable or normal flow of long-term capital, its exchange rate will eventually change in a predictable direction. This is the message of the monetary approach to balance of payments as formalised in the late 1960s by economists at the University of Chicago (Frenkel and Johnson, 1974).

A third theory which was formerly popular was that the higher interest rate currencies were inherently weak whereas the low interest rate currencies had an underlying strength. This assumption became outdated with increased use of the monetary instrument by politicians as an anti-inflationary tool through the control of money supply in recent years.

This kind of theorising becomes the basis for determining the equilibrium rate upon which it is possible to decide where a currency is misaligned, and it also has a direct effect upon the short-term behaviour of exchange rates, through a phenomenon known as 'overshooting'. This takes place when, in response to minor or gradual changes in monetary policy, exchange rates repeatedly, although only temporarily, move in excess of what is required to offset concurrent inflation differentials. Two basic conditions of economic life explain this. Firstly, the variables most directly affected by a change in macroeconomic policy – national price levels, employment and output, national interest rates and exchange rates – all have different reaction times or degrees of variability, price levels being the slowest and exchange rates the fastest to react. This explains why most of the initial adjustment caused by a change in expectations is manifested through a change in exchange rates. The second condition reflects the fact that in the capital markets that we are now experiencing, with nearly instantaneous communication and with transaction costs that are trivial, the interest rates parity relationship must hold at all times.

Effective exchange rates

Discussions of these sorts of adjustments raises further fundamental questions as far as a consideration of exchange rates is concerned. The framework in which economists are trying to evaluate these issues is multilateral rather than bilateral in character. As such it will require a relative price not just against one other currency but against a whole series, or basket, of currencies. It is just this sort of consideration that led to the inception of what are known as effective exchange rates. Most of the international financial agencies have devised their own models, and some banks, notably Morgan Guaranty Trust of New York, are also active in this field. The best known model is undoubtedly that of the International Monetary Fund in Washington, known as the Multilateral Exchange Rate Model (MERM) and devised in 1973 at the time of the demise of the Bretton Woods system of fixed parities (Artus and Rhomberg, IMF Staff Papers, November 1973).

The fundamental characteristic of an effective exchange rate index is that it measures the overall value of a currency against a number of other currencies, relative to a certain base date. The measure depends upon which other currencies are included in the calculation and the relative importance (weight) attached to each of them. This means that a whole range of effective exchange rate indices can be calculated for any one currency. The base date against which exchange rates are compared can also be varied, although the adoption of a different date will influence only the scale of the index at any point, and not percentage changes in it between different dates. The IMF's model previously mentioned, for instance, is weighted according to the multilateral trade flows of eighteen major countries for 1977 (previously 1972), and the base for the indices is that average daily closing exchange rates in London for 1975 = 100 (this was previously the middle rates following the Smithsonian Agreement of December 1971).

Thus the effective exchange rate can be defined as a means of measuring movements of one currency group against a group of currencies. In theory, this could be all currencies, but in practice some trade figures are less reliable than others, and it is unlikely that the matrix could be made accurate enough. Another point is that only a handful of major currencies really influence trade flows in any worthwhile sense, so that the payoff from the extra work would be minimal. Daily calculations according to the IMF's model and Morgan Guaranty's effective model are published each day in the *Financial Times*, although not for the complete range of currencies included in each model (eighteen and sixteen respectively).

Real effective exchange rates

In considering the long-term relationship beween exchange rates and inflation rate differentials, the nominal effective exchange rate is going to be insufficient. A further component will need to be introduced into the effective exchange rate model, namely an inflation rate measure for each currency. This provides the real effective exchange rate which, at least in theory, makes it possible to assess the degree to which a currency is either under- or overvalued in terms of other currencies, with regard to the inflation rate differential. The best known model for this measure is published by the Morgan Guaranty Trust Company of New York in its monthly *World Financial Markets*. The US Federal Reserve Board also maintains an index, which featured in the 1983 Annual Report of the Council of Economic Advisers.

It is worth emphasising that there can be a large degree of discrepancy between different real exchange rate models. This arises as a result of the large number of variables that can be introduced into the equation. Added to the choice of base and weighting in the nominal effective calculation is the selection of which index of inflation to employ. There are numerous published and unpublished aggregate indices of prices for each country, ranging from retail prices through wholesale prices to GNP deflators. There is an even greater choice of disaggregated indices. Indeed, Morgan Guaranty uses wholesale prices of non-food manufactures. A good practice is to calculate real effective indices using a wide variety of price measurements, bearing in mind that one does not always have objective comparative indices for each of the countries in the model, submit the results to some form of correlation test, and then perhaps include the successful candidates in some form of averaging process. Research findings on this subject were published in September 1983 by the Institute for International Economics, Washington (John Williamson, *The Exchange Rate System*).

CHAPTER SEVEN

Futures and Options

The financial futures and options markets which now encircle the globe have risk as their keynote. They attract two basic types of user – 'hedgers' and 'traders'. The former are the risk averse, who use such contracts to 'insure' against the more extreme changes in foreign exchange and interest rates or stock market prices. The latter, meanwhile, use them as a means of gearing up their exposures at low cost with a view to profit. Inevitably, linked quite closely to the latter are the arbitrageurs, whose existence is about the exploitation of opportunities for profit which may be thrown up by price anomalies between different instruments or markets. Such activity performs an essential function in helping to perfect the global financial markets. Financial futures and options are creatures of the 1970s and 1980s and, although they are traded on the floors of the same exchanges, and have become to a large extent interdependent, their two quite distinct origins are not always well understood.

In common with foreign exchange markets, futures and options markets differ in one other fundamental respect from straightforward equity and bond markets. Since, instead of raising capital or seeking liquidity for industry or government, they are only initiating and trading hedging positions, they are not divided into primary and secondary sectors.

Futures Trading

Contracts in financial futures are really a direct development of the principles and practices which had been used in the markets for basic commodities for more than a hundred years, ever since farmers and traders had originally organised them in order to protect themselves against future price fluctuations, and which indeed are still used today.

Futures trading offers at least four advantages over dealing in cash or forward markets. These are as follows:

1. Instruments which trade on the floors of commodity exchanges are not assets which confer an instant ownership in return for payment of the purchase price; instead they are binding contracts which, in return for a deposit of a fraction of the nominal value of that contract, call for the future delivery of an asset.

2. They entitle their holders to buy or sell at some specific date in the future, at a price fixed at the time of contracting on the floor of the exchange, a multiple of a defined commodity which is standardised as to the amount and deliverable grade. Because one can go long (buy) or go short (sell) in any market with equal facility, this makes it far easier to establish and liquidate an open position.

3. Because all trading is effected 'on the margin', dealing is relatively cheap and simple, and investors are enabled to make large profits on small outlays.

4. There is no obligation on the buyer or seller in a futures market to sustain a contract, or 'leave the position open' through to its maturity date, which would entail the making or taking of actual physical delivery. He can merely cancel, or 'close', his position by reversing the deal. That is to say, he will sell or buy the same number of contracts at any time before maturity.

Most trading in futures during market hours is transacted on exchanged floors by 'open outcry'. While such trading is under way in the 'pits' or 'rings' of the individual exchanges, information on actual trades and prices is transmitted, usually by hand signal, to exchange officials who duly record and display it on electronic display boards for all to see. It is simultaneously reported by various information broadcasting systems, which disseminate it worldwide through their networks, thereby perfecting the international dimension of the markets.

Another activity crucial to trading in futures is the function of the clearing house. In London, for example, this role is performed by the International Commodities Clearing House Ltd, which is owned by six leading British banks and is quite independent of any individual market's regulatory body. By contrast, in New York, clearing house membership is usually confined to exchange members themselves.

Such clearing houses provide three main functions: the provision of central clearing facilities for all deliveries; the extension, through the collection and dispersal of margins and matching trades, of banking arrangements to members of the various exchanges; and a guarantee of the fulfilment of contracts to their clearing members, whether buyers or sellers. This is done by demanding initial and variation margins for all deals, with daily settlement in cash by both buyers and sellers, thereby enabling the clearing house, depending upon the adequacy of its own capital resources, to cover all the losses of its members at all times and thereby protect its own interests.

Investors in futures contracts are faced by two main types of margin. The first is the 'initial' or 'original' margin, and the second is the 'variation' margin. The minimum initial margin represents the 'deposit' which each investor must put up before any futures contract is entered into. It is only a small percentage of the nominal value of each open contract, and is calculated by the respective exchanges so as to cover that movement in the price of each commodity which can be expected in any one day. The more volatile the markets, the higher will be the initial margin and vice versa. It may also be varied by the exchanges at relatively short notice. In contrast, the variation margin is calculated at the close of each day, as all open positions are revalued or 'marked to market'. If the open position shows a loss against the settlement price for that day, then a 'variation' margin equal to that day's loss will be payable. If, on the other hand, an open position is showing a profit, then the account of the investor will be credited by the extent of that profit. This means that the investor is constantly kept aware of profits or losses.

Options Trading

In common with the futures contract, an option contract is a risk management or control tool designed to mitigate the effects of possible adverse movements in the price of a security or commodity. Depending upon his expectations of future market trends and the performance of a particular security, a market player will buy either a call option (if he believes the price of the security or commodity will rise) or a put option (if he believes the price will fall), thereby placing a limit on the effect any adverse price movement will have on his transaction or portfolio.

Although an option is a negotiable contract involving both a buyer and a seller, it will avoid some confusion if these are hereafter referred to in the terms by which they are more commonly known, the 'taker' and 'writer' of the option respectively. This is because the right which each taker acquires can be to either purchase or sell a specific quantity of the commodity or security at the specified price within an agreed time period in consideration of the payment of a premium. But it must be emphasised that this is the point where the taker's obligation stops. By paying the premium he has fulfilled his obligation, whereas on the other side of the contract the obligation upon the writer to grant such rights in return for the premium remains. In the sense that the contract is thereafter only binding upon the writer, it may be viewed as unilateral. This contrasts with the futures contract which, because the buyer is still obliged to buy and the seller to sell, remains bilateral.

Some writers of options are holders of the underlying commodity or security, and use the premiums they receive to enhance their portfolio return. Others, who do not hold such commodities or instruments, are known as 'naked' holders. To the extent that this practice entails the carrying of an unlimited loss prospect and the likelihood of being exercised at any time, while only in receipt of a fixed premium, it is a high-risk area. The usual counter to being exercised in this way is to cover the exposure by dealing in the underlying market, using either options or futures.

As has already been explained, options are known as 'calls' and 'puts', dependent upon the right acquired by the taker. A call option gives the taker the right (but not the obligation) to buy at a fixed price, while a put option confers upon him the right (but not the obligation) to sell at a fix price. The fixed price at which the taker may buy or sell the underlying commodity or security, a procedure known as exercising the option, is called the striking price. If that striking price is identical to the current market price of the commodity or security (i.e. the prevailing price for delivery and payment on expiration date), the option is said to be at the money. When the striking price of a call option is lower than the current market price it is in the money, and when it is higher than the current market price it is out of the money. In contrast, the put option is in the money when the striking price is higher than the current market price out of the money when the striking price is lower than the current market price.

It will by now be clear that there are two basic prices in an options contract, the price paid for the purchase of the actual option, which is the premium, and the fixed price at which the option may be exercised, which is the striking price. In turn, the price of the premium is itself made up of two component parts, the intrinsic value and the extrinsic value (often known as the time value). Intrinsic value may be defined as the amount by which an option is in the money. The calculation of a proper time value for an option is far more complex. It is influenced by four different factors – the duration of the option, the historical price volatility of the underlying commodity or security, current interest rates, and the supply of and demand for the option.

In common with the trading of futures contrasts, most dealing in options is usually conducted on an open outcry basis, where the market for each class of option is made by a 'crowd', which consists of a Board official, market makers in options and broker-dealers from members of the Stock Exchange. All interchanges between market participants must be audible to the remainder of the crowd. Only at the end of all this are price display screens altered to reflect the latest business, solely on a historical basis.

The recently developed markets in financial option contracts are really little more than an extension of similar markets in share options, which were themselves only conceived as recently as the beginning of 1973. It was then that the Chicago Board Options Exchange (CBOE) developed the listed option concept to replace the more traditional private contracts of a type now known as London or European options. These traditional options, which had existed for many years in the major equity markets around the world, and had always been organised along over-the-counter lines without a central trading location in their respective financial centres, were more restricted in scope, only offering at the money strikes with no possibility of reselling or repurchasing the option before expiration.

Although both types of option, the traditional and the Chicago type, confer the right to buy or sell an exact quantity of the security at a predetermined price and date, the Chicago innovation had the effect of standardising the options in terms of size, expiry date, right of exercise, striking or exercise prices and, perhaps most important of all, interposing a guarantor of substance, effectively the exchange itself, to eliminate any danger of non-performance.

When the CBOE originally began such operations, all its options business was in calls. Puts were only introduced in 1977. Since then, at least four other traded share options markets have started in the United States, all based on shares listed on the New York Stock Exchange. By 1986 the market share of the CBOE, which traded 180 million contracts on 163 equity options, that is an average of 33,100 contracts per month per equity option, had declined to 62.4 per cent of total US business compared with 22.6 per cent for AMEX, 8.4 per cent for the Philadelphia Stock Exchange, 4.9 per cent for the Pacific Stock Exchange in San Francisco and a mere 1.7 per cent for the New York Stock Exchange.

The London market in traded share options, which was founded in April 1978 on the floor of The International Stock Exchange (then known as The London Stock Exchange), and is the largest such market outside the United States, traded by comparison a mere 5.4 million contracts in 1986. This is only 3 per cent of the CBOE level, despite a growth rate of 100 per cent per annum between 1982 and 1986. Traded options in 59 equities had been listed on The International Stock Exchange in London by the end of 1987, accounting for about 92 per cent of the business. To these must be added the FTSE 100 Index option (which accounts for nearly all the remainder), three gilt options and two currency options. This represented some 11 per cent of the total business done on the domestic equity market.

The oldest of the other traded options markets which have developed in Europe in recent years is the so-called European Options Exchange in Amsterdam, which also opened in 1978. Virtually all the contracts on foreign stocks which were the feature of its early days, and which justified the 'European' prefix, have gradually been phased out. Nevertheless its volume has still increased in each year since its inception, with some 9.8 million contracts from 33 listed share options traded in 1986, an increase of 40 per cent over the previous year.

Financial Futures

The financial futures markets comprise several distinct types of contract, such as currency contracts, interest rate contracts and stock index contracts. Each is designed to cover a different specific type of risk, and has emerged gradually as the need for risk cover in a new sector has arisen.

As has already been stated, the financial futures markets were a direct development from the commodity markets, which had long been equally vulnerable to price volatility and which had long experience of the economic benefits of futures contracts in the mitigation of the ensuing risks. It was not altogether surprising therefore that the two major Chicago exchanges which traded in commodities futures, the Chicago Board of Trade (CBOT) and Chicago Mercantile

Futures and options

Table 7.1   Deutschmark (IMM)
DM125,000 $US per DM

	Close	High	Low	Previous
June	0.5994	0.6019	0.5991	0.5997
September	0.6055	0.6079	0.6051	0.6058
December	0.6116	0.6130		0.6119
March	0.6179			0.6182

Source: Financial Times 27 April 1988

Exchange (CME), should have responded to the challenge by extending their activities into the financial sector.

Trading in financial futures first began on 16 May 1972 within a new division of the Chicago Mercantile Exchange (CME), the IMM (International Money Market), and initially embraced seven currency contracts.

Currency Futures Contracts

The introduction of trading in currency futures contracts followed on naturally from the unprecedented volatility in exchange and interest rates which resulted from the collapse of the Bretton Woods System in 1971 and the limited durability of the Smithsonian Agreement which followed it. The need for better management of the increased foreign exchange risks which arose as a consequence of this more than justified the creation of such instruments.

Currency futures contracts are rather like highly standardised forward contracts in the currencies concerned. In keeping with commodity price practice, each is quoted against the US dollar, and all price quotations reflect the dollar value of one unit of the currency. This is identical to the North American convention in foreign exchange markets, where a Deutschmark/dollar rate of 2.50, for example, is quoted at its reciprocal value of 0.40. An example is given in Table 7.1.

Interest Rate Futures Contracts

An underlying trend towards higher interest rates, and increased volatility, was already evident in 1970, following a gradual relaxation during the 1960s, in response to rising inflation rates, of interest rate

Table 7.2   Three-month Sterling (LIFFE)
£500,000 points of 100%

	Close	High	Low	Previous
June	91.24	91.33	91.22	91.22
September	90.83	90.92	90.83	90.83
December	90.60	90.69	90.61	90.59
March	90.41	90.48	90.46	90.42

Estimated volume (inc. figures not shown): 13069 (13950)
Previous day's open int: 30102 (30936)

Source: Financial Times 27 April 1988

restrictions and regulations which had existed in the United States since the end of the Second World War. State usery laws had been brought into question, the 4.25 per cent coupon ceiling on Treasury bonds had been removed, and Regulation Q on large commercial accounts and prohibitions against interest paid on demand deposits had both been relaxed. Ultimately, on 6 October 1979, the Federal Reserve switched its monetary policy from one of controlling monetary aggregates to one of controlling interest rate levels directly. It was in the context of these developments, when in 1978 the realisation came about that this was going to be a permanent phenomenon, that attention turned to interest rate futures, and a contract based on 'Ginnie Maes' (Government National Mortgage Association) collateralised depositary receipts was introduced at the Chicago Board of Trade. The necessity of maintaining a strong housing sector in the face of higher rates of interest and inflation had been one of the principal reasons for the relaxation in interest rate restrictions. It had also been in an attempt to facilitate a flow of funds into the housing industry that the US government had established the GNMA a couple of years previously.

The IMM responded a few weeks later with a futures instrument based on 90-day US Treasury Bills, and this very successful contract was followed in turn over the next five years on the CBOT by contracts based on US Treasury bonds and notes and on the IMM by contracts based on three-month Eurodollars and domestic CDs.

Prices of short-term interest rate futures are quoted on the basis of an index which is calculated by subtracting from 100 the annual interest rate on the instrument concerned. These prices move in increments of 0.01 per cent and the cash value associated with such a

Table 7.3   20-year 12% notional gilt (LIFFE)
£50,000 32nds of 100%

	Close	High	Low	Previous
June	120–13	120–18	120–05	120–06
September	96–12	96–13	96–05	96–06

Estimated volume: 24980 (33382)
Previous day's open int: 27546 (27666)

Source: Financial Times 27 April 1988

Table 7.4   US Treasury bonds 8% (LIFFE)
£100,000 32nds of 100%

	Close	High	Low	Previous
June	88–27	88–28	88–09	88–13
September	87–27			87–13
December				

Estimated volume: 12092 (1889)
Previous day's open int: 194 (201)

Source: Financial Times 27 April 1988

price change is $25 for US dollar denominated contracts and £12.50 for the LIFFE short sterling contract. This is illustrated in Table 7.2, which gives an example of the price quotation as published daily in the *Financial Times*.

The design of the longer-term fixed interest futures contracts is more in keeping with traditional commodity market practice, in that for each contract there is defined a set of cash market instruments which can be delivered into a maturing short futures position. Each futures instrument is based upon a notional bond or gilt (with coupons of 8 per cent and 12 per cent respectively) to which the various deliverable instruments trading in the cash market are related by a system of price factors. Price quotations are for $100 or £100 nominal, in line with convention in the cash market, and prices move in increments of 1/32 per cent, giving minimum price movements of $31.25 and £15.625 respectively. Tables 7.3 and 7.4, which are again examples of the price quotations published daily in the *Financial Times*, illustrate this.

Futures contracts such as these, based on government bonds, are undoubtedly the most successful product yet devised by the financial futures markets. Growth in volume has gone very much in parallel with the underlying cash markets, although it has frequently been the futures markets which have determined the extent of price movements.

Stock Index Futures Contracts

The first Stock Index contract was introduced on the IMM in April 1982, based on the Standard and Poors 500 Index. The rationale behind such a contract, which now has many counterparts throughout the world, is that aspect of modern portfolio theory which argues in favour of passive management. That is to say, because a weight of evidence exists supporting the view that active management through the selection of individual stocks does not necessarily produce results which are in any way superior to straightforward investment across a broad market, all that is necessary is to replicate as closely as possible indices such as the Standard and Poors 500, the FTSE 100, the Nikkei Dow Jones, the Hang Seng, and the Australian Ordinaries indices, according to their weighted mathematical formulae. While prices in London are quoted on the basis of one-tenth of the average level of the FTSE 100 stock index between 11.10 and 11.20 on the last trading day, as Table 7.5 shows, those in Chicago are more directly related to the Standard and Poors 500 index. Table 7.5 also illustrates that the unit of trading in London is £25 per full index point. Meanwhile, that in Chicago is $500 times the index value.

It was contracts such as these, based on the Standard and Poors Index, and their linkages with the stock markets in the technique known as portfolio insurance, which gained considerable notoriety immediately following the October 1987 stock market crash.

Global Expansion

On 30 September 1982 the London International Financial Futures Exchange (LIFFE) opened its doors in the Royal Exchange building in the City of London, offering the first fully-fledged market in financial futures in the European time zone. Within six months, it was trading two short-term interest rate contracts based on Eurodollar and domestic sterling time deposits, a long-term gilt contract, and four IMM-style currency contracts in sterling, the Deutschmark, the Swiss franc and the Japanese yen – each quoted against the US dollar.

Table 7.5 FT-SE 100 Index (LIFFE)
£25 per full index point

	Close	High	Low	Previous
June	180.40	180.40	178.80	178.50
September	181.90			180.00
December				
Estimated volume: 1007 (1808)				
Previous day's open int: 10406 (10345)				

Source: Financial Times 27 April 1988

Since then, LIFFE has also introduced a contract based on the Financial Times Stock Exchange 100 Index, further interest rate contracts based on long-term US Treasury Bonds and short-dated gilts and, most recently, contracts based on a long-term Japanese Government Bond and medium-dated gilts.

After two years of careful preparation, the Singapore International Monetary Exchange (SIMEX) opened for business on 5 September 1984 incorporating an innovative link with the IMM by means of which positions initiated on one exchange could be closed out by offsetting trades transacted on the other. This 'mutual offset' arrangement had considerable attractions for many multilateral organisations which now used futures to manage risk on a worldwide basis. In spite of the considerable technical and regulatory problems which have to be overcome, it seems likely that further links between other exchanges will be developed along similar lines over the coming years.

The Sydney Futures Exchange, which was launched in January 1985, has always been at the forefront of the trend towards the globalisation of markets in risk instruments, along with its options counterpart. The development of this exchange has been an attempt to take advantage of Australia's time zone advantage. The Eurodollar and Treasury bond contracts are a manifestation of this. Also unique to Australia, because it is only sanctioned there, is futures trading in individual stocks.

The New Zealand Futures Exchange, also introduced in January 1985, is unique in that it has no trading floor of dealer pits. Its seventeen members (all of whom are shareholders) are instead linked by computer in an automatic trading system. Dealers in towns and cities throughout New Zealand enter their offers, and transactions are almost instantaneously enacted as soon as a matching bid is put in by another dealer.

On 19 October 1985, the Tokyo Stock Exchange introduced a contract based on long-term domestic Japanese yen bonds, which was greeted with enormous enthusiasm. Unfortunately, a few days later, the Bank of Japan announced its intention to allow interest rates to rise in order to promote the appreciation of the yen/US dollar exchange rate, and the subsequent collapse of the Japanese bond market had serious consequences for many small investors who had been encouraged to support the new futures instrument. Even so, there are many who see tremendous long-term potential in this contract and the eve of trading in Tokyo saw the respective chairmen of the CBT and LIFFE signing a memorandum of intent to develop an identical contract on each exchange as the first step towards the creation of a 24-hour market in Japanese bond futures.

The Matif, the Paris Financial Futures Exchange, was launched in February 1986 with a long-bond contract based on a notional French government bond with a 10 per cent coupon and a life of seven to ten years, a great success, and with a second contract based on a 90-day French Treasury bill. There are now plans to launch a contract based on the three-month Paris Interbank Offered Rate (PIBOR), which would fulfil a role which the Treasury bill has never been able to satisfy, namely to hedge short-term positions. During 1987, Treasury bill volume averaged only 429 contracts a day compared with 47,837 for the long bond. Another proposal, which has been received with indifference by dealers, is for an Ecu/dollar contract. The much smaller traded share options market, the Marché des Options Négociables de Paris (Monep), was only launched in September 1987. It is hoped that it will be able to offer fifteen options by the end of 1988, although there is still substantial doubt about which exchange will be offering futures and options contracts based on the PI40 index of stock issues, which will probably appear in the autumn of 1988. Both the Matif and the Monep claim the derivatives to the index and it is likely that the Finance Ministry will award the futures contract to the Matif and the option contract to the Monep.

The expansion of the Hong Kong Futures Exchange into a financial futures market in May 1986, with a contract based on the Hang Seng Stock Index, was followed by an astronomic thirty-fold increase in first-month daily average up to the end of summer 1987, when 30,000 contracts per day were traded. This was brought to an abrupt halt by the world stock market crash, which exposed the inadequacy of the exchange's management and capital resources. Over forty futures traders were suspended, many facing legal action, and its Futures Guarantee Corporation was left with liabilities outstanding amounting to $HK 1.8 billion.

The Swiss initiative is another attempt to launch a fully computerised national exchange, integrating trading and clearing operations into a single automated system. It was perhaps for this reason that technical difficulties should have prevented the new Swiss Options and Futures Exchange (Soffex) from meeting its original opening target of March 1988. Soffex is a joint venture of the three bourses – in Zürich, Geneva and Basle – and the five largest banks, Union Bank of Switzerland, Swiss Bank Corporation, Crédit Suisse, Swiss Volksbank and Bank Leu. The initial plan is of a three-stage development. Options contracts would first be offered on 11 chosen Swiss stocks. There would then be a Swiss share index contract, and finally financial futures.

Apart from the opening up of markets in financial futures in new centres around the globe, there are three further important areas of development worthy of some comment.

The first is the increasing number of contracts which are now being traded at more than one centre in different time zones. Apart from trading in the United States, three-month Eurodollar interest rate contracts are now traded across three other time zones, in London, Sydney and Singapore. The US Treasury bond is meanwhile traded in London and Sydney only, and the Japanese Government bond is now traded in London as well as Tokyo. Three CME currency contracts are also traded in Singapore. The links between CME and Simex are, of course, in the context of the mutual offset agreement formalised in 1984, which has been rather limited in its success and is one reason why the CME is now looking at alternative routes to trading around the clock.

The second is the tendency towards longer trading hours in certain important centres. Not least of these is Chicago, which has more than 70 per cent of the world's futures and options trading business. While the CME has formed an agreement with Reuters to develop an automated trading system (PMT – Post (Pre) Market Trade) to take over when its floor is closed, the Chicago Board of Trade has preferred instead to increase its open outcry activity into the evening, from 6 p.m. to 9 p.m. The Philadelphia Stock Exchange is the only other US exchange yet to introduce such 'night trading', but both initiatives have their supporters elsewhere.

The third interesting development is the challenge offered to the recognised US exchanges by off-exchange or over-the-counter trading. This comes in the shape of a fast-expanding range of financial products displaying the characteristics of futures and options contracts which have been introduced by the various Wall Street securities houses and banks in apparent defiance of the Commodity Exchange Act 1936. The exchanges have argued that such instruments compete unfairly with their own products, are not subject to the same regulatory constraints and can be offered more cheaply, but the Commodity Futures Trading Commission, the US regulatory body for such transactions, has so far adopted an equivocal stance.

Traded Financial Options

Traded currency options were first introduced to the foreign exchange markets in the early 1980s in response to pressures from the customers of major banks for a product which would both provide a new risk management capability and be better suited to the handling of their foreign exchange exposures. At first, a few banks began offering such options, but only on a limited basis. Then several major banks adopted them as part of their regular foreign exchange service. Finally, in 1982, currency option trading was introduced on publicly quoted exchanges. This had a significant impact on the market's development, in the sense that it had now become possible for foreign exchange and option traders to interact and close the knowledge gap between the two markets.

This evolution in option markets was not restricted merely to contracts in currencies alone. Options on other instruments soon followed, with cash options offering the right to buy or sell a specified quantity of a financial instrument at a fixed price in the future and futures options offering the right to buy or sell a specified futures contract at a fixed price in the future. It was not long before options could be taken on the basis of corresponding futures contracts at major exchanges in several cities around the world. Traded options were first introduced on LIFFE in June 1985.

Option instruments can be used in several ways that are impossible with futures. They are particularly useful to those who will prefer to mitigate the risks associated with contingent liabilities. Take the example of a corporation which had reservations about tendering for a contract in dollars, because it feared that an appreciation in sterling would reduce or eliminate its profit margin. It could always obtain cover by hedging in the futures or forward currency market, but that would be conditional upon being successful in the tender. A failure to win would leave a high risk outright position which would need to be reversed. If the corporation used an exchange traded option in similar circumstances, its risk would be limited to the option premium.

Another advantage of the option is that it enables the trader to fine-tune his risk exposure in a way that is impossible with futures or forwards. The range of exercise prices, some in-the-money, some at-the-money, and others out-of-the-money, allow the trader to choose whichever risk he wishes to accept. While the high cost deep in-the-money option will provide complete protection against all price movements, however adverse, the cheap out-of-the-money option will provide cover against only part of them.

Appendix B lists the financial futures and options markets throughout the world, together with the instruments which traded on them at the beginning of 1988.

London's 'Big Bang'

Rather than being an actual physical happening, 'Big Bang' described the method by which a number of radical changes took place simultaneously in the procedures of The London Stock Exchange on 27 October 1986. The original objective – stimulated by an agreement in 1983 between Cecil Parkinson, then Secretary of State for Trade and Industry, and Sir Nicholas Goodison, chairman of The Stock Exchange, was about the need to bring competition into The Stock Exchange, with the focus on its scales of fixed minimum commissions. As time passed, the emphasis moved onto bringing London into line with international practice, as securities markets became internationalised and 24-hour global trading became an imminent reality on the back of the revolution in electronic technology. The aim was to assume the leading position in the European time zone in a seamless market stretching from Tokyo to San Francisco. This market was already well established in US treasury bonds, and was becoming important for several hundred leading equities of international grade. The first goal was to be the secondary market. The second would be the fees, commissions and trading profit which went with primary market financing.

One major change had already been taken prior to the 'Big Bang', in March 1986, when corporate members were first accepted into The Stock Exchange, opening the way for firms of stockbrokers to become part of larger groupings, including banks and other financial institutions. The highest price paid for a stockbroking firm was the £100 million by the Hong Kong and Shanghai Banking Corporation for the renowned firm, James Capel. Integrated firms such as Barclay de Zoete Wedd (BZW), Morgan Grenfell and others emerged. Typically these would have three arms, focusing upon securities, merchant banking and investment management respectively. By the same token, large international firms of share dealers have become members of The London Stock Exchange. Among outstanding examples have been the American firms, Salomon Brothers, Goldman Sachs and Merrill Lynch and Shearson Lehman, and the Japanese securities firm, Nomura International.

Rather than bring in the remaining changes piecemeal, it was decided to introduce the majority of them overnight, on 27 October, hence the 'Big Bang' concept.

The changes which took place were as follows:

1. The adoption of the 'dual capacity' dealing system
    This involved an abolition of the traditional demarcation between brokers and jobbers in favour of a dual capacity 'broker/dealer'. Some members continued to specialise as market-makers, buying and selling shares continuously under a strict code of conduct, with the market-makers linked through so-called inter-dealer brokers. Others continued to offer the same services as previously, pledged always to deal to the client's 'best advantage'. Many firms, especially the larger ones, adopted a 'dual capacity' of market-maker and broker. This led to a large increase in the number of market-makers, from the 13 jobbers prior to 'Big Bang' to 33 registered market-makers. This was thought likely to cut the margins of the market-makers, particularly in the gilts market, where three jobbers were initially replaced by 27 market-makers. This was all consistent with the original Parkinson-Goodison objective of making the market more competitive. The result has been a marked enhancement in market depth.

2. The abolition of fixed commissions
    The major criticism aimed at the traditional fixed minimum commissions had been that they tended to favour the less efficient brokers. And besides, investors paid twice, once in commission and again in the jobber's spread (the margin between 'bid' and 'offer' prices). Sometimes this would be justified by research advice, but at other times there was no differential between a full service and an execution-only service. Moreover, the commissions did not properly reflect the underlying costs of transactions. For instance, it cost a broker very little more to transact a £1m bargain than a £100 one.
    The institutional investor now has the option of going direct to

a market-maker and paying no commission. This is called net dealing, the market-maker merely taking his turn. It has already become clear that a large proportion of business by institutional investors is being conducted in this way. Indeed it had been claimed that over 50 per cent by value of all business and up to 80 per cent of institutional transactions were done in this way. A survey carried out by the International Stock Exchange, the findings of which were published in the Autumn 1987 edition of *Quality of Markets Quarterly*, discovered that over a quarter of customer business by value in the domestic equities markets (10 per cent by number of transactions) was being dealt net of commission. This compared with virtually 90 per cent of gilt turnover, which represented only a third of customer transactions in the gilt market, although almost all deals over £100,000 are dealt net. A mere 20 per cent of trade options transactions were not being charged a commission, mostly for components of strategies which involved the simultaneous buying of put and call options and transactions in underlying securities. Finally, almost one-half of transactions on the foreign equity market were dealt on a net basis, mainly conducted by UK and overseas institutions.

This method does deny investors the benefits of research, and many will undoubtedly want to continue to pay commissions, perhaps reduced, for this facility. It was often feared that this new negotiable system might not be to the advantage of the private investor with his more modest turnover and that the trends following the 1976 US deregulation could be repeated, with the private investor finding himself paying more. This has been borne out by the recent survey, for whereas the overall average commission charge including net deals has reduced from 0.43 per cent to 0.33 per cent, the upward shift, in absolute minimum commission charged has raised that paid by individuals from 0.88 per cent to 1.09 per cent, or 0.91 per cent if net deals are included.

3. Rules which will make new issues easier
Since 'Big Bang', companies coming to the market for the first time have been able to raise up to £15 million by having their shares placed directly with institutions. Previously an issue of more than £3 million had to be made through an offer for sale to the public. The placing limit in the USM (unlisted

securities market) was also moved up, from £3 million to £5 million.

These rules contributed to an increased buoyancy in the primary market, with UK companies raising nearly £21 billion in the twelve months from October 1986 to September 1987. Privatisation issues represented a further £8.9 billion. Some 193 new companies, including 40 from overseas, sought a listing on the ISE since 'Big Bang', with a further 87 companies admitted to the USM and 28 companies on the newly-established Third Market. On the gilts market, the British Government raised a gross total of £15.8 billion against redemptions of £8.8 billion.

4. The introduction of new and sophisticated electronic dealing systems
This was effected through a system called SEAQ (Stock Exchange Automated Quotation) which adapted existing systems, such as the TOPIC viewdata system and the TALISMAN computer settlement system, and added some sophisticated new facilities. It categorised the securities into four separate categories:

(a) Alpha: the most actively traded stocks, where market-makers have to show firm, continuous two-way prices; all trades being published immediately.

   The number of domestic equities subject to five minute trade publication, that is to say 'alphas', accordingly rose from 62 to 126 stocks, which represents an increase from 40 per cent to 55 per cent of domestic equity turnover value. However, these figures exclude two further groups now subject to the five minute rule, that is ADRs (American Depositary Receipts) on UK stocks which are now traded on SEAQ – of which 12 were covered at the end of September 1987 – and takeover stocks, now designated as temporary alphas so as to ensure that sensitive trades are published immediately, of which 42 were covered.

(b) Beta: Somewhat less actively traded stocks, where market-makers still have to show firm, continuous two-way prices, but trades are not immediately published.

(c) Gamma and delta: Relatively inactive stocks, where prices may be indicative rather than firm.

This meant that a market-maker was able to display his current prices on terminals accessible anywhere in Britain, or indeed the world. The latest prices and the volume of business being done were to be, if not instantly at least promptly available, since all deals must be reported to the central computer within five minutes. Obligatory firm quotation now covers some 721 UK equities, that is alphas and betas plus takeover stocks, and quotations in gamma stocks are now firm for sizes above 1000 shares.

Apart from enhanced real-time visibility, the SEAQ system has also allowed for this information on trading and prices to be stored and available for later inspection. In theory, this has enabled The Stock Exchange to build up a more complete surveillance system, so as to give the investor greater assurance that all deals were done to his best advantage.

5. This enhanced visibility has also, in turn, provoked a transfer of dealing away from the traditional floor of The Stock Exchange and 'upstairs' into the offices of the brokers.

Initially, some market makers and brokers decided to continue trading from the floor. A notable example was Smith New Court, one of the largest of the market makers. But that did not last for long, and it was subsequently announced that all trading on the floor was to cease, quickly provoking a response from the New York Stock Exchange that The London Stock Exchange is no longer a proper stock exchange.

A survey conducted by MIL Research Group and published in the *Financial Times* on the first anniversary of 'Big Bang' asked several important questions of some 120 leading UK institutional fund managers. Some 93 per cent felt that the principal gain had been the reduction in dealing costs, and more than 50 per cent argued that the speed of response and liquidity of markets have improved and that access to foreign securities has been made easier. On the other hand, most agreed that internal costs had been increased and admitted problems from conflicts of interest. On the speculative question of which firms they expected to emerge as the most successful by 1990, the twelve most highly rated were as follows:

Warburg Securities	50%
James Capel	43%
Barclays de Zoete Wedd	41%
Phillips & Drew	26%
Hoare Govett	18%
Nomura	11%

Citicorp Scrimgeour Vickers	8%
Cazenove	8%
Salomon Bros	7%
Smith New Court	7%
Goldman Sachs	5%
Kleinwort Grieveson	5%

The first three of these are under British management, although James Capel is a subsidiary of the Hong Kong and Shanghai Banking Corporation. A relatively high rating for the Japanese firm, Nomura, suggests that the fund managers are more impressed by a patient methodical build-up than by the sort of aggressive but erratic policies deployed by the top US investment banks, some of which have recently announced substantial staff cuts.

The regulation of markets (investor protection)
A further development in London, almost parallel with the 'Big Bang' was the agreement between The Stock Exchange and ISRO (the International Securities Regulatory Organisation), a body representative of the Eurobond houses, to form a single self-regulatory organisation (SRO) to cover the securities activities of both memberships, although a separate recognised investment exchange (RIE) would cover the trading of gilts, domestic and foreign equities and options. While the latter would still be known as The Stock Exchange, its official name would become the International Stock Exchange of the United Kingdom and the Republic of Ireland. The Eurobond market, which overshadowed the UK equity and government securities markets at the time, with a market capitalisation (£500 billion) and turnover (£2000 billion), would be kept apart from the traditional activities of The Stock Exchange through a separate RIE in the context of the Financial Services Act. This would be set up by the Swiss-based Association of International Bond Dealers.

This new International Stock Exchange would, in due course, be a self-regulating organisation under the new regulatory network guided by the Securities and Investments Board as a recent enactment of the Financial Services Act. In the broader context this will mean that common regulatory and investor protection standards will be applied to all forms of securities trading to a greater extent than at any time since the beginnings of the Eurobond market in London in the mid-1960s.

A network of rules and regulations to protect the public from unscrupulous company promoters and from fraudulent dealers already existed within The Stock Exchange. For instance, before being admitted to the status of 'listing', companies were required to submit themselves to extensive security, and then undertake to keep both actual and potential shareholders properly informed about their progress. Member firms of The Stock Exchange were also strictly supervised, and they were backed by the Compensation Fund, which meant that since 1951 no investor had lost money through fraud or financial failure of a member.

A series of additions to these regulations have been introduced as a result of the 'Big Bang', and these have been formalised within the Financial Services Act. The lynchpin of this new process will be the Securities and Investments Board. Initially, it will be concerned with propagating rules guiding the conduct of securities business in the United Kingdom to conform with the general principles laid down in the Act. In due course, originally thought to have been the third quarter of 1987, the SIB was to have recognised those SROs (Self-Regulatory Organisations) which it considered capable of providing at least equivalent standards of regulation the power to authorise their own members to conduct securities-related business.

One of these additions, the 'best execution' rule, has already been mentioned. It simply puts on to paper the principle that the broker will have to take all reasonable steps to ensure that the price obtained by the client is as good, or better, than the best price displayed in that security in a comparable size on the SEAQ system. As already mentioned, SEAQ itself has enhanced the work of the surveillance division of The Stock Exchange. Another new rule is the 'excessive trading rule' which says that any member company should not transact deals which are excessive in size or frequency in relation to the financial situation and investment objectives of the client. Yet another is the so-called 'client agreement letter', the basic idea of which is that each investor will formally advise the broker of his instructions. 'Chinese Walls' are a device intended to control the activities of the 'integrated firms' in the interests of the investor. An early response by many of the stockbroking firms was to appoint special compliance officers to ensure that many of these new regulations were enforced, and the Collier case of insider trading by an executive of Morgan Grenfell was an example of their success.

Of course, the Financial Services Act 1986 is just one example of a worldwide process which is taking place in the wake of the internationalisation of markets in securities. Flows of capital across national borders impose new requirements if the interests of investors as consumers are to be adequately protected.

The following is a non-exhaustive list of financial futures and options markets throughout the world, together with the instruments which traded on them at the beginning of 1988.

North America

IMM (Chicago Mercantile Exchange)

Futures	*Unit*
Three-month Eurodollar interest rate	$US 1 million
US dollar/Sterling	£25,000
US dollar/Canadian dollar	$CA 100,000
US dollar/Deutschmark	125,000 Deutschmarks
US dollar/Japanese yen	12.5 million yen
US dollar/Swiss franc	125,000 Swiss francs
US dollar/French franc	250,000 French francs
US dollar/Australian dollar	$A 100,000
US dollar/Ecu (European Currency Unit)	125,000 Ecus
Standard and Poors 500 Share Index	$US 500 times index
90-day US Treasury bills	$US 1 million

Options	Unit
Three-month Eurodollar interest rate	$US 1 million
US dollar/Sterling	£25,000
Us dollar/Canadian dollar	$CA 100,000
US dollar/Deutschmark	125,000 Deutschmarks
US dollar/Japanese yen	12.5 million yen
US dollar/Swiss franc	125,000 Swiss francs
Standard and Poors 500 Share Index	$US 500 times index
90-day US Treasury bills	$US 1 million

Chicago Board of Trade (CBOT) | **Launched: October 1975**

Futures	*Unit*
US Treasury bonds	$US 100,000
US Treasury note	$US 100,000
Corporate Bond Index	$US 1000 times index
Municipal Bond Index	$US 1000 times index
Institutional Index	$US 500 times index
Major Market Index	$US 250 times index

Options	*Unit*
US Treasury bond futures	$US 100,000
US Treasury note futures	$US 100,000
Silver futures	1000 troy oz

Chicago Board Options Exchange (CBOE)

Options	*Unit*
Standard & Poors 100 Index	$US 100 times index
Standard & Poors 500 Index	$US 100 times index
US Treasury bonds	$US 100,000
US Treasury notes	$US 100,000

New York Stock Exchange

Options	*Unit*
New York Stock Exchange Composite Index	$US 500 times index

Philadelphia Stock Exchange

Futures	*Unit*
National OTC Index	$US 500 times index
US dollar/Sterling	£25,000
US dollar/Canadian dollar	$CA 100,000
US dollar/Deutschmark	125,000 Deutschmarks
US dollar/Swiss franc	125,000 Swiss francs
US dollar/European Currency Unit (Ecu)	125,000 Ecus
US dollar/French franc	250,000 French francs
US dollar/Japanese yen	12.5 million yen
US dollar/Australian dollar	$A 100,000

Options	*Unit*
National OTC Index	$US 100 times index
Value Line Composite Index	$US 100 times index
Utility Index	$US 100 times index
Sterling spot option	£12,500
Canadian dollar spot option	$CA 50,000
Deutschmark spot option	62,500 Deutschmarks
European currency unit	62,500 Ecus
French franc spot option	25,000 French francs
Japanese yen spot option	6.25 million yen
Swiss franc spot option	62,500 Swiss francs
Australian dollar spot option	$A 50,000

Toronto Futures Exchange

Futures

Toronto 35 Index	$CA 500 times index
TSE 300 Composite Index	$CA 10 times index
TSE Oil and Gas Index	$CA 10 times index
Long-term Canadian Government bond	$CA 100,000
91-day Canadian Treasury bills	$CA 1 million
US dollar/Canadian dollar	$US 50,000

Options	*Unit*
Toronto 35 Index	$CA 500 times index
Long-term Canadian Government bond	$CA 100,000

Montreal Stock Exchange

Options	*Unit*
Canadian Government bond	$CA 25,000
91-day Canadian Treasury bills	$CA 250,000

MidAmerica Commodity Exchange

Futures	*Unit*
US Treasury bond	$US 50,000
US Treasury bill	$US 500,000
US dollar/Sterling	£12,500
US dollar/Deutschmark	62,500 Deutschmarks
US dollar/Japanese yen	6.25 million yen
US dollar/Swiss franc	62,500 Swiss francs
US dollar/Canadian dollar	$CA 50,000

New York Futures Exchange (NYFE)   **Launched: 1978**

Futures	*Unit*
NYSE Composite Index	$US 500 times index
CRB Index	$US 500 times index
Russell 2000 Index	
Russell 3000 Index	

Options	*Unit*
NYSE Composite Index	$US 500 times index

Pacific Stock Exchange, San Francisco

Options	*Unit*
FNCI Composite Index	$US 100 times index

American Stock Exchange   **Launched: 1978**

Options	*Unit*
Major Market Index	$US 100 times index
Institutional Index	$US 100 times index
Computer Technology Index	$US 100 times index
Oil Stock Index	$US 100 times index
13-week US Treasury bill	$US 1 million
10-year US Treasury note	$US 100,000

New York Cotton Exchange (FINEX)

Futures	*Unit*
US Dollar Index	$US 500 times index
5-year US Treasury note	$US 100,000
European Currency Unit	100,000 Ecus

Options   *Unit*

US Dollar Index $US 500 times index
5-year US Treasury note $US 100,000

New York Coffee, Sugar and Cocoa Exchange

Futures   *Unit*

Consumer Price Index $US 1000 times index

Kansas City Board of Trade

Futures   *Unit*

Value Line Index $US 500 times index
Mini Value Line Index $US 100 times index

Commodity Exchange Inc, New York (COMEX)

Futures   *Unit*

Corporate Bond Index $US 500 times index

Elsewhere

LIFFE   **Launched: September 1982**

Futures   *Unit*

FT-SE 100 Share Index   £25 per index point
Long gilt   £50,000 with 12% coupon
US Treasury bond $US 100,000 with 8% coupon
Three-month Eurodollar interest $US 1 million
rate
Sterling/US dollar   £25,000
US dollar/Deutschmark $US 50,000
Deutschmark/US dollar   125,000 Deutschmarks
Swiss franc/US dollar   125,000 Swiss francs

Japanese yen/US dollar	12.5 million yen
Short gilt	£100,000 with 10% coupon
Three-month Sterling interest rate	£500,000
6% Notional Japanese Government bond	100 million yen
Medium gilt	£50,000

Options	*Unit*
FT-SE 100 Share Index	All on basis of one corresponding
Long gilt	futures contract.
US Treasury bond	
Three-month Eurodollar interest rate	
Sterling/US dollar	
Deutschmark/US dollar	

The International Stock Exchange, London   **Launched: April 1978**

Traded Options	*Unit*
FT-SE 100 Share Index	£10 times index
Short gilt	£50,000
Medium gilt	£50,000
Long gilt	£50,000
Sterling/US dollar	£12,500
Deutschmark/US dollar	62,500 Deutschmarks

European Options Exchange, Amsterdam   **Launched: 1978**

Options	*Unit*
EOE Dutch Stock Index	DFL 100 times index
American Major Market Index	$US 100 times index
Dutch Government bonds	DFL 10,000
US dollar/Dutch guilder	$US 10,000
US dollar/Deutschmark	$US 10,000
Sterling/Dutch guilder	£10,000
European Currency Unit/US dollar	ECU 10,000

Gold	10 troy ounces
Silver	250 troy ounces
Stock options	100 shares

Singapore International Monetary Exchange (SIMEX)   **Launched: September 1984**

Futures	*Unit*
Three-month Eurodollar interest rate	$US 1 million
US dollar/Deutschmark	125,000 Deutschmarks
US dollar/Japanese yen	12.5 million yen
US dollar/Sterling	£25,000
Nikkei-Dow Jones Stock Average	500 Japanese yen times index

Options	*Unit*
Three-month Eurodollar interest rate	$US 1 million
US dollar/Japanese yen	12.5 million yen
US dollar/Deutschmark	125,000 Deutschmarks

Sydney Futures Exchange (SFE)   **Launched: 1985**

Futures	*Unit*
Sydney All Ordinaries Share Index	$A 100 times index
90-day bank bills	$A 500,000 face value
Commonwealth Government 10 year T-bond	$A 100,000 nominal coupon 12%
US Treasury bonds	$US 100,000
Three-month Eurodollar interest rate	$US 1 million
US dollar/Australian dollar	$A 100,000

Options	*Unit*
Sydney All Ordinaries Share Index	$A 100 times index
Commonwealth Government 10 year T-bond	$A 100,000
90-day bank bills	$A 500,000 face value

New Zealand Futures Exchange	**Launched: January 1985**
Futures	*Unit*
Barclays Share Price Index	$NZ 20 times index
5-year New Zealand Government bonds	$NZ 100,000
90-day bank bills	$NZ 500,000
US dollar/NZ dollar	$US 50,000

Tokyo Stock Exchange	**Launched: October 1985**
Futures	*Unit*
10-year Japanese Government bond	100 million Japanese yen

Paris – Matif	**Launched: February 1986**
Futures	*Unit*
10-year French Treasury bonds	FF 500,000
Three-month French Treasury bills	FF 5 million
Options	*Unit*
10-year French Treasury bonds	FF 500,000

Hong Kong Futures Exchange (HKFE)	**Launched: May 1986**
Futures	*Unit*
Hang Seng Stock Index	$HK 50 times index

Sweden's Options and Futures Exchange	
Futures	*Unit*
SX16 Share Index	SKR 100 times index

Options	Unit
SX16 Share Index	SKR 100 times index

Stockholm Options Market

Options

OMX Stock Index	SKR 100 times index

Index

Note: Most individual Asian, European and Latin American countries have not been entered separately, but are subsumed under major entries for continents.